Party Affiliations
in the State Legislatures

Party Affiliations in the State Legislatures

A Year by Year Summary, 1796–2006

Michael J. Dubin

McFarland & Company, Inc., Publishers
Jefferson, North Carolina, and London

LIBRARY OF CONGRESS CATALOGUING-IN-PUBLICATION DATA

Dubin, Michael J.
    Party affiliations in the state legislatures : a year by year
summary, 1796–2006 / Michael J. Dubin.
        p.   cm.
    Includes bibliographical references.

    ISBN-13: 978-0-7864-2914-1
    softcover : 50# alkaline paper ∞

    1. Legislative bodies — United States — States.   2. Legislative
bodies — United States — States — Registers.   3. Party affiliation —
United States — States.   4. Elections — United States — States.
I. Title.
JK2488D83   2007
328.73'0769 — dc22   2007018479

British Library cataloguing data are available

Cover photograph ©2007 PhotoSpin; artwork by Kate Irwin

Manufactured in the United States of America

McFarland & Company, Inc., Publishers
    Box 611, Jefferson, North Carolina 28640
    www.mcfarlandpub.com

To Mom and Pop,
who started it all

Acknowledgments

This volume was in large part made possible by many individuals and institutions whose assistance was critical in locating and compiling the data. Of special significance was Philip Lampi of Gilbertville, Massachusetts, whose collection of early American election data (pre–1825) is incomparable. He generously provided me with much of the material that appears here for the earliest period covered by this volume. Without his contribution this volume would be far less complete. The interlibrary loan departments of the public libraries of Glendale, Peoria, Phoenix and Surprise, Arizona, were particularly helpful in obtaining microfilm and other materials that significantly aided the research.

Table of Contents

Table of Contents   x

Introduction

State legislatures have long been a crucial part of the American political process. In addition to their lawmaking function, state legislatures in the past have elected presidential electors, governors,[1] U.S. senators until 1913, and many state and local officials.

The purpose of this volume is to provide the party totals in each of the 50 state legislatures by election. The earliest such information dates back to the late 1790s. However, the beginning date varies from state to state. Individual state factors determined the advent of partisan contests for the legislature, but usually such contests emerged only after parties had begun to appear in contests for statewide offices or congressional seats. In addition the period of 1817–1828 is largely a period of one- or no-party contests, where for the most part partisan elections were nonexistent.[2] While the coming of the second party system in the 1830s ushered in an era of partisan contests — a system of contests that, with changes, exists to this day — the reader will note that for brief periods in some states, information on these contests could not be located.

I began compiling these data more than 35 years ago. Newspapers were the major source in almost all the states, primarily prior to 1860. Political almanacs were particularly important during the last half of the 19th and the first third of the 20th century. See sources listed with the individual states for details.

In 2002 I decided to compile data for all the states and present this information in one source. I undertook additional research, filling in gaps, rechecking some existing data, and going back even further than the earlier research. Again, newspapers and political almanacs were important sources, along with some individual states' compilations.[3]

I hope that the end product of this research will provide researchers, students and general readers with a useful source on the subject of party politics in the state legislatures.

1

Format

Material for each state is presented in three parts; the first part summarizes the development of the state's electoral process. This part covers seven areas:

- statehood (or constitutional origins, for the first 13 states)
- terms (of the legislature)
- districts/elections
- membership/size
- reapportionment/redistricting[4]
- election dates
- constitutions

The second part provides figures, election by election, for the party affiliations in the legislature.[5] The third part lists the sources for the information.

The size of a legislative body is indicated within parentheses in bold type to the left of the party affiliation figures and is indicated only when there was change from the previous election.

NOTES

1. The last state legislature to cast their state's electoral votes was Colorado in 1876. Six states provided for the election of the governor by the legislature; the last such election occurred in South Carolina in 1864. Eight states provided for legislative election if no candidate received a majority of the votes cast. Two states, Vermont and Mississippi, still retain this provision, last used in the latter state in 1999.

2. For a discussion of the development of the party organizations and partisan contests of the second party system the reader should consult Richard P. McCormick, *The Second American Party System*, Chapel Hill: University of North Carolina Press, 1966. This work offers not only a state by state discussion of the development of the second party system but reviews aspects of the Democratic-Republican v. Federalist era.

3. Although official election returns do survive in many cases, they almost never indicated party affiliation until the adoption of the publicly printed ballot starting in the last decade of the 19th century or later. The same can be said of state manuals and similar publications.

4. In some instances this information is incomplete and is indicated as such. Reapportionments were determined by each state's formula until the decision of the U.S. Supreme Court in the case of *Reynolds v. Sims* (377 U.S. 633) 1964 mandated that all legislative districts had to be equal in population. (This mandate is

best known as the "one person, one vote" principle.) As a result, reapportionments have routinely occurred in all states following each federal census. See each state for more information.

5. In some instances this information is not complete. Where members' affiliations could not be determined, the listing will show only the total number of members followed by a question mark. In some instances the information shows only the majority party.

An x indicates the town(s) or county (counties) did not elect one or more members. This was primarily found in the New England states.

GENERAL SOURCES

Although sources differ from state to state, some sources were used for nearly every state; these sources are listed here rather than being repeated in each state's chapter. In a few instances they are listed in a state's "sources" section to clarify matters. But where no source is listed for a state for a given time period, the reader can assume that the applicable source(s) listed below were used: *Tribune/Whig Almanac* 1838–1914, *Evening Journal Almanac,* 1859–92, 1895, 1896; *World Almanac,* 1868–1876, 1884–1912, 1950–1971; *Daily News Almanac,* 1885–1935; *New York State Legislative Manual* 1925–1950; *Book of the States,* 1938 —1952; secretaries of state (or other applicable sources of state election returns) 1972–1996; state legislative affiliation, National Conference of State Legislatures, 1998 —(Internet website).

Abbreviations

A	American	Csts	Constitutionalists
Ab	Abolitionist	Ct	Constitution
A Cu	Anti-Caucus	CU	Constitutional Union
Ad	Administration	Cv	Conserver
AdD	Administration Democrat	D	Democratic
af	anti-federalist	DI	Democratic Independent
A-J	Anti-Jackson	DD	Douglas Democrat
All	Alliance	DPg	Democratic Progressive
A-L	Anti-Lecompton Democrat	D-R	Democratic-Republican
A-M	Anti-Masonic	F	Federalist
AML	Anti Maine Law	f	Federalist (New York only, 1788–1789; supported ratification of the federal constitution. Opposed to anti-federalists [af].)
AMn	Anti Monopoly		
Anti-KN	Anti-Know Nothing		
ao	all others		
A-R	Anti Rent		
A-TrD	Anti Trust Democrat		
AW	American Whig	FA	Farmers Alliance
Bk	Bucktail	FD	Free Democrat
BkD	Breckinridge Democrat	FL	Farmer Labor
Bu	Burrite	Fm	Farmers
C	Conservative	FS	Free Soil
Cit	Citizens	FS-D	Free Soil-Democrat
CitU	Citizens Union	Fus	Fusion
Cl	Clintonian	FusD	Fusion Democrat
CLU	Central Labor Union	G	Greenback
Co	Coalition	GL	Greenback Labor

G-R	Greenback-Republication	Nat	Nationalist
I	Independent	n ch	no choice
ICit	Independent Citizens	NCt	New Court
ID	Independent Democrat	ND	National Democrat
IL	Independence League	NP	Non Partisan
In	Independence	NPty	No Party
Ip	Independent Prohibition	NR	National Republican
IPg	Independent Progressive	OCt	Old Court
		OLW	Old Line Whig
IR	Independent Republican	Opp	Opposition
		OSR	Old School Republican
I-Sil	Independent Silver	oth	others
IVA	Independent Voters Association	P	Prohibition
		Pe	Peoples'
IW	Independent Whig	Pe&All	People's and Alliance
J	Jacksonian	Pg	Progressive
(J)D	(Jacksonian) Democrat*	PgCo	Progressive Coalition
		PgD	Progressive Democrat
K	Keystone	PgR	Progressive Republican
L	Lecompton Democrat	PO	Public Ownership
Lab	Labor	Pop	Populist
LabR	Labor Republican	PR	Prohibition Republican
Lbt	Libertarian		
Lew	Lewisite	Q	Quid
Lib	Liberal	R	Republican
LI	Liberal Independent	Rad	Radical
L&O	Law & Order	Rdj	Readjuster
LR	Liberal Republican	Rf	Reform
Lr	Liberation	RfR	Reform Republican
Lty	Liberty	RMd	Republican Moderate
MOL	Municipal Ownership League	Rs	Roosevelt
		S	Socialist
		SD	Social Democrat

Over a period of time, the Jacksonians — i.e., those loyal to U.S. president Andrew Jackson — adopted the formal name "Democratic Party." But the name was not uniformly used in all states, and the terms "Jacksonian" and "Democrat" became interchangeable. Eventually, the former term fell away in favor of the latter. In this book, "(J)D" is used for the years in which both terms were employed.

Sil	Silver	**UL**	Union Labor
SilR	Silver Republican	**UMAB**	Upper Manhattan
SoR	Southern Rights		Apartment Building
StR	States Rights	**vac**	vacancy(ies)
StRD	States Rights	**W**	Whig
	Democrat	**WD**	War Democrat
STx	Single Tax	**w-iD**	write-in Democrat
T	Temperance	**w-iI**	write-in Independent
Tol	Toleration	**Wk**	Workingmen
U	Union	**x**	did not elect
UD	Union Democrat	**?**	unknown affiliation

Summary of Party Affiliation

Listed below is a summary of party affiliation by year. From 1834 through 1880 the summary is listed annually; thereafter, bi-annually. Through 1900 two sets of statistics are listed for the Legislatures columns: the overall total and then, in parentheses and italics, those legislators elected that year. The data in parentheses ceases after 1900 because relatively few legislatures were elected in odd numbered years. For the Senates and Houses columns only the overall totals are listed.

Election of	Legislatures				Senates				Houses			
	D	W	oth[1]	Ex[3]	D	W	oth[2]	Ex[3]	D	W	oth[2]	Ex[3]
1834	6 (6)	6 (5)	5 (5)	7?[3]	8	8	0	7?[3]	6	8	3	7?[3]
1835	7 (7)	7 (4)	6 (6)	7?	10	7	2	5?	7	9	2	7?
1836	9 (9)	6 (5)	8 (8)	3?	11	9	3	3?	13	8	1	4?
1837	9 (6)	10 (8)	6 (5)	1?	10	13	1	2?	11	11	2	2?
1838	9 (7)	11 (10)	5	1?	11	12	2	1?	10	14	1	1?
1839	11 (8)	10 (8)	4	1?	12	11	2	1?	12	12	1	1?
1840	7 (5)	14 (13)	5	1?	10	14	1	1?	7	18		1?
1841	11 (7)	8 (7)	7 (5)	1?	13	10	2	1?	14	11		1?
1842	14 (13)	5 (5)	6 (1)	1?	16	8	3	1?	17	7	1	1?
1843	15 (13)	7 (5)	3 (2)	1?	16	8	1	1?	16	8	1	1?
1844	10 (9)	10 (9)	5	1?	13	10	2	1?	10	15		1?
1845	13 (11)	9 (8)	4	2?	14	10	2	2?	15	11		2?
1846	13 (9)	9 (8)	5	2?	16	10	1	2?	13	13	1	2?
1847	9 (6)	14 (12)	4	2?	11	15	1	2?	10	17		2?
1848	12 (10)	11 (9)	5	2?	13	13	2	2?	12	14	2	2?
1849	13 (8)	8 (7)	7	2?	16	10	2	2?	14	10	4	2?
1850	16 (14)	5	8 (1)	2?	19	6	2	2?	19	6	4	2?
1851	14 (5)	4 (1)	11	2?	17	5	7	2?	16	6	7	2?
1852	13 (11)	6 (4)	10	2?	15	9	5	2?	18	8	3	2?
1853	21 (14)	4 (1)	4	3?	24	5		2?	21	7	1	2?

Election of	Legislatures					Senates					Houses				
	D	W	A	oth[1]	Ex[3]	D	W	A	oth	Ex[3]	D	W	A	oth	Ex[3]
1854	10 (6)	4 (3)	3	11(10)	3?	18	7	3	3	3?	11	10	2	5	3?

9

Election of	Legislatures					Senates					Houses			
	D	W	A	oth[1]	Ex[3]	D	W	A	oth	Ex[3]	D	W	A	oth	Ex[3]
1855	12 *(8)*	2 *(1)*	5 *(4)*	10 *(7)*	2?	14	4	6	4	3?	13	2	9	5	2?
1856	12 *(11)*	10 *(9)*	2 *(0)*	5 *(4)*	2?	12	12	2	2	3?	15	10	3	1	2?
1857	16 *(12)*	8 *(7)*	1	5 *(1)*	2?	17	9	2	1	3?	18	9	1	2	2?
1858	16 *(10)*	7 *(6)*	1	7	2?	17	9	2	2	3?	16	14	1		2?

Election of	Legislatures				Senates				Houses			
	D	R	oth[1]	Ex[3]	D	R	oth	Ex[3]	D	R	oth	Ex[3]
1859	15 *(8)*	14 *(13)*	2 *(1)*	3?	16	14	1	3?	15	15	1	3?
1860	12 *(5)*	15 *(12)*	3	4?	13	17		4?	13	16	1	4?
1861	3 *(1)*	14 *(10)*	6		4	15	3		5	15	3	
1862	4	13 *(12)*	6		4	16	3		5	13	5	
1863	4 *(1)*	17 *(13)*	3		4	18	2		4	17	3	
1864	1	20 *(16)*	4		2	20	3		1	21	2	
1865	1	22 *(16)*	3		1	22	3		1	24	1	
1866	3	25 *(21)*	1		3	25	1		3	25	1	
1867	6 *(4)*	21 *(13)*	2		6	22	1		8	21		
1868	6 *(3)*	25 *(23)*	3*(1)*		6	27	1		7	26	1	
1869	8 *(6)*	27 *(14)*	2		9	28			8	28	1	
1870	12 *(8)*	22 *(18)*	3		13	24			13	24		
1871	10 *(4)*	23 *(13)*	4		11	25	2		12	25		
1872	10 *(9)*	23 *(21)*	3	1?	11	24	1	1?	10	25	1	1?
1873	11 *(5)*	23 *(11)*	2	1?	11	25		1?	12	23	1	1?
1874	14 *(8)*	13 *(11)*	10		15	19	3		21	14	2	
1875	15 *(9)*	14 *(9)*	8 *(6)*		16	17	4		19	15	3	
1876	21*(17)*	11 *(9)*	6		24	12	2		21	14	3	
1877	20 *(9)*	13 *(7)*	5 *(4)*		22	14	2		20	17	1	
1878	19 *(13)*	16 *(15)*	3		20	17	1		19	16	3	
1879	16 *(4)*	20 *(10)*	2		17	20	1		16	20	2	
1880	16 *(12)*	20 *(17)*	2		16	21	1		17	21		
1882	17 *(13)*	16 *(14)*	5 *(4)*		17	19	2		20	17	1	
1884	18 *(13)*	18 *(17)*	2		18	19	1		18	19	1	
1886	15 *(11)*	20 *(18)*	3 *(2)*		18	20			15	23		
1888	17 *(13)*	20 *(18)*	1		17	20	1		18	20		
1890	19 *(13)*	14	11*(10)*		22	19	3		22	18	4	
1892	21 *(17)*	13 *(12)*	10 *(9)*		22	17	5		22	16	6	
1894	12 *(8)*	27 *(24)*	5		14	27	3		12	30	2	
1896	12 *(10)*	22 *(20)*	11		14	23	7		13	24	7	
1898	15 *(11)*	22 *(21)*	8		16	24	5		16	25	4	
1900	15 *(11)*	25	5 *(4)*		18	26	1		15	27	3	
1902	14	28	3		16	28	1		14	30	1	
1904	13	30	2		14	30	1		13	32		
1906	14	29	2		14	29	2		14	30	1	
1908	14	27	5		15	31			18	28		
1910	21	21	4		22	23	1		23	23		
1912	24	18	6		26	20	2		26	21	1	
1914	19	22	5		20	24	3		20	25	2	
1916	20	22	5		20	25	2		23	24		
1918	15	28	4		18	28	1		15	31	1	

Election of	*Legislatures* D	R	oth[1]	Ex[3]	*Senates* D	R	oth	Ex[3]	*Houses* D	R	oth	Ex[3]
1920	12	29	6		14	31	2		14	32	1	
1922	16	24	7		17	29	1		20	25	2	
1924	15	28	4		17	29	1		16	30	1	
1926	15	28	4		17	28	2		15	30	2	
1928	15	30	2		16	30	1		15	31	1	
1930	16	24	7		17	29	1		21	25	1	
1932	28	11	8		30	15	2		34	13		
1934	31	10	6		32	12	3		34	12	1	
1936	29	8	9		32	13	1		34	10	2	
1938	21	18	7		24	19	3		23	23		
1940	21	17	8		23	23			26	19	1	
1942	19	24	3		19	26	1		21	25		
1944	19	23	4		20	26			21	24		
1946	17	25	4		18	27	1		19	27		
1948	20	16	10		22	22	2		28	18		
1950	19	22	6		23	24			22	24	1	
1952	16	27	4		18	29			18	29		
1954	19	20	8		20	26	1		26	21		
1956	22	17	8		23	22	2		27	19	1	
1958	30	7	11		30	18			40	7	1	
1960	27	14	8		31	17	1		31	17	1	
1962	25	19	5		28	21			27	21	1	
1964	32	7	10		34	14	1		39	10		
1966	24	18	7		29	19	1		25	24		
1968	20	20	9		25	23	1		23	25	1	
1970	23	18	8		26	20	3		27	22		
1972	25	17	7		26	21	2		30	18	1	
1974	37	4	8		39	8	2		41	8		
1976	35	4	10		38	9	2		39	8	2	
1978	29	11	9		33	15	1		33	13	3	
1980	30	14	5		32	17			33	16		
1982	34	11	4		34	15			38	11		
1984	27	14	8		31	18			31	17	1	
1986	29	10	10		32	16	1		35	13	1	
1988	29	8	12		32	17			37	11	1	
1990	32	8	9		35	12	2		38	11		
1992	27	8	14		31	16	2		36	12	1	
1994	19	19	11		24	25			24	24	1	
1996	20	18	11		24	24	1		26	22	1	
1998	20	17	12		26	22	1		25	22	2	
2000	16	18	15		22	24	3		24	24	1	
2002	15	22	13		19	28	2		22	26	1	
2004	19	20	10		24	24	1		23	25	1	
2006	23	15	11		26	22	1		30	18	1	

[1]This column includes legislatures where no party had a majority in both houses or where another party had a majority.   [2]This column includes those bodies where there was a tie, or no party had a majority, or control was held by another party.   [3]Party affiliation cannot be determined in one or more cases.

Length of Term

At ten-year intervals, a summary of the length of term of members of the state legislatures:

Year	Senate One year	two years	three years	four years	House six months	one year	two years	four years	total states
1790	6	1	2	4	2	12			14[1]
1800	6	2	2	5	2	13	1		16
1810	6	3	2	5[2]	2	14	1		17
1820	7	3	5	8[2]	1	19	4		24
1830	7	3	5	8[2]	1	18	5		24
1840	9	3	4	9[3]	1	16	7		26
1850	6	8	4	13		16	15		31
1860	6	10	3	15		15	19		34
1870	5	10	2	19		12	25		37
1880	2	11	1	24		5	32	1	38
1890	2	12	1	29		4	38	2	44
1900	2	12	1	30		4	39	2	45
1910	2	12	1	31		4	39	3	46
1920		15	1	32		2	43	3	48
1930		14	1	33		2	42	4	48
1940		14	1	33		1	42	4	48
1950		14		34			43	4	48
1960		13		37			45	4	50
1970		12		38			45	4	50
1980		12		38			45	4	50
1990		12		38			45	4	50
2000		12		38			44	5	50

[1]Includes Vermont, which was not admitted until 1791 but had an unrecognized but functioning state government. [2]Includes Maryland, whose senators served a five-year term. [3]Includes Maryland, whose senators served a six-year term. Vermont had a unicameral legislature until 1836. Since 1936 Nebraska has had a unicameral legislature called the Senate.

ALABAMA

Statehood: President Monroe signed the Alabama enabling act on March 2, 1819. A constitutional convention met in Huntsville, the capital, and on August 2 completed work on the first constitution of the state and proclaimed it in effect. On September 20 and 21, 1819, the first legislature was elected. The legislature began its first session on October 25, 1819. Statehood was achieved on December 14, 1819. The capital was moved to Cahaba in 1820 and then to Tuscaloosa in 1826. Montgomery became the capital in 1847.

Term: Senators were elected for three years, one third annually, until 1845 when the term was increased to four years, one half every second year. Since 1902 the entire Senate has been elected at the same time. The House was elected annually until 1845 when the term was increased to two years. In 1902 the term was increased again, this time to four years.

Districts/Elections: Senators have been elected from single-member districts since statehood. But up until 1966, no county could be divided in the formation of a district. The House was apportioned among the counties of the state, with every county entitled to at least one. In counties entitled to more than one member all were elected at-large. Since 1966 all members of the legislature have been elected from single-member districts.

Membership/Size: The Senate originally had 17 members. This number increased to 20 by 1821 and 33 in 1834. There was no further increase until 1902 when two more members were added. The total of 35 has remained in effect ever since. The House originally has 51 members and increased to 62 members in 1821 and 100 in 1834. The 1901 constitution added five members effective the following year. Between the elections of 1906 and 1970 membership totaled 106. Since 1974 the total has been 105.

Reapportionment/Redistricting: Enacted in 1821, 1834, 1845, 1853, 1868, 1876, 1882 (House only) and 1892. After the constitutional convention reapportioned the state effective in 1902 there was no valid reapportionment until 1966. Reapportionments have occurred since in 1974, 1983, 1994 and 2002.

Election Dates: Initially the first Monday in August, changed to the first Tuesday after the first Monday in November, effective in 1870. The election of 1868 was held on February 1–5. Changed back to the original date in 1876 and finally back to the November date in 1902.

Constitutions: There have been six Alabama constitutions, written in 1819, 1861, 1865, 1868, 1875 and 1901.

Affiliations	Senate D / W / oth	House D / W / oth
1834	(33) ?	(100) ?
1835	?	?
1836	12 / 18 / 3 ?	44 / 46 / 10 ?
1837	?	45 / 33 / 22 ?
1838	19 / 9 / 5 ?	66 / 31 / 3 ?
1839	23 / 10	67 / 33
1840	20 / 13	54 / 46
1841	20 / 13	52 / 48
1842	21 / 12	67 / 33
1843	19 / 14	62 / 38
1844	D majority	D majority
1845	20 / 13	61 / 37 / 2 ?
1847	17 / 16	65 / 35[1]
1849	16 / 17	57 / 43
1851	/ / 22 U, 11 SoR	/ / 62 U, 38 SoR
1853	20 / 13	59 / 41
1855	20 / / 13 A	61 / / 39 A
1857	27 / / 6 A	84 / / 16 A
1859	27 / / 6 Opp	85 / / 15 Opp
	D / R / oth	D / R / oth
1865[2]	—	—
1868	1 / 32	3 / 97
1870	—[3]	65 / 35
1872	19 / 14[4]	54 / 46[4]
1874	20 / 13	60 / 40
1876	33 / 0	80 / 20
1878	31 / 2	91 / 3 / 4 ID, 2 G
1880	33 / 0	94 / 1 / 4 ID, 1 G
1882	31 / 2	77 / 5 / 17 I, 1 G
1884	30 / 3	93 / 7
1886	32 / 1	83 / 17
1888	32 / 1	92 / 8
1890	33 / 0	97 / 3
1892	26 / 0 / 7 Pop	61 / 1 / 38 Pop
1894	24 / 1 / 8 Pop	65 / 1 / 34 Pop

Affiliations	Senate D / R / oth	House D / R / oth
1896	22 / 2 / 9 Pop	74 / 3 / 23 Pop
1898	28 / 0 / 5 Pop	89 / 1 / 10 Pop
1900	32 / 0 / 1 Pop	92 /2 / 6 Pop
1902	(35) 35 / 0	(105) 103 / 2
1906	34 / 1	(106) 104 / 2
1910	34 / 1	103 / 3
1914	34 / 1	104 / 2
1918	34 / 1	100 / 5 / 1 ?
1922	35 / 0	105 / 1
1926	35 / 0	104 / 2
1930	35 / 0	103 / 3
1934	35 / 0	105 / 1
1938	35 / 0	105 / 1
1942	35 / 0	105 / 1
1946	35 / 0	105 / 1
1950	35 / 0	105 / 1
1954	35 / 0	105 / 1
1958	35 / 0	106 / 0
1962	35 / 0	104 / 2
1966	34 / 1	106 / 0
1970	35 / 0	104 / 2
1974	35 / 0	(105) 105 / 0
1978	35 / 0	101 / 4
1983[5]	29 / 3 / 3 I	90 / 12 / 3 I
1986	30 / 5	89 / 16
1990	28 / 7	82 / 23
1994	23 / 12	74 / 31
1998	23 / 12	69 / 36
2002	25 / 10	64 / 41
2006	23 / 12	62 / 43

NOTES

1. *Niles Register* lists 62 D and 38 W.

2. Most candidates ran without party labels; no totals found; election held on November 6, 1865. As a result of reconstruction there were no further legislative elections until 1868.

3. There was no election of senators.

4. This appears to be the number holding certificates of election. Both parties contested a number of seats in each house. As a result both parties initially organized the two houses separately. The protracted dispute was not settled until March when the Republicans organized both houses as several Republicans were seated in place of Democrats. The Senate briefly had, as a result of the changes, a 17–16 Republican majority. But the death of a Republican senator reversed this. The House was organized with a Republican margin of 51–49. See Fleming, *Civil War and Reconstruction*, pp. 755–761; *Tribune Almanac*, 1873, pp. 76–77; Rogers et al., *Alabama*, pp. 251–2; Wiggins, *The Scalawag in Alabama Politics*, pp. 85–86.

5. Due to litigation over reapportionment the election was delayed one year to the following November.

SOURCES

Niles Register September 10, 1836, *Jacksonville Republican*, September 7, 1837, *Selma Free Press,* September 15, 1838, *Niles Register,* August 29, 1840; for 1839 and 1840 from J. Mills Thornton III, *Politics and Power in a Slave Society Alabama, 1800–1860* (Baton Rouge: Louisiana State University Press, 1978), p. 36; *The* (Huntsville) *Democrat,* August 28, 1841; (Tuscaloosa) Independent Monitor, October 12, 1842; *Niles Register* September 2, 1843 , September 20, 1845, September, 28, 1847. The remaining pre–Civil War data came from Lewy Dorman, *Party Politics in Alabama from 1850 through 1860,* reprint ed. (Tuscaloosa: University of Alabama Press, 1995), p. 214. The 1868 data comes from William W. Rogers et al., *Alabama: The History of a Deep South State* (Tuscaloosa: University of Alabama Press, 1994), pp. 249–50. Walter Fleming, *Civil War and Reconstruction in Alabama,* reprint ed. (New York: Columbia University Press, 1905). *Weekly* (Montgomery) *Advertiser,* August 12, 1898, August 31, 1900. Also for 1906 and 1910, data was obtained from the biographies in the *Official and Statistical Register* as well as the *Birmingham Times,* November 23, 1906, November 25, 1910.

ALASKA

Statehood: An enabling act was signed by President Eisenhower on July 7, 1958. A constitutional convention meeting in Juneau had previously written a document and completed its work on February 5, 1956. The voters approved the constitution on April 24, 1956. By the terms of the enabling act a second vote was required to meet the conditions of statehood. On August 26, 1958, the voters approved the document again along with the terms of statehood, by a vote of 40,452 to 8,010. The first legislature was elected on November 25, 1958. Alaska became a state on January 3, 1959. The capital has always been Juneau.

Term: Senators have been elected since statehood for four years; terms overlap, with one-half of the Senate elected every two years. All are elected at the same time when a new apportionment occurs. Representatives serve a term of two years.

Districts/Elections: Up until 1992 members of both houses were elected from single- and multi-member districts. Since then all members of both houses have been elected from single-member districts. Alaska has no unit of government comparable to the county or parish but basically consists of cities and boroughs (municipal government); the bulk of Alaska is unorganized territory governed by the state.

Membership/Size: There has been no change in the original size of the legislature; the Senate has 20 members, the House has 40 members.

Reapportionment/Redistricting: Enacted in 1962, 1966 (Senate), 1972, 1974, 1982, 1992 and 2002.

Election Date: Always the first Tuesday after the first Monday in November.

Constitutions: The constitution written in 1956 is in effect today.

Affiliations	Senate D / R / oth	House D / R / oth
1958	(20) 18 / 2	(40) 33 / 5 / 2 I
1960	13 / 7	20 / 18 / 2 I
1962	15 / 5	20 / 20
1964	17 / 3	30 / 10
1966	6 / 14	15 / 25
1968	9 / 11	22 / 18
1970	10 / 10	31 / 9
1972	9 / 11	21 / 19
1974	13 / 7	30 / 9 / 1 I
1976	12 / 8	24 / 15 / 1 I
1978	9 / 11	25 / 14 / 1 I
1980	11 / 9	22 / 16 / 2 Lbt
1982	9 / 11	19 / 21
1984	9 / 11	21 / 18 / 1 Lbt
1986	8 / 12	24 / 16
1988	8 / 12	22 / 18
1990	10 / 10	22 / 18
1992	9 / 10 / 1 I	20 / 18 / 2 I
1994	8 / 12	17 / 22 / 1 I
1996	7 / 13	16 / 24
1998	5 / 15	14 / 26
2000	6 / 14	13 / 27
2002	8 / 11 / 1 RMd	13 / 27
2004	8 / 12	14 / 26
2006	9 / 11	17 / 23

SOURCES

America Votes through 1970. Returns supplied by the state through 1996. Internet website of the National Conference of State Legislatures, 1998–.

ARIZONA

Statehood: An enabling act was signed by President Taft on June 20, 1910. A Constitutional Convention convened in Phoenix and met from October 10 to December 9, 1910. The constitution was approved 12,584 to 3,920 on February 9, 1911. However, President Taft vetoed the admissions bill because of objections to the document. A revised document was approved on December 12, 1911, by a vote of 14,963 to 1,980. Arizona became a state on February 14, 1912. The first legislature was elected on December 12, 1911. Phoenix has been the capital since 1887.

Term: Members of both houses have always been elected for two years.

Districts/Elections: The Senate was apportioned by county, each county entitled to a minimum of one seat. Effective in 1954 this was changed to create a body where each county had equal representation with two members. All members were elected countywide. The House was also apportioned by county with each county entitled to at least one member. All members elected countywide until 1922 when single-member districts were substituted. An amendment effective in 1922 changed the basis for apportionment from population to the number of votes cast in the preceding election for governor. Additional seats were apportioned to each county for every 1,500 votes cast for governor, raised to 2,520 in 1934 and 3,520 in 1954. All members were elected from single-member districts from counties entitled to two or more members.

Since the implementation of one person, one vote apportionment the legislature has been divided into districts, each electing one senator and two representatives.

Membership/Size: The Senate originally had 19 members; it increased to 28 in 1954 and 30 in 1966. The initial membership of the House was 35. As a result of an amendment basing reapportionment on the gubernatorial vote, the House total changed frequently (see below) before being reduced to its present size of 60 in 1966.

Reapportionment/Redistricting: The House was reapportioned in 1920, 1922, 1926, 1928, 1930, 1934, 1938, 1942, 1950, 1952, 1958 and both houses have been reapportioned in 1966, 1970, 1972, 1974, 1982, 1992 and 2002.

Election Date: Always the first Tuesday after the first Monday in November.

Constitutions: Only one constitution, written in 1910.

Affiliations	Senate D / R	House D / R
1911	(19) 15 / 4	(35) 31 / 4
1914	18 / 1	35 / 0
1916	14 / 5	31 / 4
1918	14 / 5	26 / 9
1920	9 / 10	(38) 20 / 18
1922	18 / 1	(47) 41 / 6
1924	17 / 2	41 / 6
1926	17 / 2	(52) 43 / 9
1928	17 / 2	(54) 37 / 17
1930	18 / 1	(64) 52 / 12
1932	19 / 0	(63) 59 / 4
1934	18 / 1	(51) 51 / 0
1936	19 / 0	50 / 1
1938	19 / 0	(52) 51 / 1
1940	19 / 0	(53) 53 / 0
1942	19 / 0	(58) 58 / 0
1944	19 / 0	57 / 1
1946	19 / 0	53 / 5
1948	19 / 0	(59) 52 / 7
1950	19 / 0	(71) 61 / 10
1952	15 / 4	(80) 50 / 30
1954	(28) 26 / 2	61 / 19
1956	26 / 2	57 / 23
1958	27 / 1	55 / 25
1960	24 / 4	52 / 28
1962	24 / 4	48 / 32
1964	26 / 2	45 / 35
1966	(30) 14 / 16	(60) 27 / 33
1968	13 / 17	26 / 34
1970	12 / 18	26 / 34
1972	12 / 18	22 / 38
1974	18 / 12	27 / 33
1976	16 / 14	22 / 38
1978	14 / 16	18 / 42
1980	14 / 16	17 / 43
1982	12 / 18	21 / 39
1984	12 / 18	22 / 38
1986	11 / 19	24 / 36
1988	13 / 17	26 / 34
1990	17 / 13	27 / 33
1992	12 / 18	25 / 35
1994	11 / 19	22 / 38
1996	12 / 18	22 / 38

Affiliations	Senate D / R	House D / R
1998	14 / 16	20 / 40
2000	15 / 15	24 / 36
2002	13 / 17	21 / 39
2004	12 / 18	22 / 38
2006	13 / 17	27 / 33

SOURCES

All data was obtained from the journals of the respective houses of the legislature as well as a compilation provided by the State Archives. Internet website: National Conference of State legislatures, 2000–.

ARKANSAS

Statehood: In August, 1835, the voters approved (1,942 to 908) a call for a convention to write a constitution. On October 23, 1835, a bill was enacted providing for the convening of a constitutional convention. Delegates were elected on December 14, 1835. The proposed constitution of Arkansas was completed on January 10, 1836. Statehood was achieved on June 15. The election of the first legislature occurred on August 1, 1836. The capital has always been Little Rock.

Term: Senators have always been elected for four-year terms; terms overlap so that one-half the Senate is elected every two years. Representatives have always been elected for a term of two years.

Districts/Elections: Senators for the most part were elected from single-member districts; there was one two-member district under the original constitution. Essentially no county could be divided into districts even where the county was entitled to more than one member.

The House was apportioned among the counties, each county entitled to a minimum of one member. All members were elected countywide. Since the one person, one vote reapportionment, all members have been elected from single-member districts.

Membership/Size: The Senate originally had 18 members and has been increased five times, reaching 35 members in 1902. The House had 54 members at its inception and reached its current size of 100 in 1892.

Reapportionment/Redistricting: Enacted in 1840, 1844, 1848 (Senate), 1850, 1852, 1856 (Senate), 1860 (House), 1868, 1874, 1902 (Senate) 1938, 1952, 1962, 1966, 1972, 1982, 1992, 2002.

Election Dates: Originally the first Monday in October. Changed to the first Monday in August in 1848. In 1870 the first Monday after the first Tuesday in November became election day, changed to the first Monday in September in 1876. In 1908 the date was changed to the second Monday in September and back to the November date in 1916.

Constitutions: There have been five constitutions in the state's history, written in 1836, 1861, 1864, 1868 and 1874.

Affiliations	*Senate* *D / W / oth*		*House* *D / W / oth*
1836	**(17)** 12 / 5[1]		**(54)** 35 / 18 / 1 ?[1]
1838	D majority		D majority
1840	**(21)** 16 / 5		**(64)** 42 / 22
1842	15 / 6		**(66)** 45 / 20 / 1 ?
1844	**(25)** 21 / 4		**(75)** 62 / 13
1846	22 / 3		52 / 23
1848	20 / 5		56 / 19
1850	21 / 4		50 / 25
1852	19 / 6		48 / 27
1854	17 / 8		57 / 15 / 3 I
1856	21 / / 2 A, 1 AW, 1 OLW		65 / / 9 A, 1 W
1858	20 / / 2 A, 3 oth[2]		D majority
1860	?		?
	D / R / oth		*D / R / oth*
1865[3]	—		—
1866	25 / 0		56 / 19
1868	**(26)** 1 / 21 / 4 ?		**(82)** 1 / 79 / 2 ?
1870	8 C / 18		29 C / 44 / 9 L
1872[4]	5 / 20		27 / 52 / 3 ?
1874	**(31)** 29 / 2		**(93)** 82 / 11
1876	29 / 2		75 / 17 / 1 OLW
1878	29 / 1 / 1 G		83 / 3 / 6 G, 1 ?
1880	30 / 0 / 1 GL		80 / 10 / 1 G
1882	28 / 1 / 2 GL		78 / 1 / 5 oth[5]
1884	**(32)** 31 / 1		**(95)** 80 / 15
1886	30 / 2		73 / 14 / 8 oth[6]
1888	30 / 2		69 / 11 / 15 UL
1890	29 / 1 / 2 UL		81 / 10 / 4 UL
1892	29 / 1 / 2 Pop		**(100)** 85 / 6 / 9 Pop
1894	31 / 1		88 / 3 / 9 Pop
1896	30 / 1 / 1 Pop		85 / 2 / 13 Pop
1898	32 / 0		98 / 2

Affiliations	*Senate* D / R / oth	*House* D / R / oth
1900	32 / 0	97 / 2 / 1 Pop
1902	(35) 35 / 0	100 / 0
1904	34 / 1	95 / 5
1906	34 / 1	96 / 4
1908	35 / 0	97 / 3
1910	34 / 1	95 / 5
1912	33 / 1 / 1 Pg	96 / 4
1914	35 / 0	97 / 3
1916	34 / 0 / 1 I	97 / 3
1918	35 / 0	95 / 5
1920	35 / 0	96 / 4
1922	35 / 0	96 / 4
1924	35 / 0	97 / 3
1926	35 / 0	96 / 4
1928	35 / 0	98 / 2
1930	35 / 0	99 / 1
1932	35 / 0	100 / 0
1934	35 / 0	100 / 0
1936	35 / 0	98 / 2
1938	35 / 0	98 / 2
1940	35 / 0	98 / 2
1942	35 / 0	98 / 2
1944	35 / 0	98 / 2
1946	35 / 0	96 / 3 / 1 I
1948	35 / 0	98 / 2
1950	35 / 0	98 / 2
1952	35 / 0	97 / 3
1954	35 / 0	97 / 3
1956	35 / 0	98 / 2
1958	35 / 0	100 / 0
1960	35 / 0	99 / 1
1962	35 / 0	99 / 0 / 1 I
1964	35 / 0	99 / 1
1966	35 / 0	98 / 2
1968	35 / 0	98 / 2
1970	34 / 1	98 / 2
1972	34 / 1	99 / 1
1974	34 / 1	97 / 3
1976	34 / 1	96 / 4
1978	35 / 0	94 / 6
1980	34 / 1	94 / 6
1982	32 / 3	93 / 7
1984	31 / 4	91 / 9
1986	31 / 4	91 / 9
1988	31 / 4	88 / 11 / 1 I
1990	31 / 4	88 / 11 / 1 I
1992	30 / 5	89 / 10 / 1 I
1994	28 / 7	88 / 12

Affiliations	Senate D / R / oth	House D / R / oth
1996	28 / 6 / 1 vac	86 / 14
1998	29 / 6	76 / 24
2000	27 / 8	72 / 28
2002	27 / 8	70 / 30
2004	27 / 8	72 / 28
2006	27 / 8	75 / 25

NOTES

1. Whigs and those unknown.
2. 1 OSD, 1 StRD., 1 OLW
3. Most candidates ran without party labels.
4. 39 members of the legislature, mainly Republicans, resigned after the first session of the legislature adjourned on April 25, 1873. As a result of special elections the Democrats won control of the next session.
5. 2 GL, 2 IR, 1 ID
6. 4 I, 3 Wheeler, 1 G

SOURCES

Much of the pre–Civil War information was obtained from Margaret Ross, *Arkansas Gazette: The Early Years, 1819–1866* (Little Rock: Arkansas Gazette Foundation, 1966). "First State Election in Arkansas 1836," *Arkansas Historical Quarterly*, 1961, p. 142. Brian Walton, "Arkansas Politics During the Compromise Crisis 1848–1852," *Arkansas Historical Quarterly*, Vol. 36, 1977. The period 1865–1872 was taken from Thomas S. Staples, *Reconstruction in Arkansas 1862–1874*, reprint edition, Gloucester: Peter Smith, 1964). D. A. Stokes, Sharon Priest, Secretary of State, *Historical Report of the Arkansas Secretary of State*, 1998, Little Rock. (Little Rock) *Arkansas Gazette*, August 23, 1836, November 4, 1840, November 9, 1842, November 27, 1844, August 30, 1850, October 29, 1852; (Little Rock) *Arkansas True Democrat*, December 30, 1856, February 9, 1859, *Arkansas Gazette*, November 19, 1870, January 19, 31, 1877; *Arkansas True Democrat* January 29, February 8, 1879; *Arkansas Gazette*, November 22, 1916, January 8, 1917, November 22, 1922; Arkansas History Commission for 1918 and 1946.

CALIFORNIA

Statehood: On June 3, 1849, the military governor of California, Bennet Riley, issued a call for a convention to establish government of the area. The delegates were elected on August 1, 1849, and convened at Monterey on September 3. They wrote a constitution and adjourned on October 11. The document was approved by popular vote on November 13, by a vote of 12,872 to 811, and on the same day the first legislature was elected. Meeting in San Jose, the first legislature convened on December 15, but statehood was not achieved until September 1, 1850. The legislature met successively at San Jose (1849–51), Vallejo (1852–3) and Benecia (1854) until establishing Sacramento as the permanent capital in 1854. They had also had met in Sacramento in 1852.

Term: Senators were initially elected for a term of two years, with overlapping terms so that half the body was elected annually. Effective in 1863 the term was increased to four years, half the body every two years. Assemblymen were elected annually until 1863 when term was increased to two years.

Districts/Elections: Senators were elected from both single- and multi-member districts made up of one or more whole counties. In 1883 all senators were elected from single-member districts, but under a plan adopted in 1926 representation was radically changed. No county could elect more than one senator and no district could contain more than three counties. Assemblymen were also elected from single- and multi-member districts made up of one or more whole counties. In 1874 San Francisco was divided into five four-member districts. Since 1884 all members have been elected from single-member districts. However, only counties entitled to two or more members could be divided. Under one person, one vote reapportionment these restrictions disappeared in 1966.

Membership/Size: The Senate originally consisted of 16 members. There were seven early changes producing a body of 40 members in 1861. The Assembly started off with 36 members and there were two early increases to 80 members in 1853.

Reapportionment/Redistricting: Enacted in 1851,1852, 1853, 1854, 1855, 1856, 1857, 1861, 1862, 1863, 1866, 1874, 1884, 1892, 1902, 1912, 1930, 1932, 1942, 1952, 1962, 1966, 1972, 1974, 1982, 1992 and 2002.

Election Dates: First Monday in October in 1850, changed to the first Wednesday in September in 1851, and finally, in 1880, to the first Tuesday after the first Monday in November.

Constitutions: There have been two constitutions in state history: 1849 and 1879.

Affiliations	Senate D / W / oth	House D / W / oth
1849[1]	(16) —	(36) —
1850	10 / 4 / 2 I	17 / 18 / 1 I
1851	26 / 2	(63) 41 / 21 / 1 I
1852	(27) 20 / 7	41 / 22
1853	(34) 26 / 8	(80) 68 / 12
1854	(33) 26 / 7	42 / 36 / 2 I
1855	16 / 1 / 16 A	23 / / 56 A, 1 I
1856	19 / / 11 A, 3 R	61 / / 8 A, 11 R
	D / R / oth	D / R / oth
1857	(35) 27 / 5 / 3 A	66 / 9 / 4 A, 1 I
1858[2]	30 / 4 / 1 I	72 / 8
1859[3]	33 / 2	78 / 2
1860[4]	(36) 30 / 6	60 / 19 / 1 CU
1861[5]	(40) 23 / 17	41 / 39
1862[6]	9 / 31	17 / 63
1863	5 / 35	10 / 70
1865	9 / 31	19 / 61
1867	19 / 21	52 / 28
1869	26 / 12 / 2 I	67 / 10 / 3 I
1871	22 / 17 / 1 I	25 / 54 / 1 I
1873	14 / 18 / 8 I	27 / 19 / 34 I
1875	20 / 6 / 11 I, 3 ID	64 / 12 / 4 I
1877	27 / 10 / 2 I, 1 Wk	55 / 24 / 1 Wk
1879	7 / 23 / 10 Wk	18 / 46 / 16 Wk
1880	7 / 23 / 10 Wk	33 / 42 / 4 Wk, 1 G
1882	32 / 8	61 / 19
1884	20 / 20	20 / 60
1886	26 / 14	39 / 41
1888	22 / 18	42 / 38
1890	12 / 28	19 / 60 / 1 A
1892	18 / 22	45 / 31 / 2 Pe, 2 I
1894	15 / 25	14 / 64 / 2 Pe
1896	12 / 28	8 / 47 / 16 Fus, 9 Pop
1898	14 / 26	20 / 59 / 1 I
1900	6 / 34	20 / 60
1902	7 / 33	19 / 60 / 1 UL
1904	3 / 33 / 4 UL	4 / 71 / 4 UL, 1 vac
1906	6 / 33 / 1 NP	6 / 73 / 1 IL
1908	9 / 30 / 1 NP	20 / 60
1910	8 / 32	11 / 69
1912	10 / 30	25 / 54 / 1 S
1914	10 / 21 / 9 Pg	15 / 33 / 28 Pg, 3 S, 1 P
1916	11 / 20 / 8 Pg, 1 I	9 / 69 / 1 P, 1 Pg
1918	7 / 32 / 1 I	10 / 70
1920	7 / 33	7 / 73
1922	3 / 36 / 1 I	4 / 76

Affiliations	Senate D / R / oth	House D / R / oth
1924	3 / 37	5 / 75
1926	5 / 35	6 / 74
1928	5 / 35	7 / 71 / 2 I
1930	4 / 36	7 / 73
1932	5 / 35	25 / 55
1934	8 / 31 / 1 I	37 / 42 / 1 I
1936	15 / 25	47 / 33
1938	19 / 21	44 / 36
1940	16 / 24	42 / 38
1942	16 / 24	36 / 44
1944	13 / 27	37 / 42 / 1 I
1946	13 / 27	32 / 48
1948	14 / 26	35 / 45
1950	12 / 28	33 / 47
1952	11 / 29	27 / 53
1954	18 / 22	33 / 47
1956	20 / 20	38 / 42
1958	26 / 14	47 / 33
1960	30 / 10	47 / 33
1962	27 / 13	52 / 28
1964	27 / 13	49 / 31
1966	21 / 19	42 / 38
1968	20 / 20	39 / 41
1970	21 / 19	43 / 37
1972	20 / 20	51 / 29
1974	25 / 15	55 / 25
1976	28 / 12	57 / 23
1978	26 / 14	50 / 30
1980	26 / 14	47 / 33
1982	25 / 15	48 / 32
1984	25 / 15	47 / 33
1986	24 / 15 / 1 I	44 / 36
1988	24 / 15 / 1 I	47 / 33
1990	25 / 14 / 1 I	46 / 34
1992	23 / 14 / 2 I, 1 vac	48 / 32
1994	21 / 17 / 2 I	39 / 40 / 1 I
1996	24 / 15 / 1 I	44 / 36
1998	25 / 15	48 / 32
2000	26 / 14	50 / 30
2002	26 / 14	48 / 32
2004	25 / 15	48 / 32
2006	25 / 15	48 / 32

NOTES

1. Chosen without party labels.
2. Divided Democrats, as follows: *Senate*: L-25, A-L5; *Assembly*: L-56, A-L 16
3. Divided Democrats, as follows: *Senate*: L-28, A-L5; *Assembly*: L-70 A-L 8

4. Divided Democrats, as follows: *Senate*: DD-20, BkD-10; *Assembly*: DD-37, BkD-23

5. Divided Democrats, as follows: *Senate*: UD-16, BkD-7; *Assembly*: UD-32, BkD-9

6. Divided Democrats, as follows: *Senate*: UD-5, BkD-4; *Assembly*: UD-10, BkD-7

SOURCE

All data through the election of 1964 was obtained from Don A. Allen Sr., *Legislative Sourcebook the California Legislature and Reapportionment 1849–1965* (Assembly of the State of California: n.d.).

COLORADO

Statehood: An enabling act was signed by President Grant on March 3, 1875, calling for the election of a constitutional convention. The delegates convened in Denver on December 20, 1875. The constitution of the state of Colorado was written in March 1876 and approved by popular vote (15,443 to 4,062) on July 1. The state capital has always been Denver. Statehood was achieved on August 1, 1876, and election of the first legislature occurred on October 3, 1876.

Term: Senators have been elected for a term of four years, with overlapping terms (one-half elected every two years). The House of Representatives is elected for a term of two years.

Districts/Elections: Members of the Senate were elected from both single- and multi-member districts that included one or more counties, but counties could not be divided in the creation of districts, nor could part of one county be attached to another county to form a district. House members were chosen from similar-type districts. This remained the basis for apportionment until the U.S. Supreme Court decision in *Reynolds v. Sims* which mandated equal population districts. Ever since then legislators have been elected from single-member districts.

Membership/Size: In 1892 the Senate was increased from 26 to 35 members and the House from 49 to 65 members. It was the only time in state history that the size of the legislature has been changed.

Reapportionments/Redistricting: Occurred in 1882, 1892, 1902, 1914, 1932 (by initiative), 1953, 1962 (by initiative), 1964, 1966, 1972, 1982, 1992 and 2002.

Constitution: The original constitution of 1876 is still in effect today.

Affiliations	Senate D / R / oth	House D / R / oth
1876	(26) 7 / 19	(49) 18 / 31
1878	7 / 19	12 / 36 / 1 G
1880	3 / 23	13 / 36
1882	9 / 17	13 / 36
1884	7 / 19	13 / 35 / 1 ?
1886	8 / 18	23 / 25 / 1 I
1888	6 / 20	6 / 43
1890	10 / 16	17 / 32
1892	(35) 8 / 15 / 12 Pop	(65) 5 / 33 / 27 Pop
1894	1 / 16 / 18 Pop	10 / 41 / 14 Pop
1896	4 / 16 / 14 Pop, 1 Sil	20 / 11 / 33 Pop, 1 Sil
1898	9 / 2 / 15 Sil, 9 Pop	21 / 6 / 20 Pop, 16 Sil
1900	19 / 2 / 14 oth[1]	37 / 7 / 21 oth[1]
1902	24 / 11	29 / 36
1904	16 / 19	29 / 36
1906	11 / 24	16 / 49
1908	20 / 15	53 / 12
1910	26 / 9	40 / 25
1912	24 / 11	48 / 17
1914	17 / 18	29 / 36
1916	18 / 17	45 / 20
1918	21 / 14	24 / 41
1920	11 / 24	7 / 58
1922	11 / 23 / 1 vac	32 / 33
1924	14 / 21	12 / 53
1926	15 / 20	22 / 43
1928	11 / 24	19 / 46
1930	13 / 22	34 / 31
1932	26 / 9	54 / 11
1934	29 / 6	50 / 15
1936	29 / 6	50 / 15
1938	23 / 12	28 / 37
1940	18 / 17	28 / 37
1942	12 / 23	10 / 55
1944	8 / 27	19 / 46
1946	8 / 27	19 / 46
1948	16 / 19	39 / 26
1950	15 / 20	18 / 47
1952	12 / 23	20 / 45
1954	15 / 20	29 / 36
1956	21 / 14	38 / 27
1958	22 / 13	44 / 21

Affiliations	*Senate*	*House*
	D / R / oth	*D / R / oth*
1960	19 / 16	33 / 32
1962	15 / 20	24 / 41
1964	15 / 20	42 / 23
1966	15 / 20	28 / 37
1968	11 / 24	27 / 38
1970	14 / 21	27 / 38
1972	13 / 22	28 / 37
1974	16 / 19	39 / 26
1976	17 / 18	30 / 35
1978	13 / 22	27 / 38
1980	13 / 22	26 / 39
1982	13 / 22	25 / 40
1984	11 / 24	17 / 48
1986	10 / 25	24 / 41
1988	11 / 24	25 / 40
1990	12 / 23	27 / 38
1992	16 / 19	31 / 34
1994	16 / 19	24 / 41
1996	15 / 20	24 / 41
1998	14 / 21	26 / 39
2000	18 / 17	27 / 38
2002	17 / 18	28 / 37
2004	18 / 17	33 / 32
2006	20 / 15	39 / 26

NOTES

1. 7Pop, 6SilR, 1STx in the Senate and 13 Pop and 8 SilR in the House.

SOURCE

For the elections of 1884, 1900, 1918, 1920, 1922, the State Archives provided a list of members taken from the journals of the legislature.

CONNECTICUT

Constitutional Origins: Connecticut was one of two self-governing colonies; all officials were directly elected. On October 2, 1776, the legislature made the existing colonial charter the instrument of state government. Elections continued as before, and in April 1777 the state conducted its first elections under the charter as the governing document of the state of Connecticut. The state had two capitals, Hartford and New Haven. The legislature alternated sessions between the two cities until 1875 when a constitutional amendment made Hartford the sole capital.

Term: The upper house — called the Assistants until 1819, when it was changed to the Senate — served a one-year term. This was increased to two years in 1876, with one-half the body elected annually. Beginning in 1886 all senators were elected at the same time. The lower house, the Assembly, was elected for six months until 1819 when the term was made one year. It became two years in 1886.

District/Elections: The assistants were elected statewide under the charter, and this was continued until 1830 when the members were chosen from single-member districts. This has been the case ever since. The town was the basis for representation in the Assembly until 1966. All towns were entitled to one member, but no town, under a variety of formulas, could have more than two. Towns entitled to two members elected both at large. With the advent of population-based reapportionment the Assembly since 1966 has been elected from single-member districts.

Membership/Size: The Senate has had relatively few increases in its number. Its original membership (since its beginnings as the Assistants) was 12 and this was first increased to 21 in 1830, in 1881 to 24, and to 35 in 1904; since 1942 it has had 36 members. The Assembly, on the other hand, changed frequently as towns were created and others met the qualification for a second representative. In addition there are instances where towns failed to send a member to the Assembly for a given session. The body reached 294 in 1960 before one person, one vote apportionment led to a reduction in its size: 177 in 1968, and since 1972, 151 members.

Reapportionment/Redistricting: Since the Senate was elected at large no reapportionment occurred until the introduction of districts in 1830. Subsequent reapportionments occurred in 1881, 1904, and 1942.[1] All reapportionments of the House have only occurred since the *Reynolds v. Sims* decision. As a consequence there was redistricting of both houses in 1966, 1972, 1982, 1992 and 2002.

Election Dates: Until 1819 elections were held twice a year, the second Thursday in April and the third Monday in September. Beginning with 1819 only the former date was used. In 1836 elections were changed to the first Monday in April. In 1876 the date was changed to its present time, the first Tuesday after the first Monday in November.

Constitutions: In addition to the Charter there have been two constitutions: 1818 and 1965.

Affiliations	*Senate* *D-R / F*	*House* *D-R / F / oth*
1799 (April)	—	F majority[2]
(September)	—	F majority
1800 (April)	0 / 12	**(189)** F majority
(September)	—	27 / 162
1801 (April)	0 / 12	36 / 153
(September)	—	40 / 149
1802 (April)	0 / 12	**(191)** 55 / 136
(September)	—	66 / 125
1803 (April)	0 / 12	**(193)** 48 / 145
(September)	—	63 / 130
1804 (April)	0 / 12	**(195)** 78 / 117
(September)	—	63 / 132
1805 (April)	0 / 12	68 / 127
(September)	—	61 / 134
1806 (April)	0 / 12	72 / 123
(September)	—	**(197)** 61 / 136
1807 (April)	0 / 12	63 / 131 / 3 vac
(September)	—	**(198)** 76 / 121 / 1 vac
1808 (April)	0 / 12	61 / 136 / 1 vac
(September)	—	**(199)** 54 / 144 / 1 vac
1809 (April)	0 / 12	43 / 156
(September)	—	50 / 148 / 1 vac
1810 (April)	0 / 12	56 / 143
(September)	—	65 / 134
1811 (April)	0 / 12	60 / 139
(September)	—	F majority
1812 (April)	0 / 12	52 / 147
(September)	—	38 / 161
1813 (April)	0 / 12	**(200)** 37 / 163
(September)	—	F majority[2]
1814 (April)	0 / 12	F majority
(September)	—	39 / 161
1815 (April)	0 / 12	60 / 140
(September)	—	57 / 143

	Tol[3] / F	*Tol / F*
1816 (April)	0 / 12	**(201)** 85 / 116
(September)	—	90 / 111
1817 (April)	0 / 12	105 / 96
(September)	—	128 / 73
1818 (April)	7 / 5	129 / 72
(September)	—	115 / 86

	Senate	
1819	12 / 0	119 / 82
1820	12 / 0	**(202)** 129 / 73

Affiliations	*Senate* *Tol[3] / F*	*House* *Tol / F*
1821	12 / 0	Tol majority
1822	12 / 0	?
1823	12 / 0	?
1824	12 / 0	?
	(J)D / NR / oth	*(J)D / NR / oth*
1828	—	—
1829	—	—
1830	**(21)** —	—
1831	—	—
1832	—	—
1833	17 / 4	129 / 35 / 24 A-M, 14 ?
1834	5 / 16	80 / 82 / 30 A-M, 9 NPty
	D / W / oth	*D / W / oth*
1835	16 / 5	126 / 80
1836	17 / 4	130 / 71
1837	14 / 7	110 / 79
1838	1 / 20	42 / 158 / 6 Cv
1839	8 / 13	87 / 107 / 2 Cv
1840	3 / 18	63 / 143 / 8 ?
1841	1 / 20	57 / 116 / 41 vac
1842	14 / 7	124 / 55
1843	16 / 5	113 / 75
1844	6 / 15	83 / 104
1845	5 / 16	77 / 112 / 1 Lty
1846	11 / 10	116 / 103 / 1 Lty
1847	8 / 13	100 / 119 / 1 I
1848	8 / 13	102 / 117 / 1 Lty
1849	11 / 6 / 4 FS	95 / 108 / 19 FS
1850	12 / 6 / 3 FS	111 / 97 / 14 FS
1851	8 / 12 /1 FS	110 / 107 / 5 FS, 2I
1852	14 / 6 / 1 FS	130 / 85 / 7 FS, 3I
1853	15 / 6	144 / 77 / 4 FS, 2 x
1854	5 / 16	89 / 119 / 10 FS, 1 I
1855	4 / /16 A, 1 W	65 / / 163 ao
1856	8 / / 13 Opp	105 / / 127 Opp
	D / R / oth	*D / R / oth*
1857	6 / 15	93 / 139
1858	6 / 15	88 / 146
1859	8 / 13	109 / 125
1860	7 / 14	88 / 147
1861	8 / 13	86 / 149
1862	0 / 21	57 / 187
1863	7 / 14	96 / 139 / 1 I, 1 ?

Affiliations	*Senate* D / R / oth	*House* D / R / oth
1864	3 / 18	79 / 155
1865	0 / 21	77 / 158
1866	8 / 13	94 / 141
1867	10 / 11	(238) 111 / 127
1868	9 / 12	109 / 129
1869	7 / 14	106 / 132
1870	10 / 11	(239) 109 / 127 / 3 I
1871	8 / 13	110 / 129
1872	6 / 15	(241) 111 / 130
1873	7 / 14	132 / 108 / 1 I
1874	17 / 4	(242) 99 / 143
1875	15 / 6	(245) 137 / 107 / 1 I
1876 (April)	18 / 3	(246) 161 / 85
(November)	10 / 11	105 / 141
1877	8 / 13	109 / 137
1878	7 / 14	99 / 143 / 1 G, 1 I, 2 x
1879	5 / 16	83 / 162 / 1 G
1880	5 / 16	(248) 80 / 166 / 1 G, 1 I
1881	(24) 7 / 17	(249) 89 / 160
1882	11 / 13	110 / 139
1883	9 / 15	96 / 153
1884	7 / 17	100 / 148 / 1 G
1885	11 / 13	116 / 131 / 2 I
1886	10 / 14	109 / 137 / 2 I, 1 vac
1888	7 / 17	96 / 152 / 1 I
1890	17 / 7	(251) 116 / 133 / 1 I, 1 vac
1892	12 / 12	113 / 137 / 1 P
1894	1 / 23	46 / 204 / 1 Pop
1896	0 / 24	(252) 29 / 218 / 5 ND
1898	4 / 20	69 / 180 / 3 ND
1900	2 / 22	(255) 52 / 201 / 1 ND, 1 I
1902	6 / 18	68 / 187
1904	(35) 6 / 29	36 / 219
1906	8 / 27	66 / 189
1908	4 / 31	47 / 208
1910	14 / 21	(258) 98 / 160
1912	21 / 14	120 / 130 / 6 Pg, 2 PgR
1914	5 / 30	60 / 196 / 1 Pg, 1 I
1916	10 / 25	64 / 194
1918	11 / 24	69 / 189
1920	1 / 34	(262) 13 / 248 / 1 I
1922	8 / 27	52 / 210
1924	2 / 33	23 / 239
1926	1 / 34	24 / 238
1928	13 / 22	42 / 220
1930	15 / 20	(267) 85 / 182
1932	18 / 17	72 / 195
1934	17 / 15 / 3 S	85 / 180 / 2 S

Affiliations	Senate D / R / oth	House D / R / oth
1936	26 / 9	100 / 167
1938	17 / 16 / 2 S	63 / 202 / 2 S
1940	21 / 14	(272) 87 / 185
1942	(36) 15 / 21	70 / 202
1944	21 / 15	76 / 196
1946	8 / 28	45 / 227
1948	23 / 13	92 / 180
1950	19 / 17	(277) 87 / 190
1952	14 / 22	(279) 58 / 221
1954	20 / 16	92 / 184 / 3 I
1956	5 / 31	30 / 249
1958	29 / 7	141 / 138
1960	24 / 12	(294) 118 / 176
1962	23 / 13	111 / 183
1964[4]	—	—
1966	25 / 11	(177) 117 / 60
1968	24 / 12	110 / 67
1970	19 / 17	99 / 78
1972	13 / 23	(151) 58 / 93
1974	29 / 7	118 / 33
1976	22 / 14	93 / 58
1978	26 / 10	103 / 48
1980	23 / 13	83 / 68
1982	23 / 13	89 / 62
1984	12 / 24	66 / 85
1986	25 / 11	91 / 60
1988	23 / 13	88 / 63
1990	19 / 17	89 / 62
1992	20 / 16	87 / 64
1994	17 / 19	90 / 61
1996	19 / 17	97 / 54
1998	19 / 17	96 / 55
2000	21 / 15	100 / 51
2002	21 / 15	94 / 57
2004	24 / 12	99 / 52
2006	24 / 12	106 / 45

NOTES

1. Limited to creating one additional district from an existing district.

2. Purcell citing usually the (Connecticut) *Courant* and/or the *American Mercury* gives a total for the Democratic-Republicans without giving the Federalist total, as follows: 1799 (April) 15 or 16, 1801 (1813) (Sept) D-R gained a few seats.

3. In the late winter of 1816 the Dem-Rep and Episcopalian leaders, previously Federalists, met to form a new political party that generally became known as the Toleration Party. This party for the next several years was the opposition to the Federalists, indeed eventually emerging as the only party by the early 1820s.

4. Due to litigation over reapportionment the courts cancelled the 1964 election and held over the previously elected legislature.

SOURCES

Research was done at the State Archives in Hartford. Most of the data through 1824 was provided by Philip Lampi citing several Connecticut newspapers, the most frequent were Hartford papers; *American Mercury, Connecticut Courant* and the *Connecticut Herald*. A significance source of party data was found in the (Connecticut) *Register & Manual,* published by the state since 1889 but privately published under a variety of titles back to 1799. This is probably the oldest publication of this type in the nation. The *Register* was used continuously for data since the 1840s. Several editions of the *Register* contain a summary of party affiliations back to 1886, about the time the state began publishing the *Register*. Also consulted were various political almanacs. Several other books containing data about Connecticut politics include Richard J. Purcell, *Connecticut in Transition: 1775–1818,* revised ed. Middletown: (Wesleyan University Press, 1963); Jarvis M. Morse, *A Neglected Period of Connecticut's History, 1818–1850* (New Haven: 1933), and Norman L. Stamps, *Political Parties in Connecticut, 1789–1818* (Ph.d. dissertation, Yale University, 1952). *The Niles Register*, April 24, 1841. (Concord) *Patriot,* April 20, 1835.

DELAWARE

Constitutional Origins: The first constitution of Delaware was written in August–September 1776 and was the first written by delegates specifically elected for that purpose. The initial elections were held in October of the same year. Then as now, the legislature met in Dover.

Term: The Legislative Council, as the upper house was originally called, was elected for a term of three years until 1832 when it was increased to four years, the present length of service. The Assembly — the name initially given to the other house — was elected annually until 1832 when the term became two years, which it has remained ever since. The legislative chambers took their present names, Senate and House of Representatives, in 1792.

Districts/Elections: Both houses were elected on a countywide basis until 1898, when all members were elected from single-member districts, which has been the case ever since. One-third of the Senate and all of the House was elected annually until 1832, when, as a result of an increase in the term of all members, half the Senate and all of the House was elected every second year; that has been the procedure ever since.

Membership/Size: The Council consisted of nine members, three from each county, until 1898 when that body was increased to 17, five per county plus two for the city of Wilmington. Since the one person, one vote ruling the Senate has been increased three times: in 1964 to 18, in 1968 to 19, and in 1972 to 21 members, the present number. The Assembly was a larger version of the Council, consisting of 21 members, seven from each county, until 1988 when it was increased to 35, ten per county plus five for Wilmington. There have been two increases in the size of the House: in 1968 to 39 and in 1972 to its present total of 41.

Reapportionment/Redistricting: Have been enacted in 1898 (by constitutional convention), 1964 (as a consequence of litigation), 1968 (as a consequence of litigation), 1972, 1982, 1992 and 2002.

There was no provision in the Delaware constitution for reapportionment. When the courts invalidated the relevant part of the constitution in 1964, statutes were enacted to carry out the process.

Election Dates: Initially the first Tuesday in October until 1832. Changed to the second Tuesday in November; however, beginning in 1848, in presidential years the first Tuesday after the first Monday in November. Starting in 1866 all elections were held on the later date.

Constitutions: There have been three: 1776, 1792 and 1896.

Addenda: Delaware was unique in two respects. First, its electoral system — county wide election for all legislators — remained in effect for 122 years (until 1898) with no real changes, except for the increase in member terms in 1832. Second, the first party system — Democratic-Republicans and Federalists — remained in effect longer than any other state, more than 30 years. In fact, the two parties' names continued to be used long after the Federalist Party disappeared in all other states. As late as the election of 1826 these two names were still used throughout the state. Only the necessity of adapting to the realities of the emerging second party system resulted in the end of the old names as generally the Federalist became supporters of John Quincy Adams and the Democratic-Republicans became identified with Andrew Jackson.

Affiliations	*Senate*	*House*
	D-R / F	*D-R / F*
1796	(9) F majority	(21) 7 / 14
1797	F majority	F majority
1798	F majority	F majority
1799	F majority	7 / 14

Affiliations	Senate D-R / F	House D-R / F
1800	3 / 6	7 / 14
1801	3 / 6	7 / 14
1802	3 / 6	7 / 14
1803	3 / 6	7 / 14
1804	3 / 6	7 / 14
1805	3 / 6	7 / 14
1806	3 / 6	7 / 14
1807	3 / 6	7 / 14
1808	3 / 6	7 / 14
1809	3 / 6	7 / 14
1810	3 / 6	7 / 14
1811	3 / 6	7 / 14
1812	3 / 6	7 / 14
1813	3 / 6	7 / 14
1814	3 / 6	7 / 14
1815	2 / 7	7 / 14
1816	2 / 7	7 / 14
1817	3 / 6	7 / 14
1818	3 / 6	7 / 14
1819	3 / 6	7 / 14
1820	3 / 6	7 / 14
1821	4 / 5	11 / 10
1822	5 / 4	13 / 8
1823	4 / 5	7 / 14
1824	4 / 5	8 / 13
1825	4 / 5	14 / 7
1826	5 / 4	8 / 13

	(J)D / NR / oth	(J)D / NR / oth
1827	3 / 5 / 1 ?	10 / 11
1828	4 / 5	7 / 14
1829	4 / 5	7 / 14
1830	2 / 7	5 / 16
1831	2 / 7	7 / 14
1832	2 / 7	7 / 14

	D / W	D / W / oth
1834	3 / 6	7 / 14
1836	3 / 6	7 / 14
1838	6 / 3	13 / 8
1840	5 / 4	0 / 21
1842	2 / 7	7 / 14
1844	3 / 6	7 / 14
1846	4 / 5	10 / 11
1848	3 / 6	7 / 13 / 1 ?
1850	5 / 4	14 / 7
1852	5 / 4	8 / 13

Affiliations	*Senate* *D / A / oth*	*House* *D / A*
1854	2 / 6 / 1 W	2 / 19
1856	5 / 4	21 / 0
1858	7 / / 2 Opp	14 / / 7 Opp
	D / R	*D / R*
1860	5 / 4	10 / 11
1862	5 / 4	14 / 7
1864	6 / 3	14 / 7
1866	6 / 3	15 / 6
1868	9 / 0	21 / 0
1870	9 / 0	21 / 0
1872	8 / 1	21 / 0
1874	8 / 1	21 / 0
1876	9 / 0	21 / 0
1878	9 / 0	21 / 0
1880	8 / 1	14 / 7
1882	7 / 2	21 / 0
1884	9 / 0	21 / 0
1886	9 / 0	21 / 0
1888	4 / 5	7 / 14
1890	7 / 2	7 / 14
1892	5 / 4	21 / 0
1894	5 / 4	6 / 15
1896	5 / 4	20 / 1
1898	(17) 9 / 8	(35) 12 / 23
1900	8 / 9	15 / 20
1902	7 / 10	15 / 20
1904	7 / 10	14 / 21
1906	6 / 11	10 / 25
1908	6 / 11	18 / 17
1910	8 / 9	13 / 22
1912	8 / 9	21 / 14
1914	8 / 9	16 / 19
1916	7 / 10	19 / 16
1918	7 / 10	12 / 23
1920	5 / 12	18 / 17
1922	6 / 11	18 / 17
1924	9 / 8	13 / 22
1926	9 / 8	17 / 18
1928	8 / 9	9 / 26
1930	5 / 12	13 / 22
1932	8 / 9	22 / 13
1934	7 / 10	12 / 23
1936	6 / 11	21 / 14
1938	6 / 11	15 / 20
1940	7 / 10	15 / 20
1942	7 / 10	11 / 24

Affiliations	Senate D / R	House D / R
1944	6 / 11	13 / 22
1946	6 / 11	11 / 24
1948	8 / 9	17 / 18
1950	9 / 8	16 / 19
1952	7 / 10	17 / 18
1954	12 / 5	27 / 8
1956	13 / 4	19 / 16
1958	11 / 6	26 / 9
1960	11 / 6	20 / 15
1962	10 / 7	24 / 11
1964	(18) 13 / 5	30 / 5
1966	9 / 9	12 / 23
1968	(19) 6 / 13	(39) 13 / 26
1970	6 / 13	16 / 23
1972	(21) 10 / 11	(41) 20 / 21
1974	13 / 8	25 / 16
1976	13 / 8	26 / 15
1978	13 / 8	21 / 20
1980	12 / 9	16 / 25
1982	13 / 8	25 / 16
1984	13 / 8	19 / 22
1986	13 / 8	19 / 22
1988	13 / 8	18 / 23
1990	15 / 6	17 / 24
1992	15 / 6	18 / 23
1994	12 / 9	14 / 27
1996	15 / 6	18 / 23
1998	13 / 8	15 / 26
2000	13 / 8	15 / 26
2002	13 / 8	12 / 29
2004	13 / 8	15 / 26
2006	13 / 8	18 / 23

SOURCES

Research was conducted at the Hall of Records (Archives) in Dover, the Delaware Historical Society and the Wilmington Public Library, both in Wilmington, in addition to the New York Public Library.

Newspapers published in Wilmington were the main source for data through the Civil War; those consulted were *Delaware and Eastern Shore Advertiser* 1794–1799, *Mirror of the Times* 1800–1806, *American Watchman* 1809–1820, *Delaware Gazette 1820–1860* and *Delaware Republican* 1820–1860. Thereafter the Wilmington *Every Evening* from 1871 and the *Journal* from 1887 until its merger with *Every Evening* in the mid–1930s. The reliance on newspapers even well into the 20th century was primarily due to a lack of any volume equivalent to a legislative manual until the appearance of *The Delaware State Manual* beginning in 1940.

The *Manual* was used until 1966; in that year, the State Board of Election began publishing a booklet of returns, and that source was used for data from 1966 on.

For some of the years during the Federalist/ Democratic-Republican period, the party totals are estimates because no source gave party totals or a list of the members of the legislature. In these instances the county vote was used for other officials (governor and/or Congressman). Also used were the affiliation of the presiding officer of each house and when applicable the vote by the legislature for U.S. senator. One helpful factor during this period was the consistency of the voting habits of each of the state's three counties. Sussex always voted Federalist and New Castle always voted Democratic-Republican — in most cases by wide margins. Kent was also traditionally Federalist but by smaller margins than Sussex. In the few years where the Sussex vote was close or even went Democratic-Republican in a state race, I have used the vote for members of the legislature. What made this method effective was the fact that all members were elected on a countywide basis. In most years the available returns showed straight party vote by an overwhelming number of voters. Also House membership changed little from year to year. Estimates for senator were usually necessitated by the fact that only ⅓ were elected each year. Estimates pertaining to the House were primarily made necessary by a lack of returns from Kent County, the most partisan of the state's counties. For the elections of 1796–1799 the party affiliations were most likely the same as the later years but there is little actual evidence to support this conclusion; hence here, with one exception, I do not give party totals but simply note that the Federalists were in the majority.

Estimates were made for the elections of 1800, 1801, 1804, 1810 1818 and 1819 based solely on returns for statewide race. No returns for legislator were located for Sussex County for 1809, 1810, 1812, 1813 and 1817. No data was available for the election of 1806.

Starting with the election of 1820 a complete record of legislative returns exists.

FLORIDA

Statehood: A referendum was approved (2,214 to 1,274) in May 1839 calling for a constitutional convention. The convention meeting at Tallahassee from December 3, 1838, to January 4, 1839, wrote the document that would become the state's first constitution when statehood was achieved on March 3, 1845. The proposed constitution was approved (2,071 to 1,958) in 1839. The first legislative elections were held on May 26, 1845, and the legislature convened on June 23, 1845, at Tallahassee, the capital.

Term: Senators were initially elected for a term of two years (one-half the body elected every year) until 1848 when the term was increased to four years one-half elected every two years). House members were originally elected every year; the term was increased to two years in 1848.

Districts/Elections: With one exception, senators were initially elected from single-members districts, there was one two-member district. Thereafter all senators have been elected from single-member districts of one or more counties. In 1924 a provision was added preventing the division of any county in the formation of a district, and no county could have more than one member. In 1962 Dade was given a second district.

The House was apportioned among the counties, each county guaranteed at least one member and all members elected on a countywide basis. In 1868 no county could have more than four members, reduced in 1885 to three. A 1924 amendment divided the state into three groups; the five most populous were entitled to three members, the next 18 counties were given two, the remainder one. Single-member districts became universal in 1972.

Membership/Size: The Senate originally had 17 members; this number was raised to 32 in 1880 and 38 in 1928, and three changes between 1962 and 1972 raised the total to 40. The House had 41 members at the outset, 76 in 1880, a reduction to 68 in 1896, and 95 in 1926; four changes between 1962 and 1972 brought the total to 120.

Reapportionment/Redistricting: In 1925, 1945, 1955 (House), 1962, 1964, 1966 (two elections) 1972, 1982, 1992 and 2002. No information could be found on apportionments prior to 1925.

Election Dates: First Monday in October until 1872 when it was changed to the first Tuesday after the first Monday in November.

Constitutions: There have been six constitutions in the state's history: 1839, 1861, 1865, 1868, 1886 and 1968.

Affiliations	Senate D / W / oth	House D / W / oth
1845	(17) 11 / 6	(41) 30 / 10 / 1 ?
1846	(19) 12 / 7	(39) 22 / 17
1847	7 / 12	11 / 21 / 7 ?
1848	7 / 12	(40) 16 / 24
1850	10 / 9	21 / 19
1852	12 / 6 / 1 I	26 / 13 / 1 vac
1854	11 / 7 / 1 vac	(41) 23 / 17 / 1 ?
	D / A	D / A
1856	(21) 13 / 7 / 1 ?	(45) 29 / 16

Affiliations	Senate D / Opp	House D / Opp
1858	15 / 6	35 / 10
1860	13 / 8	37 / 10
1865[1]	—	—

	D / R / oth	D / R / oth
1868[2]	8 / 16	15 / 37
1870[3]	10 / 11	20 / 23
1872	11 / 13	23 / 29
1874	12 / 12	28 / 24
1876	15 / 9	31 / 21
1878	(32) 25 / 7	(76) 46 / 28 / 1 I, 1 tie
1880	27 / 5	58 / 18
1882	17 / 6 / 9 I	34 / 27 / 15 I
1884	17 / 7 / 8 I	48 / 25 / 3 I
1886	24 / 5 / 3 I	55 / 13 / 8 I
1888	27 / 5	58 / 9 / 9 I
1890	31 / 1	76 / 0
1892	31 / 1	76 / 0
1894	31 / 0 / 1 Pop	74 / 1 / 1 I
1896	31 / 0 / 1 Pop	(68) 63 / 3 / 2 I
1898	32 / 0	68 / 0
1900	32 / 0	68 / 0
1902	32 / 0	67 / 1
1904	32 / 0	68 / 0
1906	32 / 0	67 / 0 / 1 S
1908	32 / 0	67 / 0 / 1 S
1910	32 / 0	68 / 0
1912	32 / 0	(71) 71 / 0
1914	32 / 0	(73) 73 / 0
1916	32 / 0	(75) 74 / 1
1918	32 / 0	(77) 77 / 0
1920	32 / 0	77 / 0
1922	32 / 0	77 / 0
1924	32 / 0	(87) 84 / 0 / 3 vac[4]
1926	32 / 0	(95) 95 / 0
1928	(38) 37 / 1	93 / 2
1930	38 / 0	95 / 0
1932	38 / 0	94 / 1
1934	38 / 0	95 / 0
1936	38 / 0	95 / 0
1938	38 / 0	95 / 0
1940	38 / 0	95 / 0
1942	38 / 0	95 / 0
1944	38 / 0	95 / 0
1946	38 / 0	94 / 1
1948	38 / 0	95 / 0
1950	38 / 0	92 / 3

Affiliations	Senate D / R / oth	House D / R / oth
1952	37 / 1	90 / 5
1954	37 / 1	89 / 6
1956	37 / 1	89 / 6
1958	37 / 1	92 / 3
1960	37 / 1	88 / 7
1962[5]	37 / 1	90 / 5
1962[5]	(43) 41 / 2	(125) 109 / 16
1964	41 / 2	(112) 102 / 10
1966[5]	(48) 37 / 11	(117) 91 / 26
1966[5]	28 / 20	(119) 70 / 49
1968	32 / 16	77 / 42
1970	33 / 15	81 / 38
1972	(40) 25 / 14 / 1 I	(120) 77 / 43
1974	27 / 12 / 1 I	86 / 34
1976	31 / 9	92 / 28
1978	29 / 11	89 / 31
1980	27 / 13	81 / 39
1982	33 / 7	85 / 35
1984	32 / 8	78 / 42
1986	25 / 15	75 / 45
1988	23 / 17	73 / 47
1990	22 / 18	74 / 46
1992	20 / 20	71 / 49
1994	19 / 21	63 / 57
1996	17 / 23	59 / 61
1998	15 / 25	48 / 72
2000	15 / 25	43 / 77
2002	14 / 26	39 / 81
2004	14 / 26	36 / 84
2006	14 / 26	41 / 79

NOTES

1. Election largely without party labels.

2. As a result of Congressional reconstruction, no election in the intervening period.

3. The legislature rejected returns from nine counties and refused to seat the members (3 senators and 9 representatives) from these counties. According to the (Tallahassee) *Weekly Floridian*, December 27, 1870, the full body as elected was a Senate of 12–12 and a House with 28 Conservatives, 23 Republicans and 1 Independent.

4. Three additional members served during the special session as a result of the creation of three new counties.

5. Because of litigation over reapportionment there were two elections in this year.

SOURCES

(St. Augustine*) Florida News*, April 26, 1845, (St. Augustine) *Herald,* May 6, 20, 1845, November 13, 1846, *Niles Register* December 5, 1846, (Tallahassee) *Florida*

Sentinel, October 19, 1847, October 19, November 20, 1852, (Tallahassee) *Floridian,* October 16, December 11, 1847, November 20, 1852, November 11, 1854, November 15, 26, 1856, November 13, 1858, November 17, 1860, December 27, 1870, January 7, 1879, (Marianna) *Florida Whig,* December 2, 1848, (Jacksonville) *Florida Republican,* November 26, 1856, (Fernandina) *East Floridian,* November 17, 1860.

Also consulted were Edward C. Williamson, *Florida Politics in the Gilded Age 1877–1893* (Gainesville: University of Florida Press, 1976) and Charlton W. Tebeau, *A History of Florida* (Coral Gables: University of Miami Press, 1971). Historical list of legislators supplied by the Florida Archives.

GEORGIA

Constitutional Origins: Between September 1 and 10, 1776, delegates were elected to write Georgia's first constitution. The delegates met from October 1776 until February 5, 1777. They established a unicameral legislature called the House of the Assembly. The first legislature met in Savannah, the first of five capitals. The capital was moved to Augusta in 1786, to Louisville in 1795, to Milledgeville in 1807, and to the present location, Atlanta, in 1868.

Term: Members of the unicameral legislature served a one-year term. When a bicameral legislature was established in 1789, the House of Representatives, as the lower house was called, was also elected for a one-year term. The term was changed to its present length of two years in 1843. Senators (the Senate was established by the constitution of 1789) served a three-year term, reduced to one year in 1795 but increased to four years by the constitution in 1868. The constitution of 1877 established the present term of two years.

Districts/Elections: The county was the basis for election until the impact of the U.S. Supreme Court's one person, one vote ruling in 1964. Even when a county elected more than one member, all members were elected countywide. Prior to the reapportionment revolution of the 1960s no Georgia county was ever divided into districts to elect members of either house of the legislature. Senators have always been elected from single-member districts. They were originally apportioned one to a county until an 1843 constitutional amendment created a body solely of districts consisting of two counties. But in 1852 the Senate reverted to one-per-county representation and this continued until 1861 when a new constitution established districts all containing three counties. Some modification was made in 1918 although most districts (41 of 52) continued to contain three counties the others ranged from one to five counties. By 1962, 52 of 54 districts were made up three counties; the other two districts contained one and two counties respectively. In 1962 the legislature radically reapportioned the Senate, largely on a population basis, dividing counties entitled to more than one member into single-member districts. No county previously had had more than one member.

The county was always the basis for apportioning members of the House and every county had at least one member. However there had always been a ceiling on representation except under the 1777 constitution when Liberty County had 14 members. Under the 1789 constitution representation ranged from a minimum of two to a maximum of five. In 1798 the minimum was reduced to one and the maximum to four. Under an 1843 amendment representation was fixed at either one or two per county. Beginning in 1868, House counties were divided into three categories with a fixed number of counties entitled to no less than one nor more than three members. Except for slight modifications in the number of counties in each category, this system of representation remained in effect until 1965.

Under court order, Georgia created equal population districts, with the Senate all single-member districts as before but the House, until 1992, made up of both single- and multi-member districts. In the multi-member districts, candidates ran for a specific seat in each case. Since 1992 all House members have been elected from single-member districts.

Membership/Size: The unicameral body consisted of 72 members. The 1789 constitution set a membership for the House at 34. The 1798 Constitution did not fix a number, and as new counties were created the body grew in size. A constitutional amendment fixed the number at 130, but that was repealed in 1851 and as new counties were created the House increased. The constitution of 1861 restored the 1843 formula which produced a House of 168. The 1868 constitution fixed the number at 175 but constitutional amendments between 1904 and 1920 increased the body to 206 members to allow for representation for newly created counties. By 1930 the House totaled 207 members. The consolidation of three Atlanta area counties into one reduced the House in 1932 by two and the number remained in effect until the one person, one vote apportionment resulting in four changes in the size of the House, which reached its present total of 180 in 1978.

The Senate originally was made up of 11 members, and that body grew as new counties were created until 1843 when the number was fixed at 47. But a constitutional amendment restoring the one-member-per-county formula in 1851 saw the body grow rapidly, so that by 1861 the Senate had 131 members, the largest number of any similar body in the U.S. Thereafter the 1861 constitution fixed Senate representation at 44, and that remained unchanged until 1918 when it was increased to 51 members. There have been three additional increases in the Senate, with the membership in 1968 reaching 56, its present total. The Georgia Senate is the fourth largest such body in the nation; the House is exceeded in size by only two other states.

Reapportionment/Redistricting: Until the 1960s reapportionment was largely accomplished by either constitutional amendment or a constitutional convention as the formulas enacted made significant reapportionment impossible.[1] But since the implementation of one person, one vote this has occurred on regular basis. There have been such enactments in 1962, 1964 (Senate) 1965 (House), 1967 (Senate) 1968, 1972, 1974, 1976, 1978, 1982, 1992, 2002, and 2004.

Election Dates: Elections were held on the first Tuesday in October until 1865 when the date was changed to the first Wednesday in October. Effective in 1916 the date was changed to the first Tuesday after the first Monday in November.

Constitutions: The state has had ten constitutions, second only to Louisiana: 1777, 1789, 1798, 1861, 1865, 1868, 1877, 1945, 1976 and 1982.

Affiliations	*Senate*	*House*
	U / SoR / oth	*U / SoR / oth*
1835	54 / 31	102 / 68
1836	?	?
1837	42 / 50	88 / 103
1838	50 / 37	96 / 76
1839	28 / 46 / 1 tie	102 / 94 / 1 ?
	D / W / oth	*D / W / oth*
1840	44 / 48	88 / 118
1841	51 / 38 / 1 tie	109 / 91
1842	55 / 36 / 2 ties	118 / 87 / 2 ties
1843	49 / 43 / 1 ?	81 / 124
1845	(47) 25 / 22	(130) 69 / 60 / 1 tie
1847	21 / 25 / 1 I	62 / 68
1849	25 / 22	61 / 65 / 1 tie, 3 ?
1851	/ / 39 U, 8 SoR	/ / 104 U, 29 SoR

Affiliations	*Senate* D / W / oth	*House* D / W / oth
1853	52 / 42	66 / 59
1855	78 / / 33 A	92 / 55 / 1 ID
1857	86 / / 32 A	102 / / 51 A, 1 I, 1 ID
1859	103 / / 21 Opp	120 / / 48 Opp, 1 I, 1 ID

	D / R	*D / R*
1868	(44) 18 / 26	(175) —[2]
1870	29 / 14 / 1 I	136 / 29 / 9 I, 1 ?
1872	40 / 4	161 / 14
1874	43 / 1	168 / 7
1876	40 / 1 / 3 ID	159 / 8 / 8 I
1878	44 / 0	171 / 4
1880	43 / 1	165 / 10
1882	44 / 0	167 / 2 / 5 I, 1 P
1884	44 / 0	169 / 6
1886	39 / 2 / 2 I, 1 Lab	150 / 10 / 10 I, 5 Lab
1888	43 / 1	172 / 3
1890	44 / 0	171 / 4
1892	43 / 0 / 1 Pop	159 / 4 / 11 Pop, 1 ?
1894	38 / 1 / 5 Pop	126 / 2 / 47 Pop
1896	37 / 1 / 6 Pop	142 / 3 / 30 Pop
1898	43 / 1	170 / 0 / 5 Pop
1900	43 / 1	166 / 0 / 9 Pop
1902	40 / 2 / 2 Pop	171 / 3 / 1 Pop
1904	44 / 0	173 / 2
1906	44 / 0	(183) 170 / 3 / 2Pe, 8 ?
1908	44 / 0	(184) 184 / 0
1910	43 / 1	183 / 1
1912	43 / 1	183 / 1
1914	43 / 1	(189) D majority[3]
1916	44 / 0	D majority[3]
1918	(51) 51 / 0	(193) D majority[3]
1920	50 / 1	(206) D majority[3]
1922	51 / 0	D majority[3]
1924	50 / 1	204 / 2
1926	50 / 1	204 / 2
1928	51 / 0	(207) 204 / 3
1930	50 / 1	207 / 0
1932	50 / 1	(205) 205 / 0
1934	50 / 1	203 / 2
1936	50 / 1	204 / 1
1938	(52) 51 / 1	204 / 1
1940	51 / 1	204 / 1
1942	51 / 1	204 / 1
1944	51 / 1	204 / 1
1946	(54) 53 / 1	204 / 1
1948	53 / 1	203 / 2

Affiliations	Senate D / R	House D / R
1950	54 / 0	204 / 1
1952	53 / 1	204 / 1
1954	53 / 1	202 / 3
1956	53 / 1	202 / 3
1958	53 / 1	202 / 3
1960	53 / 1	203 / 2
1962	50 / 4	203 / 2
1964	44 / 9 / 2 I	198 / 7
1965[4]	—	188 / 17
1966	46 / 7 / 1 I	183 / 22
1968	(56) 48 / 7 / 1 I	(195) 169 / 26
1970	50 / 6	173 / 22
1972	48 / 8	(179) 152 / 27
1974	51 / 5	155 / 24
1976	52 / 4	(182) 158 / 24
1978	51 / 5	(180) 161 / 19
1980	51 / 5	157 / 23
1982	52 / 4	156 / 24
1984	47 / 9	155 / 25
1986	46 / 10	154 / 26
1988	46 / 10	145 / 35
1990	45 / 11	144 / 36
1992	41 / 15	128 / 52
1994	35 / 21	114 / 66
1996	34 / 22	106 / 74
1998	34 / 22	102 / 78
2000	32 / 24	105 / 74 / 1 I
2002	26 / 30	106 / 73 / 1 I
2004	22 / 34	86 / 94
2006	22 / 34	74 / 106

NOTES

1. There were reapportionments of the Senate within the limits of the existing formulas in 1906, 1946 and 1962 prior to one person, one vote.

2. Although I was not able to find a party breakdown for the House, there is an estimate based on voting records in C. Mildred Thompson, *Reconstruction in Georgia* (New York: Columbia University Press, 1915; reprint edition (Gloucester: Peter Smith, 1964, pp. 207–212). The author estimates the party breakdown as 84 Republicans (75 Radicals and 9 Moderates) and 88 Conservative Democrats.

3. Although the exact party breakdown could not determined, the Democratic total was near 100 percent for each election. The Republican membership probably was 1–4 members per session.

4. Court-ordered election as a result of reapportionment suit concerning the House of Representatives held on May 26, 1965. See decisions in *Fortson v. Dorsey* (379 U.S. 433) 1965 and *Reynolds v. Sims* (377 U.S. 533) 1964.

SOURCES

Niles Register, November 21, 1835. (Milledgeville) *Federal Union*, October 17, 1837, October 23, 1838, October 22, 1839, October 24, 1840, October 19, 1841, October 25, 1842, October 24, 1843, October 21, 1845, November 9, 1847, October 16, 1849, October 21, 1851, October 18, 1853, October 16, 1855, October 20, 1857, October 25, 1859. *The* (Atlanta) *Constitution*, October 18, 1876, November 3, 1880, October 19, 1882. Richard Scammon, ed., *America Votes*, Volumes 1–8 (Pittsburgh: Macmillan/Congressional Quarterly, annually since 1955). Information about past apportionments and other constitutional issues taken largely from Albert B. Saye, *A Constitutional History of Georgia 1732–1968* (Athens: University of Georgia Press, 1970). The Georgia Archives supplied a list of Republican state senators from 1868 through the election of 2000.

HAWAII

Statehood: Before an enabling act was passed by Congress, the territorial legislature, in the fall of 1949, authorized the calling of a constitutional convention. The delegates met in Honolulu from April 4 to July 22, 1950, and the document was approved on November 7, 1950 (82,788 to 27,109). Congress did not pass an enabling act until March 18, 1959, subject to a further vote of the people, which occurred on June 27, 1959. Statehood was achieved on August 21, 1959, and the constitution went into effect on the same day. The capital has always been Honolulu.

Term: Senators since statehood, have served terms of four years, part of the body elected every two years.[1] Representatives have served a two-year term since statehood.

Districts/Elections: Initially the Senate was elected from six multi-member districts electing from two to five members. Multi-member districts continued to be the predominant method of election through the reapportionment of 1974, which created eight districts electing one to four members. The House was similarly apportioned into mainly multi-member districts but there were some single-member districts as well. Since 1982 all legislators have been elected from single-member districts.

Membership/Size: The legislature has always been made up of 25 senators and 51 representatives.

Reapportionment/Redistricting: 1966 (Senate), 1974, 1982, 1992 and 2002.

Election Date: Always the first Tuesday after the first Monday in November.

Constitution: The original constitution, written in 1950 and effective with statehood, is still in effect today.

Affiliations	Senate D / R	House D / R
1959	(25) 11 / 14	(51) 33 / 18
1962	15 / 10	40 / 11
1964	16 / 9	39 / 12
1966	15 / 10	39 / 12
1968	—	38 / 13
1970	17 / 8	34 / 17
1972	—	35 / 16
1974	17 / 8	34 / 17
1976	—	41 / 10
1978	18 / 7	42 / 9
1980	17 / 8	39 / 12
1982	17 / 8	43 / 8
1984	22 / 3	40 / 11
1986	20 / 5	40 / 11
1988	22 / 3	45 / 6
1990	22 / 3	45 / 6
1992	22 / 3	47 / 4
1994	23 / 2	44 / 7
1996	23 / 2	39 / 12
1998	23 / 2	39 / 12
2000	22 / 3	32 / 19
2002	20 / 5	36 / 15
2004	20 / 5	41 /10
2006	20 / 5	43 / 8

NOTES

1. The entire Senate was elected in 1966, 1970, 1974 and 1978.

IDAHO

Statehood: On April 2, 1889, territorial governor George Shoup called for the election of delegates to a constitutional convention. The delegates met in Boise from July 4 to August 2 and produced Idaho's constitution. The document was submitted to the voters on November 5, 1889, and was approved by a vote of 12,126 to 6,282. The statehood bill was signed by President Harrison on July 3, 1890. The initial election of the legislature took place on October 1, 1890. The first legislature convened on December 8. The capital has always been located at Boise.

Terms: Members of both houses have always been elected for a term of two years.

Districts/Elections: The Senate was initially made up mainly of single-member and a few two-member districts plus floterial districts. By amendment in 1911 every county had one member.

The House of Representatives initially had the same setup as the Senate, but each county was entitled to at least one member. No county could be divided in the formation of districts; that rule applied to both houses.

In 1966, in response to one person, one vote apportionment, the legislature was divided into 35 districts electing one senator and two representatives, each elected separately. Except for the apportionment of 1984, this system has been used ever since. The 1984 apportionment provided for a few districts that elected as many as three senators and six representatives, each elected separately.

Membership/Size: The Senate was initially 18 members. By 1922 the total had increased to 44 due to the creation of new counties. The total was changed again when it was reduced to 35 in 1966, increased to 42 in 1984 and reduced again to 35 in 1992. The House increased from 36 at statehood to 59 by 1910. In 1962 the House was increased to 63; members since then there have been four changes. The most recent change, in 1992, reduced the body from 84 to 70 members.

Reapportionment/Redistricting[1]: Enacted in 1894 (House) 1896, 1902 (House) 1906 (House) 1908, 1910(House), 1912, 1914, 1916, 1918, 1920, 1922, 1924, 1926, 1928, 1934, 1942, 1952, 1964, 1966, 1972, 1974, 1984, 1992 and 2002.

Election Date: Always the first Tuesday after the first Monday in November.

Constitutions: The original constitution of 1889 is in use today.

Affiliations	Senate	House
	D / R / oth	D / R / oth
1890	(18) 4 / 14	(36) 5 / 31
1892	8 / 6 / 4 Pop	9 / 20 / 7 Pop
1894	2 / 10 / 5 Pop, 1 I	(35) 1 / 25 / 8 Pop, 1I
1896	(21) 7 / 7 / 7 Pop	(48) 15 / 17 / 16 Pop

Affiliations	*Senate* D / R / oth	*House* D / R / oth
1898	3 / 9 / 7 Fus, 2 Pop	(49) 14 / 12 / 17 Fus, 6 Pop
1900	10 / 7 / 3 Pop, 1 SilR	16 / 20 / 7 Sil, 6 Pop
1902	6 / 14 / 1 I	13 / 36
1904	2 / 19	(50) 2 / 48
1906	6 / 15	(51) 12 / 38 / 1 I
1908	(23) 10 / 13	(53) 9 / 44
1910	9 / 14	(59) 25 / 34
1912	(24) 3 / 21	(60) 4 / 56
1914	(33) 11 / 19 / 2 Pg, 1 S	(61) 28 / 32 / 1 Pg
1916	(37) 21 / 16	(65) 36 / 29
1918	(41) 12 / 29	(64) 18 / 46
1920	(44) 5 / 39	(54) 3 / 51
1922	14 / 25 / 5 Pg	(65) 22 / 37 / 6 Pg
1924	5 / 32 / 7 Pg	(62) 5 / 45 / 12 Pg
1926	11 / 29 / 4 Pg	(68) 7 / 52 / 8 Pg, 1 I
1928	12 / 32	(59) 9 / 50
1930	21 / 23	27 / 32
1932	35 / 9	55 / 4
1934	36 / 8	53 / 6
1936	33 / 11	50 / 9
1938	17 / 27	20 / 39
1940	23 / 21	38 / 21
1942	13 / 31	(59) 27 / 32
1944	20 / 24	29 / 30
1946	15 / 29	18 / 41
1948	23 / 21	24 / 35
1950	15 / 29	23 / 36
1952	11 / 33	14 / 45
1954	20 / 24	23 / 36
1956	25 / 19	27 / 32
1958	27 / 17	35 / 24
1960	21 / 23	28 / 31
1962	21 / 23	(63) 29 / 34
1964	19 / 25	(79) 37 / 42
1966	(35) 13 / 22	(70) 32 / 38
1968	15 / 20	32 / 38
1970	16 / 19	29 / 41
1972	12 / 23	19 / 51
1974	14 / 21	27 / 43
1976	15 / 20	22 / 48
1978	16 / 19	20 / 50
1980	12 / 23	14 / 56
1982	14 / 21	19 / 51
1984	(42) 14 / 28	(84) 17 / 67
1986	16 / 26	20 / 64
1988	19 / 23	20 / 64
1990	21 / 21	28 / 56
1992	(35) 12 / 23	(70) 20 / 50

Affiliations	*Senate* D / R / oth	*House* D / R / oth
1994	8 / 27	13 / 57
1996	5 / 30	11 / 59
1998	4 / 31	12 / 58
2000	3 / 32	9 / 61
2002	7 / 28	16 / 54
2004	7 / 28	13 / 57
2006	7 / 28	19 / 51

NOTES

1. Several of the early reapportionments affected only a few counties, and between 1912 and 1964 reapportionments were of the House only.

SOURCES

For all elections from 1894 through 2000 data was obtained from the *Idaho Blue Book 2001–2002* published by the Idaho Secretary of State.

ILLINOIS

Statehood: On April 18, 1818, an enabling act was signed by President James Monroe calling on the citizens of the territory of Illinois to elect delegates to a constitutional convention. The delegates met at the capital, Kaskaskia, August 3–26, 1818, and wrote a constitution. The first state elections were held September 17–19, 1818. Illinois formally became a state on December 3, 1818. The capital was moved to Vandalia in 1820 and to Springfield in 1839.

Term: Senators were elected for a term of four years until 1872; with overlapping terms, one-half the body was elected every two years. In 1872 senators were divided into three classes with two out of three elections for a four-year term and one for a two-year term. At the beginning of a new apportionment cycle all senators are elected. Thereafter ⅓ and then ⅔ of the Senate are elected followed by ⅔ and ⅓ again. However, in 1966 all senators were elected for four years. House members have always served a term of two years.

Districts/Elections: Senators have always been elected from single-member districts, except in 1870, when each district elected two members.

House members until the constitution of 1870 were elected from both single- and multi-member districts on a countywide basis, no county being divided into districts. In 1872 the House, using the same districts as the Senate, elected three members per district, and cumulative voting was introduced.[1] This method remained in effect until 1982 when single-member districts were established, except for 1964, when the entire House was elected statewide.

Membership/Size: The Senate initially consisted of 14 members, increased to 18 in 1822, to 40 in 1836, and to 42 six years later. The membership was reduced to 25 under the constitution of 1848 but doubled to 50 in 1870. There have been three increases since: to 51 in 1872, 58 in 1956 and 59 in 1972. The House consisted of 28 members in 1818 and 36 in 1822. By 1846 the total had reached 123. After a reduction to 75 in 1848, there were two increases: to 85 in 1862 and to 177 in 1870. In 1872 the total was reduced to 153 and that remained unchanged until 1956 when it was increased to 177. In 1982 once again the membership was decreased, this time to 118.

Reapportionment/Redistricting: Enacted in the years 1822, 1826, 1832, 1836, 1842, 1848, 1854 1862, 1870, 1872, 1884, 1894, 1902, 1956, 1964, 1966, 1972, 1982, 1992 and 2002.

Election Dates: Elections were originally held on the first Monday in August. In 1850 the date was changed to the first Tuesday after the first Monday in November.

Constitutions: The state's four constitutions were written in 1818, 1848, 1870 and 1970.

Affiliations	Senate D / W / oth	House D / W / oth
1836[2]	(40) 22 / 18	(91) 57 / 24 / 10 ?
1838	20 / 20	40 / 46 / 5 I
1840	26 / 14	51 / 40[3]
1842	(41) 30 / 12	(121) 84 / 37
1844	26 / 15	78 / 40 / 3 ?
1846	29 / 13	(123) 76 / 44 / 3 ?
1848	(25) 17 / 7 / 1 ?	(75) 54 / 21
1850	17 / 8	46 / 29
1852	20 / 5	56 / 18 / 1 FS
1854	14 / 11	34 / 41
	D / R / oth	D / R / oth
1856	13 / 12	38 / 31 / 6 A

Affiliations	*Senate* *D / R / oth*	*House* *D / R / oth*
1858	14 / 11	40 / 35
1860	12 / 13	34 / 41
1862	13 / 12	(85) 55 / 30
1864	11 / 14	34 / 51
1866	9 / 16	25 / 60
1868	7 / 18	27 / 58
1870	(50) 20 / 30	(177) 76 / 98 / 3 I
1872	(51) 18 / 33	(153) 67 / 86
1874	18 / 24 / 9 I	42 / 69 / 41 I
1876	22 / 21 / 8 I	67 / 79 / 7 I
1878	24 / 26 / 1 I	60 / 80 / 10 G, 3 S
1880	18 / 32 / 1 S	71 / 82
1882	20 / 31	75 / 77 / 1 I
1884	25 / 26	76 / 76 / 1 I
1886	18 / 32 / 1 Lab	64 / 79 / 9 Lab, 1 P
1888	15 / 35 / 1 Lab	72 / 80 / 1 Lab
1890	24 / 27	77 / 73 / 3 FA
1892	29 / 22	78 / 75
1894	18 / 33	61 / 92
1896	11 / 39 / 1 Pop	62 / 89 / 2 Pop
1898	16 / 34 / 1 Pop	71 / 81 / 1 P
1900	19 / 32	72 / 81
1902	15 / 36	62 / 88 / 2 PO, 1 P
1904	10 / 41	57 / 91 / 3 P, 2 S
1906	7 / 44	60 / 90 / 3 P
1908	13 / 38	65 / 88
1910	17 / 34	68 / 82 / 2 I, 1 P
1912	24 / 25 / 2 Pg	71 / 52 / 27 Pg, 3 S
1914	25 / 25 / 1 Pg	70 / 79 / 2 S, 1 I, 1 Pg
1916	18 / 33	67 / 85 / 1 I
1918	17 / 34	63 / 90
1920	8 / 43	58 / 95
1922	9 / 42	63 / 89 / 1 I
1924	13 / 38	59 / 94
1926	10 / 41	60 / 93
1928	11 / 40	62 / 91
1930	18 / 33	72 / 81
1932	33 / 18	80 / 73
1934	35 / 16	84 / 69
1936	34 / 17	86 / 67
1938	30 / 21	73 / 80
1940	23 / 28	74 / 79
1942	23 / 28	69 / 84
1944	17 / 34	75 / 78
1946	14 / 37	66 / 87
1948	18 / 33	79 / 74
1950	20 / 31	69 / 84
1952	13 / 38	69 / 84

Affiliations	Senate D / R / oth	House D / R / oth
1954	19 / 32	74 / 79
1956	(58) 20 / 38	(177) 83 / 94
1958	24 / 34	92 / 85
1960	27 / 31	88 / 89
1962	23 / 35	87 / 90
1964	25 / 33	118 / 59
1966	20 / 38	78 / 99
1968	—	83 / 94
1970	29 / 29	87 / 90
1972	(59) 29 / 30	84 / 92 / 1 I
1974	34 / 25	98 / 76 / 3 I
1976	34 / 25	93 / 83 / 1 I
1978	32 / 27	88 / 88 / 1 I
1980	30 / 29	86 / 89 / 2 I
1982	33 / 26	(118) 70 / 48
1984	31 / 28	67 / 51
1986	31 / 28	67 / 51
1988	31 / 28	68 / 50
1990	31 / 28	72 / 46
1992	27 / 32	67 / 51
1994	26 / 33	54 / 64
1996	28 / 31	60 / 58
1998	27 / 32	62 / 56
2000	27 / 32	62 / 56
2002	32 / 27	66 / 52
2004	31 / 27 / 1 I	65 / 53
2006	37 / 22	66 / 52

NOTES

1. Under this system the voter had three votes, which in traditional fashion he could cast equally for three candidates. But the voter could also give his three votes for just one candidate or divide his vote equally between two candidates. In most cases as long as the system was used, this usually resulted in a 2–1 split in each district in favor of one or the other major parties.

2. Prior to 1836, party affiliation could not be ascertained.

3. *Niles Register* gives the affiliation as 49D and 42W (October 24, 1840).

SOURCES

(Vandilla) *Illinois State Register*, August 26, September 2, 1836, *Niles Register*, November 6, 1838,(Springfield) *Illinois State Register*, August 14, 1840, January 6, 1849. Theodore C. Pease, *Illinois Election Returns 1818–1848* (Springfield: Illinois State Historical Society, 1923).

From 1880 to 1968, John Clayton, *The Illinois Fact Book and Historical Almanac, 1673–1968* (Carbondale: Southern Illinois University Press, 1970).

INDIANA

Statehood: The U.S. Congress passed an enabling act on April 19, 1816, providing that the residents of the territory of Indiana write a constitution and become a state. Delegates to the convention were elected on May 13, 1816, and convened on June 10 at the capital, Corydon. On June 29 they completed their work. The first election of the legislature took place on August 5, 1816, and the legislature convened on November 4. Statehood was not officially achieved until December 11, 1816. The capital was moved to Indianapolis in 1825.

Term: Under the 1816 constitution, senators were elected for a three-year term; one-third of the body was elected each year. Under the 1851 constitution the term was increased to four years, with one-half elected every two years; this is the present procedure. The House was at first elected annually, but terms were increased to two years by the 1851 constitution.

Districts/Elections: Senators were initially elected from single-member districts, but Wayne County elected two members countywide from 1841 to 1846. This provision was restated by the 1851 constitution except that any county that was entitled to more than one member would not be divided into districts. This practice continued until the implementation of one person, one vote reapportionment in 1966 when all members were elected from single-member districts — the procedure ever since.

House members were elected countywide from a combination of single- and multi-member districts under the 1816 constitution. In 1826 partial representation was introduced. Under the 1851 constitution the apportionment provisions were modified to the extent that it was up to the legislature to determine whether to divide counties entitled to more than one member into districts. Apparently this was applicable only to counties entitled to more than one member and not multi-county districts. This combination of single- and multi-member districts continued until 1992, when for the first time all House members were elected from single-member districts.

Membership/Size: The Senate originally consisted of 16 members and increased under each of the next four reapportionments, in 1841 reaching 50, its present size. The House had 29 members at its inception. The next three reapportionments increased the House to 100 by 1836, and that number has remained the same.[1]

Reapportionment/Redistricting: Enacted in 1821, 1826, 1831, 1836, 1841, 1846, 1851, 1857, 1867, 1885, 1897, 1905, 1915, 1921, 1963, 1966, 1972, 1982, 1992 and 2002.[2]

Election Dates: The legislature was originally elected on the first Monday in August, a date changed to the first Monday in October in 1852. In 1882 election day was changed to the first Tuesday after the first Monday in November.

Constitutions: There have been two constitutions, the first written in 1816 and the other in 1851.

Affiliations	Senate	House
	J / Ad	J / Ad / oth
1826	(21) Ad majority	(58) Ad majority
1827	4 / 17	15 / 38 / 4 ?
1828	2 / 19	22 / 27 / 9 ?
	D / NR / oth	D / NR / oth
1829	(22) 3 / 18 / 1 ?	(62) 28 / 23 / 11 ?
1830	(23) 6 / 17	(61) 22 / 30 / 9 ?
1831	(30) 9 / 21	(75) 37 / 37 / 1 ?[3]
1832	9 / 20 / 1 ?	42 / 33
1833	13 / 15 / 2 ?	39 / 33 / 3 ?
	D / W / oth	D / W / oth
1834	14 / 16 / 1 ?	30 / 36 / 10 ?[4]
1835	(31) 14 / 16 / 1 ?	(81) 37 / 44
1836	(47) 20 / 27	(100) 46 / 54
1837	22 / 25	44 / 56
1838	20 / 27	43 / 57
1839	25 / 22	61 / 39
1840	14 / 33	22 / 78
1841	(50) 22 / 28	53 / 47
1842	19 / 31	54 / 46
1843	26 / 24	55 / 45
1844	25 / 25	45 / 54 / 1 ?
1845	25 / 25	56 / 44
1846	26 / 24	47 / 53
1847	25 / 25	49 / 51
1848	27 / 23	60 / 40
1849	29 / 21	59 / 41
1850	33 / 17	65 / 35
1851	39 / 10 / 1 FS	61 / 38 / 1 FS

Affiliations	*Senate* D / W / oth	*House* D / W / oth
1852	34 / 16	66 / 34
1854	26 / / 24 Pe	43 / / 57 Pe

	D / R / oth	*D / R / oth*
1856	23 / 26 / 1 A	63 / 35 / 2 A
1858	25 / 25	49 / 51
1860	22 / 28	38 / 62
1862	27 / 21 / 2 I	60 / 40
1864	25 / 25	45 / 55
1866	20 / 30	39 / 61
1868	17 / 33	43 / 57
1870	26 / 24	53 / 47
1872	23 / 27	46 / 54
1874	23 / 22 / 5 I	60 / 32 / 8 I
1876	25 / 24 / 1 I	46 / 54
1878	24 / 23 / 3 G	50 / 39 / 11 G
1880	24 / 24 / 2 G	41 / 58 / 1 I
1882	28 / 22	58 / 42
1884	33 / 17	65 / 35
1886	31 / 19	45 / 55
1888	27 / 23	57 / 43
1890	34 / 16	74 / 26
1892	35 / 15	63 / 37
1894	18 / 32	18 / 82
1896	14 / 33 / 2 Pop	39 / 52 / 9 Pop
1898	21 / 29	40 / 60
1900	17 / 33	39 / 61
1902	15 / 35	34 / 66
1904	14 / 36	21 / 79
1906	13 / 37	47 / 53
1908	23 / 27	60 / 40
1910	30 / 20	60 / 40
1912	40 / 8 / 2 Pg	95 / 4 / 1 Pg
1914	41 / 8 / 1 Pg	60 / 39 / 1 Pg
1916	25 / 24 / 1 Pg	35 / 65
1918	16 / 34	18 / 82
1920	9 / 41	11 / 89
1922	18 / 32	48 / 52
1924	18 / 32	16 / 84
1926	15 / 35	37 / 63
1928	12 / 38	20 / 80
1930	21 / 29	75 / 25
1932	43 / 7	91 / 9
1934	38 / 12	65 / 35
1936	38 / 12	77 / 23
1938	33 / 17	49 / 51
1940	18 / 32	35 / 65

Affiliations	Senate D / R / oth	House D / R / oth
1942	12 / 38	18 / 82
1944	13 / 37	31 / 69
1946	18 / 32	13 / 87
1948	21 / 29	60 / 40
1950	24 / 26	31 / 69
1952	10 / 40	19 / 81
1954	15 / 35	37 / 63
1956	17 / 33	24 / 76
1958	23 / 27	79 / 21
1960	26 / 24	34 / 66
1962	24 / 26	44 / 56
1964	35 / 15	78 / 22
1966	29 / 21	34 / 66
1968	15 / 35	27 / 73
1970	21 / 29	46 / 54
1972	21 / 29	27 / 73
1974	23 / 27	56 / 44
1976	28 / 22	47 / 53
1978	21 / 29	46 / 54
1980	15 / 35	37 / 63
1982	18 / 32	43 / 57
1984	20 / 30	37 / 63
1986	20 / 30	48 / 52
1988	24 / 26	50 / 50
1990	24 / 26	52 / 48
1992	22 / 28	55 / 45
1994	20 / 30	44 / 56
1996	19 / 31	50 / 50
1998	19 / 31	53 / 47
2000	18 / 32	53 / 47
2002	18 / 32	51 / 49
2004	17 / 33	48 / 52
2006	17 / 33	51 / 49

NOTES

1. In 1821 the Senate was increased to 16, in 1826 to 21, in 1831 to 30 and in 1836 to 47. The House was increased in 1821 to 43, in 1826 to 58, and in 1831 to 73.

2. Five reapportionments have been declared unconstitutional by the courts: 1879, 1891, 1893, 1895 and 1903.

3. *Niles Register* (September 3, 1831) gives the House breakdown as follows: 30 D / 39 NR / 6 not given.

4. The figures in the *The Pioneer Era* are Senate D 13 / W 17, and House D 30 / W 46, citing the (Indianapolis) *Indiana State Sentinel* of April 18, 25, 1843.

SOURCES

A Biographical Directory of the Indiana General Assembly, Volume 1 (Indianapolis: 1980) was used for the years 1826–1837. For the other years prior to 1850 data was obtained from Dorothy Riker and Gayle Thornbrough (compilers), *Indiana Election Returns 1816–1851* (Indiana Historical Bureau: 1960); Donald F. Carmony, *Indiana 1816–1850: The Pioneer Era* (Indianapolis: Indiana Historical Bureau and Indiana Historical Society, 1998), citing the *Directory*. Party affiliations appear in the *Indiana Year Book* beginning in 1900.

IOWA

Statehood: A constitutional convention met at Iowa City, the capital, on May 4, 1846, and drafted a constitution that was approved by the voters of Iowa (9,492 to 9,036) on August 3. On October 26 the first legislature was elected; it convened on November 30. On December 28 President Polk signed the bill formally admitting Iowa to the Union. Iowa City was the capital until 1857, when the capital was moved to Des Moines.

Term: Senators have always been elected for a four-year term; terms overlap so that one-half the body is elected every two years. Members of the House have since statehood served a two-year term.

Districts/Elections: Senators have been elected from single-member districts, but no district could include more than four counties. In 1928 an amendment limited a county to no more than one seat, nor could any county be divided in the formation of a district. House members were initially elected from single-member districts of from one to four counties. Under the 1857 constitution it would appear that a second seat was given to a county or district with more than one and one-half ratios. (A ratio is the population necessary to have a seat in a legislative body.) In 1904 the formula was changed so that each county was guaranteed one seat, leaving a remainder of nine seats to be apportioned to the nine most populous counties; thus nine two-member districts were created. The implementation of one person, one vote apportionment initially resulted in the more populous counties electing all members at large, but in 1968 these counties were divided into single-member districts. Since 1972 districts have crossed county lines.

Membership/Size: The first legislature consisted of 18 senators and 40 representatives. The Senate reached its present size of 50 in 1869 after five increases. There were temporary increases in that body in 1964 and 1966. But the Senate was returned to 50 members in 1970. The House increased to 100 members by 1867 as a result of five increases. The total was increased to 108 in 1906 and remained unchanged until an increase to 124 in 1964. The body was reduced to its present size of 100 in 1970.

Reapportionment/Redistricting: In 1857, 1865, 1876, 1886, 1906 (Senate), 1911 (Senate), 1921 (House), 1927 (House),[1] 1961, 1966 1968, 1970, 1972, 1982, 1992 and 2002.

Election Dates: Originally the first Monday in August, changed in 1857 to the second Tuesday in October. In 1884 the present date was selected: the first Tuesday after the first Monday in November.

Constitutions: There have been two constitutions, 1846 and 1857.

Affiliations	Senate D / W		House D / W	
1846	**(18)**	12 / 6	**(40)**	17 / 23
1848		11 / 8		28 / 11
1850		13 / 5		34 / 5
1852	**(31)**	20 / 11	**(63)**	40 / 23
1854		17 / 14	**(71)**	31 / 40

Affiliations	Senate D / R / oth		House D / R / oth	
1856	**(35)**	12 / 23		26 / 44
1857		14 / 22		30 / 42
1859	**(43)**	20 / 23	**(86)**	37 / 49
1861	**(46)**	14 / 32	**(94)**	34 / 60
1863		4 / 42		5 / 87
1865	**(47)**	5 / 42		15 / 83
1867		7 / 42	**(100)**	14 / 86
1869	**(50)**	7 / 43		14 / 86
1871		8 / 42		22 / 78
1873		6 / 34 / 10 I		6 / 50 / 44 I
1875		9 / 41		30 / 70
1877		12 / 38		25 / 73 / 2 G
1879		7 / 41 / 2 G		14 / 82 / 4 G
1881		2 / 46 / 2 G		22 / 71 / 7 G
1883		11 / 39		42 / 52 / 6 G
1885		19 / 31		39 / 60 / 1 I
1887		15 / 35		33 / 64 / 3 I
1889		20 / 28 / 1 I, 1 UL		45 / 50 / 4 I, 1 UL
1891		25 / 24 / 1 Pop		45 / 54 / 1I
1893		16 / 34		21 / 79
1895		7 / 43		20 / 80

Affiliations	*Senate* D / R / oth	*House* D / R / oth
1897	11 / 39	38 / 62
1899	8 / 42	19 / 81
1901	11 / 39	16 / 84
1903	8 / 42	22 / 78
1905	10 / 40	18 / 82
1906[1]	14 / 36	(108) 33 / 75
1908	16 / 34	28 / 80
1910	16 / 34	38 / 70
1912	17 / 33	42 / 66
1914	15 / 35	32 / 76
1916	10 / 40	14 / 94
1918	5 / 45	15 / 93
1920	2 / 48	6 / 101 / 1 I
1922	4 / 46	16 / 91 / 1 I
1924	4 / 45 / 1 I	7 / 101
1926	1 / 48 / 1 ID	13 / 95
1928	2 / 48	12 / 96
1930	6 / 44	37 / 71
1932	25 / 25	76 / 32
1934	28 / 22	58 / 50
1936	28 / 22	54 / 54
1938	12 / 38	19 / 89
1940	5 / 45	21 / 87
1942	5 / 45	10 / 98
1944	5 / 45	17 / 91
1946	4 / 46	10 / 98
1948	7 / 43	29 / 79
1950	9 / 41	15 / 93
1952	4 / 46	3 / 105
1954	6 / 44	18 / 90
1956	10 / 40	37 / 71
1958	17 / 33	50 / 58
1960	15 / 35	30 / 78
1962	12 / 38	30 / 78
1964	(59) 34 / 25	(124) 101 / 23
1966	(61) 32 / 29	35 / 89
1968	17 / 44	38 / 86
1970	(50) 12 / 38	(100) 37 / 63
1972	22 / 28	43 / 57
1974	26 / 24	61 / 39
1976	26 / 24	59 / 41
1978	22 / 28	43 / 57
1980	21 / 29	42 / 58
1982	28 / 22	60 / 40
1984	29 / 21	60 / 40
1986	30 / 20	58 / 42
1988	30 / 20	61 / 39
1990	28 / 22	53 / 47

Affiliations	Senate D / R / oth	House D / R / oth
1992	26 / 24	49 / 51
1994	27 / 23	36 / 64
1996	21 / 29	46 / 54
1998	20 / 30	44 / 56
2000	20 / 30	44 / 56
2002	21 / 29	46 / 54
2004	25 / 25	49 / 51
2006	30 / 20	54 / 46

NOTES

1. In both 1932 and 1942 two counties were reapportioned in the House.

SOURCES

Research was done at the Iowa State Historical Society (Archives) in Des Moines. The state returns provided much of the data for the pre–Civil War era. Editions of the *Iowa Official Register* were used from 1888. The state also supplied data since 1966.

KANSAS

Statehood: An enabling act passed in May 1858 allowed the territory to become a state under the controversial Lecompton constitution. This constitution was rejected on August 2, 1858. A new convention convened at Wyandotte on January 11, 1859, and its work was approved on October 4, 1859 by a vote of 10,421 to 5,530. The first legislature was elected on December 6, 1859, but statehood was not achieved until January 20, 1861. The first legislature convened in March, 1861. Topeka has been the capital since statehood.

Term: Senators were originally elected for two years until 1876 when the term was increased to four years. Representatives were initially elected for one year, increased to two years in 1876.

Districts/Elections: Originally members were elected from single- and multi-member districts made up of one or more counties. Beginning in 1876 senators were elected from single-member districts. In the same year each county was guaranteed at least one member in the House, leaving 20 other seats for the more populous counties. In fact no county had more than three seats, all elected countywide. Since one person, one vote apportionment all members have been elected from single-member districts without regard for county boundaries.

Membership/Size: The Senate had 25 members at its outset, increased to 33 in 1872 and 40 in 1876. The House had 75 members originally and was increased 10 times, reaching 125 in 1876.

Reapportionment/Redistricting: In 1862, 1866, 1871, 1876, 1886, 1891, 1897, 1909 1933 and 1947 (Senate), 1959, 1961 (House), 1963 (Senate), 1968 (Senate), 1972, 1974, 1982, 1992 and 2002

Election Dates: Elections have always been held on the first Tuesday after the first Monday in November.

Constitutions: The constitution written in 1859 is in effect today.

Affiliations	*Senate* D / R	*House* D / R
1859	(**25**) 3 / 22	(**75**) 11 / 64
1862	2 / 20 / 2 I, 1 ID	8 / 57[1]
1863	—	R majority[2]
1864	1 / 19 / 5[3]	(**78**) 7 / 62 / 9[4]
1865	—	10 / 61 / 7[5]
1866	5 / 22	(**82**) 13 / 69
1867	—	(**88**) 26 / 62
1868	1 / 24	(**90**) 6 / 84
1869	—	(**91**) R majority[6]
1870	0 / 25	(**98**) 16 / 82
1871	—	(**94**) R majority[7]
1872	(**33**) 1 / 27 / 5 Fm	2 / 51 / 34 Fm, 18 I
1873	—	(**107**) 3 / 57 / 47[8]
1874	3 / 21 / 9 Rf	10 / 75 / 20 Rf, 2 ?
1875	—	(**104**) 9 / 77 / 18[9]
1876	(**40**) 5 / 35	(**125**) 18 / 107
1878	—	17 / 108
1880	2 / 37 / 1 Fus	9 / 112 / 4 Fus
1882	—	26 / 86 / 13 G
1884	3 / 37	11 / 107 / 7 I
1886	—	24 / 97 / 3 I, 1 Lab
1888	1 / 39	2 / 121 / 2 UL
1890	—	7 / 26 / 92 FA
1892	2 / 15 / 23 Pop	2 / 64 / 58 Pop, 1 I[10]
1894	—	1 / 91 / 33 Pop
1896	2 / 11 / 27 Pop	8 / 47 / 67 Pop, 3 SilR
1898	—	0 / 92 / 33 Pop
1900	2 / 31 / 7 Pop	12 / 81 / 30 Pop, 2 SilR
1902	—	30 / 95

Affiliations	Senate D / R	House D / R
1904	3 / 37	15 / 110
1906	—	31 / 94
1908	6 / 34	40 / 84 / 1 I
1910	—	53 / 71 / 1 I
1912	21 / 18 / 1 S	72 / 51 / 2 S
1914	—	49 / 66 / 9 Pg, 1 S
1916	9 / 31	37 / 86 / 2 S
1918	—	15 / 110
1920	2 / 38	12 / 113
1922	—	30 / 95
1924	8 / 32	33 / 92
1926	—	33 / 92
1928	3 / 37	24 / 101
1930	—	48 / 77
1932	17 / 23	60 / 65
1934	—	50 / 75
1936	15 / 25	51 / 74
1938	—	17 / 108
1940	5 / 35	27 / 98
1942	—	12 / 113
1944	1 / 39	5 / 120
1946	—	17 / 108
1948	6 / 34	30 / 95
1950	—	20 / 105
1952	5 / 35	20 / 105
1954	—	36 / 89
1956	8 / 32	42 / 83
1958	—	56 / 69
1960	8 / 32	43 / 82
1962	—	36 / 89
1964	13 / 27	45 / 80
1966	—	48 / 77
1968	8 / 32	38 / 87
1970	—	41 / 84
1972	13 / 27	45 / 80
1974	—	53 / 72
1976	19 / 21	65 / 60
1978	—	56 / 69
1980	17 / 23	53 / 72
1982	—	53 / 72
1984	16 / 24	49 / 76
1986	—	51 / 74
1988	18 / 22	58 / 67
1990	—	63 / 62
1992	14 / 26	59 / 66
1994	—	45 / 80
1996	13 / 27	48 / 77
1998	—	48 / 77

Affiliations	Senate D / R	House D / R
2000	10 / 30	46 / 79
2002	—	45 / 80
2004	10 / 30	42 / 83
2006	—	47 / 78

NOTES

1. 7 U, 1 Ab, 1 I, 1 ?
2. Of those who could identified by party the totals were 30 R, 3 D and 42 ?
3. 2 I, 2 WD, 1 Nat
4. 1 WD, 1 I, 1 IR, 4 Ab, 2 ?
5. 1 AdD, 1 I, 1 IR, 1 W, 3 ?
6. Of those who could be identified by party the totals were 50 R, 7 D, 1 ID and 33 ?
7. Of those who could be identified by party the totals were 29 R, 3 D, 4 I, 1 IR, 1 Rf and 56 ?
8. 18 Rf, 10 I, 9 Fm, 4 Lib, 2 IR, 1 LI, 2 ?, 1 vac
9. 9 I, 4 IR, 3 Rf, 1 RfR, 1 ?
10. There was considerable controversy over a few seats that determined who would organize the House. For the figures used here I relied on the information in Wynne P. Harrington, *The Populist Party In Kansas* (Kansas State Historical Society), Vol. XVI, pp. 421–431.

SOURCES

Annals of Kansas 1862–1876, (Topeka) *State Record,* January 1, 1868. Wynne P. Harrington, *The Populist Party in Kansas* (Kansas State Historical Society), Volume XVI for the period 1890–1900. William F. Zornow, *Kansas: A History of the Jayhawk State,* (Norman: University Oklahoma Press, 1957), for much of the material between 1908–1956. Also Charles H. Titus, "Voting in Kansas, 1900–1932," *Kansas Historical Quarterly*, August 1935, for the elections of 1908–1932. Thomas Page, *Legislative Apportionment in Kansas* (Bureau of Government Research, University of Kansas; 1952).

KENTUCKY

Statehood: On December 18, 1789, the state of Virginia agreed to the separation of the area called the district of Kentucky. The U.S. Congress then provided for the admission of the area as a state on February 4,

1791, effective June 1, 1792. A constitutional convention meeting in Danville wrote the document between April 2 and 19, 1792, and proclaimed it in effect. Elections followed in May and the legislature convened on June 4, 1792, at Lexington. The first legislature selected Frankfort as the state capital, and the legislature met there for the first time in 1793.

Term: Senators have always been elected for a four-year term. Initially, one-quarter of the body was elected annually. Since the constitution of 1850, one-half of the Senate has been elected every two years. The House was elected annually until 1851, when the term was increased to two years.

Districts/Elections: Senators were initially indirectly elected by an electoral college. The electors were chosen by the voters in the same manner as the House of Representatives. These electors in turn chose the senators. At least one senator had to be chosen from each county before any county had two. Popular elections were introduced effective in 1800. The elected senators were chosen from single-member districts, but no county could be divided between districts. The 1850 constitution also provided for only single-member districts, and this has continued to the present. The 1890 constitution permitted the division of a county into districts, provided that county was entitled to two or more districts.

The House was apportioned among the counties, all members elected from countywide districts. Under the 1890 constitution counties with more than one member could be divided into districts but no district could consist of more than two counties. But in fact districts had as many four counties in effort to reconcile the matter with the constitutional provision of equal population districts; this was in fact upheld by the Kentucky Court of Appeals. All members since one person, one vote apportionment have been elected from single-member districts.

Membership/Size: The Senate initially had 11 members, increased to 15 in 1796. The constitution of 1799 created a 24-member body than soon (by at least 1824) grew to 38. The number has not changed since. The House had an original membership of 40, increasing in four successive steps to 62 in 1800. The constitution of 1799 established the number at 58 but the number soon reached 100, the present total.

Reapportionment/Redistricting: There were several early reapportionments in 1794, 1796 and 1800.[1] Reapportionments also occurred in 1891, 1919, 1942 and 1963. Since equal population apportionment, reapportionments have occurred in 1973, 1983/4, 1992, 1996 and 2002.

Election Dates: First Tuesday in May until 1801 when the date was changed to the first Monday in August. The present date, the first Tuesday after the first Monday in November, took effect in 1895.

Constitutions: There have been four constitutions: 1792, 1799, 1850 and 1891.

Addendum: In order to change legislative elections to even-numbered years, senators elected in 1981 and 1983 served a five-year term, and House members elected in 1981 served a three-year term.

Affiliations	*Senate* NCt / OCt	*House* NCt / OCt
1825	21 / 17	38 / 62
1826	16 / 22	44 / 56
	(J)D / Ad	*(J)D / Ad / oth*
1827[2]	18 / 20	46 / 54
1828	16 / 20	57 / 42 / 1 ?
1829	14 / 24	36 / 64
1830	18 / 20	44 / 55 / 1 tie
1831	20 / 18	48 / 52
1832	16 / 22	40 / 60
1833[3]	20 / 18	40 / 60
	D / W	*D / W / oth*
1834	17 / 21	25 / 75
1835[4]	15 / 23	37 / 63
1836	14 / 24	42 / 58
1837	14 / 24	29 / 71
1838	16 / 22	32 / 68
1839	16 / 22	38 / 60 / 2 ?
1840	14 / 24	24 / 76
1841	11 / 27	23 / 77
1842	9 / 29	43 / 57
1843	12 / 26	38 / 62
1844	12 / 26	35 / 64 / 1 ?
1845	14 / 24	38 / 62
1846	12 / 26	37 / 63
1847	11 / 27	41 / 59
1848	11 / 27	36 / 64
1849	11 / 27	41 / 59
1850	13 / 25	43 / 57
1851	18 / 20	45 / 55
1853	15 / 23	45 / 55
	D / A / oth	*D / A / oth*
1855	13 / 25	39 / 61

Affiliations	Senate	House
	D / A / oth	*D / A / oth*
1857	18 / 20	61 / 39
1859	24 / / 14 Opp	59 / / 41 Opp
	U / StR	*U / StR*
1861	76 / 24	27 / 11
1863	38 / 0	96 / 4
	C / Rad	*C / Rad*
1865	20 / 18	60 / 40
	D / R / oth	*D / R / oth*
1867[5]	28 / 7 / 3 UD	85 / 10 / 5 UD
1869	36 / 2	92 / 8
1871[6]	35 / 3	88 / 12
1873	31 / 7	80 / 20
1875	32 / 6	89 / 11
1877	37 / 1	87 / 13
1879	34 / 4	80 / 20
1881	26 / 8 / 4 G	72 / 20 / 4 G
1883	33 / 5	89 / 11
1885	35 / 3	80 / 20
1887	32 / 6	70 / 25 / 3 P, 2 Lab
1889	31 / 7	86 / 14
1891[7]	27 / 11	73 / 22 / 5 Pop
1893	27 / 11	76 / 22 / 2 Pop
1895	22 / 16	46 / 52 / 1 Pop, 1 IPg
1897	27 / 11	73 / 25 / 2 Pop
1899	26 / 12	60 / 40
1901	25 / 13	73 / 26 / 1 ID
1903	30 / 7 / 1 vac	77 / 23
1905	31 / 7	73 / 27
1907	22 / 16	51 / 49
1909	26 / 12	73 / 27
1911	32 / 6	76 / 24
1913	32 / 6	79 / 20 / 1 Fus
1915	28 / 10	64 / 36
1917	24 / 14	60 / 40
1919	20 / 18	45 / 55
1921	20 / 18	68 / 32
1923	25 / 13	67 / 32 / 1 I
1925	26 / 12	65 / 35
1927	24 / 14	62 / 38
1929	24 / 14	66 / 34
1931	26 / 12	74 / 26
1933	26 / 12	70 / 30

Affiliations	Senate D / R / oth	House D / R / oth
1935	26 / 12	66 / 34
1937	28 / 10	76 / 24
1939	29 / 9	73 / 27
1941	29 / 9	75 / 25
1943	23 / 15	57 / 43
1945	21 / 17	69 / 31
1947	29 / 9	75 / 25
1949	29 / 9	76 / 24
1951	28 / 10	73 / 27
1953	29 / 9	79 / 21
1955	30 / 8	77 / 23
1957	29 / 9	75 / 25
1959	30 / 8	80 / 20
1961	29 / 9	74 / 26
1963	25 / 13	63 / 37
1965	26 / 12	64 / 36
1967	24 / 14	59 / 41
1969	24 / 14	71 / 29
1971	27 / 11	73 / 27
1973	29 / 9	80 / 20
1975	30 / 8	79 / 21
1977	30 / 8	78 / 22
1979	30 / 8	75 / 25
1981	29 / 9	76 / 24
1983	28 / 10	no election (see addenda)
1984	no election (see addenda)	74 / 26
1986	29 / 9	73 / 27
1988	29 / 9	71 / 29
1990	27 / 11	68 / 32
1992	25 / 13	72 / 28
1994	21 / 17	64 / 36
1996	20 / 18	64 / 36
1998	20 / 18	66 / 34
2000	18 / 20	64 / 36
2002	17 / 21	65 / 35
2004	15 / 23	57 / 43
2006	16 / 21 / 1 I	61 / 39

NOTES

1. Reapportionments between 1800 and 1891 could not be ascertained.

2. Source is the (Frankfort) *Spirit of 76*, August 30, 1827, but the (Lexington) *Kentucky Gazette* citing the *Frankfort Argus* has the Senate 17 J / 21 Ad and the House 46 J / 54 Ad.

3. The *Frankfort Commentator*, August 19, 1834, is used here, but the *Argus*, August 20, 1834, gives a House breakdown of D 37 / NR 63 and the *Lexington Intelligencer*, August 22, 1834, has it D 41 / 59 NR.

4. The *Intelligencer*, August 25, is used for the Senate, but the *Argus* gives the

breakdown as 17 D / 21 W and the *Commentator* 16 D / 22 W, both August 22, 1835. For the House the figure cited is from the *Intelligencer*, August 22, 1835 but the *Commentator* three days earlier has 39 D / 61 W, the Argus 41 D / 59 W, same date.

5. Figures cited are from the *Tribune Almanac 1868*, but the *Evening Journal Almanac, 1868*, has 30 D / 8 R and 85 D / 11 R / 4 UD. The *World Almanac, 1868*, has 28 D / 7 R / 3 UD and 90 D / 10 R.

6. Figures cited are from the *Tribune Almanac, 1871*, but the *Evening Journal Almanac, 1871*, gives D 30 / 8 R and 91 D / 9 R.

7. Figures cited are from the *Tribune Almanac, 1892*, but the *World Almanac, 1892*, gives 28 D / 9 R / 1 Pe & All and 75 D / 16 R / 9 Pe & All.

SOURCES

Research was done at the State Archives, State Library and Kentucky Historical Society, all in Frankfort. Also the Lexington Public Library, University of Kentucky in Lexington, the Filson Club in Louisville and the Louisville Public Library.

A variety of Kentucky newspapers were used from the earliest period through 1863: (Lexington) *Reporter*, 1825, 1829, 1830, *Frankfort Argus*, 1826, 1828, 1832, 1834, 1835, (Frankfort) *Spirit of 76*, 1827, *Louisville Public Advertiser*, 1827, 1831, (Louisville) *Daily Journal* 1831, (Lexington) *Kentucky Observer*, 1832, 1849, *Frankfort Commentator*, 1833–35, 1837–40, 1844, 1857, 1861, *Lexington Intelligencer*, 1833–39, (Lexington) *Kentucky Gazette*, 1836, 1838, *Paris Western Citizen*, 1846. From 1893 to 1973 I relied primarily on the *Kentucky Directory & Manual* through 1955 and the *Kentucky Government Guide* 1959–1973 as well as the *Kentucky General Assembly Membership* Vol. 1 1900–1949, Vol. 2 1950–2000.

Since 1971 official returns have been supplied by the Kentucky Board of Elections. Secondary works used were Richard H. Collins, *History of Kentucky*, Vol. 1 (Lexington: Collins & Co. 1878, James C. Klotter and Hambleton Tapp, *Kentucky: Decades of Discord 1865–1900* (Frankfort: Kentucky Historical Society, 1977), and Thomas D. Clark, *A History of Kentucky* (Lexington: The John Bradford Press, 1960). For much of the compilation prior to 1893 multiple sources were used that on occasion resulted in conflicting totals. Generally speaking, when nothing else guided me, I used the latest dated source.

LOUISIANA

Statehood: President Madison signed an enabling act on February 18, 1811. A constitutional convention assembled at New Orleans on November 4, 1811, and finished its work on January 28, 1812. Louisiana formally became a state on April 30, 1812. The first legislature was elected June

29–July 1, 1812. The capital was moved from New Orleans to Donaldsville in 1830 and back to New Orleans in 1831. Baton Rouge became the capital in 1846 and New Orleans again in 1864. Baton Rouge again became the capital in 1880.

Term: Senators since statehood have been elected for a term of four years. Initially they served overlapping terms, one-half the body elected every two years. Since 1880 they have all been elected at the same time. The House was initially elected for two years, increased to four years in 1880.

Districts/Elections: Under the 1812 constitution the Senate was elected from single-member districts, except for Orleans parish which was divided into two districts; all the other districts were made up of one or more parishes. The 1845 constitution essentially continued the same districting system except for Orleans which was divided into four districts. The maximum number of senators allowed any parish was ⅛ of the total or four. The 1864 constitution divided the Senate into 22 districts creating both single- and multi-member districts. In 1956 a provision stated that when a district is given more than one senator that has more than one parish, no parish could elect more than one member. The House was apportioned among the parishes and in 1845 each parish was guaranteed at least one representative; this had been the practice up to that time. The 1864 constitution divided the House into 48 single- and multi-member districts. Orleans parish was divided into ten multi-member districts.

Since the implementation of one person, one vote all members have been elected from single-member districts.

Membership/Size: The original Senate had 14 members, increased to 32 by the constitution of 1845, and to 36 by the constitution of 1864. The Senate reached 41 members in 1908, reduced to its present size of 39 in 1924. The original House consisted of 35 members; three increases raised the total to 60 members in 1841. The 1845 constitution increased membership to 98. The number fluctuated on several occasions over the next three decades before again being set at 98 by the constitution of 1879. By 1912 membership stood at 118. But by virtue of the 1921 constitution the number was set at 101 and finally 105 in 1964.

Reapportionment/Redistricting: 1816, 1818, 1822, 1826, 1841,[1] 1845, 1848, 1852, 1854, 1859, 1868, 1871, 1876, 1878, 1880, 1900, 1922, 1956 (Senate), 1964,[2] 1968, 1972, 1983, 1995 and 2003.

Election Dates: Elections were originally held over a three-day period beginning on the first Monday in July. In 1846 this was changed to the first Monday in November and in 1855 to the first Tuesday after the first Monday in November. Beginning in 1884 elections were held on Tuesday after the third Monday in April. But in 1960 the date was changed to either February or March of a presidential election year, depending on whether a runoff primary was required. Under 1974 legislation, which established the open primary, the open primary took place on the first Saturday in November beginning in 1975. Runoffs were to be held on the sixth Saturday thereafter.

Constitutions: The state has had more constitutions than any other, 11 in all: 1812, 1845, 1852, 1861, 1865, 1868, 1879, 1898, 1913, 1921 and 1974.

Affiliations	*Senate*		*House*	
	D / NR		*D / NR*	
1828	6 / 11 / 1 ?		21 / 26 / 3 ?	
1830	NR majority		NR majority	
1832	?		?	
	D / W / oth		*D / W / oth*	
1834	W majority		W majority	
1836	D majority		D majority	
1838	—[3]		17 / 31 / 2 NPty	
1840	8 / 8 / 1 ?		14 / 26 / 10 ?	
1842	8 / 9		26 / 34	
1844	9 / 8		26 / 34	
1846[4]	(32) 20 / 12		(98) 55 / 43	
1847	17 / 15		47 / 51	
1849	18 / 14		(97) 43 / 54	
1851	16 / 16		44 / 53	
1852[5]	(36) 17 / 19		(91) 50 / 41	
1853	20 / 12		60 / 37	
	D / A / oth		*D / A / oth*	
1855	(32) 18 / 12 / 1 anti–KN, 1 vac		(88) 47 / 41	
1857	23 / 9		49 / 37 / 1 IW, 1 tie	
1859	21 / 6 / 3 Opp, 1 I, 1 vac		(98) 59 / 18 / 9 Opp, 9 I, 3 ?	
	D / R		*D / R*	
1865	—		—	
1868	(36) 16 / 20		(101) 45 / 56	
1870	7 / 29[6]		29 / 74 / 2 vac	
1872[7]	—		(110) —	

Affiliations	*Senate* D / R	*House* D / R
1874[8]	—	—
1876[9]	20 / 16	64 / 42 / 4 vac
1878	26 / 10	75 / 16 / 2 G, 1 I
1880	32 / 4	(98) 74 / 24
1884	31 / 5	85 / 13
1888	(38) 33 / 5	86 / 12
1892	38 / 0	96 / 2
1896	28 / 7 / 1Pop	60 / 24 / 14 Pop
1900	(39) 39 / 0	98 / 0
1904	39 / 0	98 / 0
1908	(41) 41 / 0	(114) 114 / 0
1912	39 / 0 / 2 NPty	(118) 118 / 0
1916	36 / 0 / 5Pg	106 / 0 / 12Pg
1920	41 / 0	118 / 0
1924	(39) 39 / 0	(101) 101 / 0
1928	39 / 0	101 / 0
1932	39 / 0	101 / 0
1936	39 / 0	101 / 0
1940	39 / 0	101 / 0
1944	39 / 0	101 / 0
1948	39 / 0	101 / 0
1952	39 / 0	101 / 0
1956	39 / 0	101 / 0
1960	39 / 0	101 / 0
1964	39 / 0	(105) 103 / 2
1968	39 / 0	105 / 0
1972	38 / 1	103 / 2
1975	39 / 0	101 / 4
1979	39 / 0	99 / 6
1983	38 / 1	93 / 11 / 1 NPty
1987	34 / 5	88 / 16 / 1 NPty
1991	33 / 6	86 / 17 / 1 I, 1 vac
1995	25 / 14	76 / 28 / 1vac
1999	27 / 12	75 / 30
2003	26 / 13	68 / 36 / 1 I

NOTES

1. Reapportionments until 1845 were of the House only.

2. The only change was the addition of four seats.

3. *Niles Register*, July 21, 1838, states 10 or 11 Whigs out of 17.

4. As a result of the implementation of the 1845 constitution a general election was held on January 5, 1846, and then elections were held in odd years.

5. To implement the 1852 constitution, a general election was held on December 6, 1852, and then in odd years thereafter.

6. The *Picayune* lists the totals as "7 colored Republicans, 29 white Republicans and 7 Democrats." But the total membership was 36. The State Archives

provided a list of Senators for this session, listing 36 members. It is likely that paper listed the total 29 *white* Republicans when it was the total of *all* Republicans, for 7 and 29 adds up to a total of 36 members.

7. There were essentially two sets of returns for this election. One set of returns known as the Lynch (returning) Board, listed the totals as Senate 28 R / 8 D and the House 77 R / 32 D. The Forman Board reported 75 D / 35 R in the Senate; for only that part elected in 1872, 15 D / 4 R. A total of 58 House and 8 Senate seats were disputed. For a detailed discussion of the attempt to resolve the disputed seats see Ella Lonn, *Reconstruction in Louisiana (after 1868),* reprint edition (Gloucecster: Peter Smith, 1967). Chapters VIII–XIII. For some time after the election there were two functioning legislatures in the state.

8. There were conflicting claims to many legislative seats and in reality two sets of returns. The State Canvassing Board certified 53 Democrats and 53 Republicans as winners but failed to act on the five remaining seats. The Democratic Committee gave results as 71 D / 37 R. Little mention is made of the division of the Senate. But the one reference in Lonn's work (p. 370) to the proposed "Wheeler Compromise" puts the Senate at 27 R / 9 D and the House at 63D / 47 R.

9. Two sets of returns were found. One claiming to be the "Official Returns" of the Returning Board listed the Senate as 19 R / 17 D, the House as 71 R / 43 D / 3 I, 3 ? (found in the *Picayune,* December 8, 1876). The other set of returns, from the Democratic-Conservative Executive Committee appeared in the same source on December 10, 1876, and gave the Senate as 19 D / 17 R and the House as 60 R / 52D / 3 I, 5 ?. Several of the Republican victories were challenged. The eventual figures were the result of much political manuevering where dual legislatures functioned until April 1877. These figures were found in Lonn, pp. 524–5, citing *Appleton Cyclopaedia,* 1877.

SOURCES

Some of the pre–Civil War data was taken from William H. Adams, *The Whig Party of Louisiana* (Lafayette: University of Southwestern Louisiana, 1973). For a discussion of Reconstruction Era controversies we used Ella Lonn, *Reconstruction in Louisiana (after 1868),* reprint edition (Gloucester: Peter Smith, 1967). The State Archives provided a list of members for both houses for 1871–1876. A listing of House members was obtained from the House website for the years 1878–1920. Data since 1972 was provided by the state. Also: *Niles Register,* July 21, 1838, July 25, 1840, July 30, 1842, and December 4, 1847. (Baton Rouge) *Weekly Advocate,* November 17, 1855, November 15, 22, 1857, November 27, 1859. (New Orleans) *Daily Picayune,* December 13, 1870, December 23, 1874, December 20, 1878. Emmett Asseff, *Legislative Apportionment in Louisiana* (Baton Rouge: Bureau of Government Research, Louisiana State University, 1950).

MAINE

Statehood: Maine was part of Massachusetts (known as the District of Maine) until March 15, 1820, when it became a state. The Massachusetts legislature had voted on June 19, 1819, to allow Maine residents to conduct a referendum on this issue (there had been five previous referendums), and on July 26 voters, by a vote of 17,091–7,132, approved separation. The constitutional convention convened in Portland (the capital) on October 17; after finishing their work, they submitted it to the voters. On December 6, the new constitution was approved 9,040 to 797. Following statehood (March 15, 1820) the first legislature was elected on April 3, 1820, and convened on May 20.

The capital remained at Portland until 1832, when it was moved to Augusta.

Term: Members of both houses were elected annually until 1880 when the term was increased to two years.

Districts/Elections: Senators were originally elected from single- and multi-member districts, usually of one county. Later apportionments created multi-county districts as well as districts that crossed county lines. By amendment effective in 1932, senators were apportioned among the counties and all were elected countywide based on a formula that guaranteed each county at least one member and a maximum of five. Since 1968 all members have been elected from single-member districts. The House was apportioned among the cities and towns based on a formula that limited representation to seven members for any one community. Towns falling below the minimum were formed into districts with similar communities. Towns and cities entitled to more than one member elected them at large. Similar to the Senate, single-member districts were instituted in 1968. Elections to both houses originally required a majority of votes cast. In the absence of a majority, the two houses jointly filled Senate vacancies, choosing between the top two vote-getters for each vacancy. This practice was eliminated in 1875. In the House additional elections were held until a majority vote was achieved. This practice was eliminated in 1847.

Membership/Size: The Senate initially had 20 members but reached its original maximum of 31 by 1841. It was increased to 33 in 1932 and to

34 in 1962; decreased to 32 in 1968; increased again to 33 in 1972; and finally increased to 35 in 1984. The House originally had 151 members in 1821, increased to 200 by 1841 and reduced to 151 effective in 1842. The number has remained unchanged ever since.[1]

Reapportionment/Redistricting: In 1831 (House), 1842 (House),[2] 1932 (House), 1952 (Senate), 1956 (House), 1962, 1964 (House), 1967 (Senate), 1972 (Senate), 1974 (House), 1984, 1993,[3] 1994 and 2004.

Election Dates: The second Monday in September until 1958 when it was changed to the first Tuesday after the first Monday in November. Maine was last state to switch to November elections.

Constitutions: The state has but one constitution, written in 1819.

Affiliations	Senate D-R / F		House D-R / F	
1820	(20)	—	(139)	—
1821		—	(150)	—
1822		—	(148)	—
1823		—	(147)	—
1824		—	(146)	—
1825		—	(150)	—
1826		—	(150	—
1827		—	(150)	—
	J / Ad		*J / Ad / oth*	
1828	Ad majority		(148) Ad majority	
1829	8 / 12		(146) —[4]	
1830	11 / 9		(149) 86 / 62 / 1 ?	
1831	(25) 21 / 4		(184) 100 / 58 / 24 ?, 2 x	
	D / Ad / oth		*D / Ad / oth*	
1832	15 / 10		(186) 97 / 59 / 30 ?[5]	
1833	21 / 3 / 1 A-M		(184) 79 / 39 / 63 ?[6]	
	D / W / oth		*D / W / oth*	
1834	18 / 7		(186) 94 / 66 / 26 ?	
1835	22 / 3		(186) 51 / 41 / 94 ?	
1836	21 / 4		(186) 108 / 54 / 24 ?	
1837	14 / 11		(188) 85 / 98 / 5 ?	
1838	15 / 10		(190) 107 / 73 / 9 ?, 1 x	
1839	17 / 8		(191) 123 / 63 / 5 ?	
1840	8 / 17		(190) 66 / 94 / 30 ?	
1841	(31) 27 / 4		(204) 131 / 55 / 18 ?	
1842	30 / 1		(151) 55 / 18 / 78 ?	
1843	28 / 3		72 / 33 / 2 Lty, 44 ?[7]	

Affiliations	*Senate* *D / W / oth*	*House* *D / W / oth*
1844	28 / 3	68 / 29 / 54 ?[5]
1845	27 / 4	85 / 66
1846	27 / 4	78 / 66 / 6 Lty, 1 I
1847	27 / 4	102 / 49
1848	20 / 11	85 / 66
1849	20 / 11	88 / 63
1850	26 / 4 / 1 FS	93 / 50 / 8 FS
1852[8]	9 / 22	84 / 62 / 4 FS, 1 ?
1853	14 / 17	76 / 66 / 9 FS
1854	10 / 16 / 5 FS	83 / 44 / 23 FS, 1 ?
	D / R / oth	*D / R / oth*
1855	20 / 2 / 9 W	68 / 61 / 22 W
1856	1 / 30	26 / 125
1857	1 / 30	34 / 117
1858	1 / 30	48 / 103
1859	1 / 30	32 / 119
1860	0 / 31	23 / 128
1861	5 / 26	28 / 123
1862	6 / 25	44 / 107
1863	1 / 30	31 / 120
1864	3 / 28	22 / 129
1865	0 / 31	15 / 136
1866	0 / 31	13 / 138
1867	3 / 28	46 / 105
1868	2 / 29	28 / 123
1869	3 / 28	34 / 117
1870	3 / 28	38 / 113
1871	3 / 28	39 / 112
1872	0 / 30 / 1 LR	19 / 128 / 2 I, 2 LR
1873	0 / 30 / 1 LR	41 / 103 / 7 I
1874	3 / 28	55 / 89 / 7 I
1875	11 / 20	63 / 85 / 3 I
1876	2 / 29	30 / 120 / 1 I
1877	3 / 28	47 / 99 / 3 I, 2 G
1878	1 / 20 / 10 G	27 / 65 / 57 G, 2 I
1879	1 / 19 / 11 G	11 / 90 / 50 G
1880	2 / 23 / 6 G	27 / 84 / 40 G
1882	3 / 28	43 / 108
1884	0 / 31	34 / 115 / 2 G
1886	4 / 27	29 / 122
1888	0 / 31	26 / 125
1890	4 / 27	41 / 110
1892	1 / 30	44 / 107
1894	0 / 31	5 / 146
1896	0 / 31	6 / 145
1898	0 / 31	25 / 126

Affiliations	*Senate* D / R / oth	*House* D / R / oth
1900	1 / 30	19 / 132
1902	1 / 30	23 / 128
1904	4 / 27	25 / 126
1906	8 / 23	63 / 88
1908	8 / 23	51 / 100
1910	22 / 9	86 / 65
1912	10 / 21	72 / 79
1914	14 / 17	69 / 78 / 4 Pg
1916	3 / 28	46 / 105
1918	2 / 29	41 / 110
1920	0 / 31	16 / 135
1922	3 / 28	35 / 116
1924	1 / 30	29 / 122
1926	1 / 30	22 / 129
1928	0 / 31	16 / 135
1930	0 / 31	31 / 120
1932	(33) 7 / 26	58 / 93
1934	11 / 22	55 / 96
1936	4 / 29	27 / 124
1938	2 / 31	27 / 124
1940	2 / 31	23 / 128
1942	1 / 32	15 / 136
1944	2 / 31	15 / 136
1946	3 / 30	25 / 126
1948	5 / 28	25 / 126
1950	2 / 31	24 / 126 / 1I
1952	2 / 31	24 / 127
1954	6 / 27	32 / 119
1956	8 / 25	51 / 100
1958	12 / 21	57 / 94
1960	3 / 30	38 / 113
1962	(34) 5 / 29	41 / 110
1964	29 / 5	80 / 71
1966	10 / 24	56 / 95
1968	(32) 14 / 18	66 / 85
1970	14 / 18	71 / 80
1972	(33) 11 / 22	72 / 79
1974	14 / 19	91 / 59 / 1 I
1976	12 / 21	89 / 62
1978	13 / 19 / 1 I	77 / 73 / 1 ID
1980	16 / 17	84 / 67
1982	23 / 10	92 / 59
1984	(35) 24 / 11	83 / 68
1986	20 / 15	86 / 65
1988	20 / 15	97 / 54
1990	21 / 14	97 / 54
1992	20 / 15	90 / 61
1994	16 / 18 / 1 I	77 / 74

Affiliations	*Senate*	*House*
	D / R / oth	*D / R / oth*
1996	19 / 15 / 1 I	81 / 69 / 1 I
1998	20 / 14 / 1 I	79 / 71 / 1 I
2000	17 / 17 / 1 I	88 / 63 / 1 I
2002	18 / 17	80 / 67 / 3 I, 1 Gr
2004	18 / 17	76 / 73 / 2 I
2006	18 / 17	89 / 60 / 2 I

NOTES

1. Between 1820 and 1841 the number of members fluctuated because not all towns sent members and some towns were entitled to a member for part of the time. The total for each election between 1820 and 1841 is based on a list of members for each session furnished by the State Archives.

2. No information was found on reapportionments after 1842 until 1932.

3. Divided all multi-member districts into single-member districts.

4. In the absence of party totals the vote for Speaker was 114 J / 62 NR / 1 oth.

5. In the absence of complete party totals the vote for Speaker was 73 J / 71 NR.

6. The 39 represents other than Democrats; there was no breakdown between National Republicans and Anti-Masons.

7. In the absence of the complete party totals for 1843 and 1844, the vote for Speaker: 1843, 89 D / 42 W / 2 oth; 1844, 85 D / 49 W / 2 oth.

8. Due to a constitutional change concerning the time officials took office, there were no legislative elections in 1851.

SOURCES

Research was done at the State Archives and Library in Augusta, the Maine Historical Society in Portland and the Portland Public Library.

For the period prior to 1848 I used the following; *Providence Journal*, October 6, 12, 1837, *Niles Register*, January 16, 1830, (Portland) *Eastern Argus*, August 25, November 3, 1829, November 12, 1830, September 2, 16, 20, 23, November 23, December 9, 1831, January 27, September 4, 23, 1832, September 11, 13, 16, 20, December 6, 1833, January 15, 1834, January 17, 1835, September 18, 19, November 14, 1835, December 13, 1836, January 21, 1837, January 27, 1838, September 3, 1838, January 5, 1839, September 21, November 25, 1840, January 13, September 17, October 18, 23, December 14, 1841, January 12, 1842 September 25, October 2, 3, 9, November 11, 1843, September 18, 1844, January 6, 10, 1845, *The* (Portland) *Advertiser*, August 31, September 20, November 6, 1842. Also consulted: Louis C. Hatch, *Maine: A History*, reprint ed. (Somersworth: New Hampshire Publishing Co., 1974). From 1871 until 1972 I used the issues of the *Maine Register*. Since 1972 the data has come from returns furnished by the Secretary of State.

MARYLAND

Constitutional Origins: The first constitution of Maryland was written during the summer of 1776 by 76 delegates elected on August 2, 1776, for that purpose. Following public comment, the convention reconvened and proclaimed the document in effect on November 8, 1776.

Term: Senators were initially indirectly elected (see below) for five years. The term was increased to six years in 1838, with one-third of the body up for election every two years. In 1850 the term was set at four years, the present length, one-half the body every two years, until 1926 when all legislators were elected at the same time for four years.

Members of the House of Delegates were elected annually until 1847 when the term was increased to two years. Effective with the election of 1926 the term became four years, as it remains today.

Districts/Elections: Senators were until 1838 elected by a body called the Electoral College. The electors were chosen by the voters, two per county and one each from the towns of Baltimore and Annapolis. The electors then chose nine members from the Western Shore and six from the Eastern Shore. After 1838 senators were directly elected on a countywide basis; each county plus the city of Baltimore elected one member. The city was given additional representation beginning in 1864 and divided into single-member districts. The counties continued to elect one member each.

The county was also the basis for representation in the House, with members elected at large. Initially each county elected four members to the House and the towns of Baltimore and Annapolis two each. (Annapolis eventually lost its separate representation, in 1837.) Population-based apportionment began in 1837, but no county or city could have more than six members and each county was guaranteed a minimum of two. The city of Baltimore was given additional representation in 1851 but the city was limited to four more members than the most populous county for a total of ten. In 1864 and in all subsequent reapportionments the city was divided into multi-member districts. However, until 1966, except for the city of Baltimore, members apportioned among the counties continued to be elected countywide.

In 1966 one person, one vote reapportionment produced a combination of single- and multi-member districts, but with one exception (a

Senate seat), districts were made up of all or part of a county. In 1974 the state was divided into 47 legislative districts, each electing one senator and three delegates. But in some districts the three delegates were elected from one multi-member and one two-member district or three single-member districts. This mixed system was repeated in the reapportionments of 1982, 1994 and 2002.

Membership/Size: The Senate originally consisted of 15 members. By constitutional amendment the body was increased to 21 in 1838, 22 in 1851, 24 in 1864 and 25 in 1867. Five additional increases have produced a current Senate of 47. The House was originally composed of 80 members and remained unchanged until 1837 when it was increased to 86. There have been numerous increases (see below). The House reached its present size of 141 members in 1974.

Reapportionments/Redistricting: There was no reapportionment provision in the original constitution, and no change in apportionment occurred until 1837. Essentially the subsequent reapportionments until 1966 were of the House only, except as described above to increase the city of Baltimore's Senate representation. Reapportionments have occurred in 1838, 1842, 1851, 1864, 1869, 1871, 1881, 1901, 1903, 1913, 1921, 1923, 1934, 1942, 1954 1962, 1966, 1974, 1982, 1992, 1994 and 2002. A few of the pre–1962 acts dealt solely with additional representation for the city of Baltimore.

Election Dates: Originally the elections were held on the first Monday of October, changed to the first Wednesday in November in 1853 and to the first Tuesday after the first Monday in November in 1864. When elections became bi-annual they were held in odd-numbered years beginning in 1851, which changed briefly, to even-numbered years in 1864 and 1866; back to odd years in 1867; and finally to even years in 1926.

Constitutions: There have been four constitutions: 1776, 1851, 1864 and 1867.

Affiliations	*Senate*	*House*
	D-R / F	*D-R / F / oth*
1800	—	47 / 33
1801	15 / 0	53 / 27
1802	—	47 / 33
1803	—	47 / 33
1804	—	52 / 28
1805	—	56 / 24
1806	15 / 0	54 / 25 / 1 vac
1807	—	51 / 29

Affiliations	*Senate* *D-R / F*	*House* *D-R / F / oth*
1808	—	37 / 43
1809	—	44 / 36
1810	—	48 / 32
1811	15 / 0	44 / 36
1812	—	26 / 54
1813	—	31 / 49
1814	—	21 / 59
1815	—	32 / 48
1816	0 / 15	24 / 56
1817	—	35 / 45
1818	—	45 / 35
1819	—	50 / 30
1820	—	49 / 31
1821	15 / 0	61 / 19
1822	—	67 / 13
1823	—	63 / 17
	(J)D / NR	*(J)D / NR*
1827[1]	—	31 / 49
1828	—	31 / 48 / 1 tie
1829	—	39 / 41
1830	—	16 / 64
1831	0 / 15	21 / 59[2]
1832	—	26 / 54
1833	—	42 / 36 / 2 Wk
	D / W / oth	*D / W / oth*
1834	—	18 / 62
1835	—	25 / 55
1836	0 / 15	20 / 60
1837	—	(86) 35 / 51
1838[3]	(21) 9 / 12	(79) 37 / 42
1839[4]	—	46 / 33
1840	6 / 15	19 / 60
1841[5]	—	44 / 35
1842	8 / 13	(82) 47 / 35
1843	—	35 / 47
1844	6 / 15	21 / 61
1845	—	39 / 43
1846	8 / 13	29 / 53
1847	—	28 / 54
1848	7 / 14	—
1849	—	36 / 46
1850	9 / 12	—
1851[6]	(22) 11 / 11	(74) 44 / 30
1853[7]	8 / 14	30 / 34 / 10 T

Affiliations	Senate D / A / oth	House D / A / oth
1855[8]	5 / 8 / 9 W	14 / 54 / 6 W
1857	7 / 15	30 / 44
1859	12 / 10	45 / 29

	Senate D / U	House D / U
1861[9]	9 / 13	6 / 68
1863[10]	3 / 19	18 / 56
1864[11]	(24) 12 / 12	(80) 26 / 54

	Senate D / R / oth	House D / R / oth
1866	16 / 8	59 / 21
1867[12]	(25) 25 / 0	(86) 86 / 0
1869	25 / 0	86 / 0
1871[13]	24 / 1	(82) 70 / 12
1873[14]	(26) 23 / 3	(84) 64 / 20
1875[15]	19 / 7	58 / 26
1877[16]	18 / 5 / 2 ID, 1 Rf	65 / 19
1879	19 / 7	63 / 21
1881	16 / 10	(91) 60 / 31
1883	14 / 12	63 / 28
1885[17]	22 / 4	80 / 10 / 1 Fus
1887	22 / 4	71 / 20
1889[18]	18 / 8	59 / 32
1891[19]	22 / 4	81 / 7 / 3Fus
1893	21 / 5	68 / 23
1895	14 / 12	21 / 70
1897	8 / 18	42 / 49
1899	15 / 11	65 / 26
1901	17 / 9	(95) 51 / 44
1903	(27) 19 / 8	(101) 71 / 30
1905	18 / 8 / 1 I	51 / 46 / 3 I, 1 Fus
1907	17 / 9 / 1 I	71 / 30
1909	21 / 6	70 / 31
1911	19 / 8	60 / 41
1913	18 / 9	(102) 79 / 23
1915	16 / 11	56 / 44 / 2 Pe
1917	14 / 13	47 / 55
1919	15 / 12	56 / 46
1921	21 / 6	(106) 73 / 33
1923	(29) 22 / 7	(118) 93 / 25
1926	21 / 8	82 / 36
1930	23 / 6	91 / 27
1934	18 / 11	(120) 94 / 34 / 2 Fus
1938	23 / 6	104 / 16
1942	20 / 9	(123) 101 / 22
1946	18 / 11	87 / 36

Affiliations	Senate D / R / oth	House D / R / oth
1950	18 / 11	88 / 35
1954	21 / 8	98 / 25
1958	26 / 3	116 / 7
1962	22 / 7	(142) 117 / 25
1966	(43) 35 / 8	117 / 25
1970	33 / 10	121 / 21
1974	(47) 39 / 8	(141) 126 / 15
1978	41 / 6	128 / 13
1982	41 / 6	124 / 17
1986	44 / 3	126 / 15
1990	38 / 9	116 / 25
1994	32 / 15	100 / 41
1998	32 / 15	106 / 35
2002	33 / 14	98 / 43
2006	33 / 14	106 / 35

NOTES

1. The figure listed is from *Niles Register* but is an estimate given the tentative nature of the emerging new party system. Additionally the vote for Speaker was 41–36 for a Jacksonian over an Administration candidate. *Niles* the year following stated the previous year's division was 45–35 Administration.

2. *Niles* gives the breakdown 57–23 National Republican but indicates it is an estimate.

3. The exact totals could not be determined because three seats (two in Kent and one in Frederick) ended in a tie. The *House Journal* does not clarify the matter. The figures used are from the *History of Maryland*, p.280, and also given in W. Wayne Smith, *Whig Party in Maryland* (Ph.D. diss., University of Maryland, 1967). The *Maryland Republican* gives the totals as 40 W and 35 D, 1 I and three ties, figures also found in *Niles*.

4. One tie in Calvert apparently won by a Democrat. Same totals were found in the *Maryland Republican* the following year.

5. *American* totals were 42D, 36 W, 1I. *Niles* is the same as the figure used here.

6. There was a tie in a Washington County Senate seat, eventually won by a Whig. A tie in a Frederick House seat was eventually won by a Democrat, producing the totals used here.

7. In the city of Baltimore all ten House seats were won by candidates running on the Temperance ticket. Apparently five had been Democrats and the other five Whigs. While several sources credit each of the parties with five additional seats, since these individuals ran only on the Temperance ticket they are listed as such.

8. The House figure is from the *Republican* and also the *Tribune Almanac*. Other sources do not make a distinction between Democrats and Whigs.

9. All sources list the Senate membership at 21, although 22 was the constitutional figure. No member is listed for Charles county in any of these same sources. The *Senate Journal* 1862 (which gives no party labels) lists a member from that

county. Given the heavily Democratic nature of the county in that election it is reasonable to believe the member was a Democrat (States' Rights).

10. Several sources break down the Unionist members in into three groups: In the Senate, 10 Emancipation Unionists, 6 Unionists and 3 Union State Convention. In the House, 47 Emancipation Unionists, 4 Unionists and 5 Union State Convention. All defeated Democratic opponents.

11. The totals used here are from the *American* at the beginning of the session in January. The *Tribune Almanac, 1865* gives the totals as 13U and 11D in the Senate, and in the House 52U and 28D.

12. The *Maryland Manual, 1973–74*, p. 829, contains a listing of the division of the legislature back to 1867, no sources given. For the period prior to 1895, the *Manual's* totals were the same as other sources but in a few instances (see below) other sources were likely more accurate.

13. The *Manual* says there were 84 House members but the reapportionment bill lists 82.

14. The *Manual* totals are used here but there is a lack of agreement with other sources regarding the House totals: *Tribune Almanac Evening Journal Almanac,* 59 D / 20 R / 5 I; *World Almanac* 57 D / 28 W; *Maryland Republican* 58 D / 23 W / 3 I; *Baltimore Gazette* 58 D / 21 W / 5 ID.

In the Senate the *Manual's* totals are the same as found in the *Tribune Almanac* and the *Gazette* but the *World* and *Evening Journal Almanac* give the totals as 23 D / 2 R / 1 I.

15. The *Manual's* figures are Senate 20 D / 4 W / 2 others and House 68 D / 18 R, but the *Tribune* and *American* almanacs agree on different totals and are used here.

16. Beginning with this election the *Sun Almanac* was used as an additional source to resolve differences.

17. The *Manual's* figures for the House is used here but the other sources differ by one or two for each party.

18. The *Sun's* totals for the House are the primary source because they list the affiliation for each member. The *Manual* gives the breakdown as 68 D / 24 R, one more member than the actual total. Both the *Tribune Almanac* and the *Argus Almanac* list the party totals as 60 D / 31 R.

19. Three sources give these totals: *Manual, Sun* and *Argus* almanacs. However, the *Evening Journal, Tribune* and *World* almanacs give the following: 78 D / 10 R / 3 Fus.

SOURCES

Research was conducted at the Hall of Records (Archives) in Annapolis and at the Enoch Pratt Public Library and the Maryland Historical Society, both in Baltimore.

For the years 1800–1811 I relied upon Phil Lampi's data, also William Lloyd Fox and Richard Walsh, *Maryland A History 1632–1974* (Baltimore: Maryland Historical Society, 1974) for the years 1812–1822, 1838–1861. (Annapolis) *Maryland Republican*, 1823, 1827–1840. *Niles Register* 1812–1818, 1827–33, 1838, 1839, 1842, 1846, 1847. (Annapolis) *Maryland Gazette* 1830, 1834, 1837, 1838. *Baltimore American* 1831, 1835, 1840, 1841, 1859, 1863, 1864, 1875, *Baltimore Sun*, 1844, 1853,

1855, 1863, *Whig/Tribune Almanac* 1850–1893, *World Almanac* 1867, 1891, *Evening Journal Almanac* 1871, 1873, 1877, 1891 *Argus Almanac*, 1891, *Sun Almanac*, 1877, 1879, 1885–91 and the (Maryland) *Manual, 1973–4*, 1867–1974. Returns supplied by the State 1974–.

MASSACHUSETTS

Constitutional Origins: The constitution of Massachusetts went into effect on June 15, 1780, after it had been approved by the voters. It was the first constitution that had been subject to voter approval. The legislature was elected shortly afterwards and the first legislature of the Commonwealth of Massachusetts convened on October 25, 1780, in Boston, the capital. Until 1820 Massachusetts included the present state of Maine, known as the District of Maine. All data includes Maine until Maine's statehood was achieved on March 15, 1820.

Term: Members of both houses were elected annually until 1920 when the term was increased to two years, the present length.

Districts/Elections: The Senate was elected from both single- and multi-member districts consisting of one or more whole counties until 1857 when single-member districts were mandated. But no district could consist of two or more counties or parts of two counties, nor could any town or city ward be divided between districts. In the House the town was the unit of representation and all members were elected on a town-wide basis, thus districts were originally both single- and multi-member. Originally all towns were entitled to at least one member, but in 1836 an amendment provided that towns with less than the minimum requirement would be entitled to representation proportionate to a full ratio. Beginning in 1857 the House was apportioned among the counties of the state with the county commissions empowered to draw the boundaries of the districts within the county. No town or city ward could be divided in the formation of a district and no district could elect more than three members. In 1935 this was amended to prevent any town, or for that matter any precinct of a town, with less than 12,000 from being divided.

Until 1857, election required a popular vote majority to both houses. The senators already elected, together with the House of Representatives, filled the vacant seat(s) from among the two top candidates in each Senate district. An additional election was held to determine a winner for the House. However a majority vote was still required and if no one was elected at the second election, the seat(s) remained vacant for that term. This produced significant change in the number of members of the House from one year to the next.

Membership/Size: The Senate has always consisted of 40 members[1] but the size of the House varied dramatically prior to 1857 (see above), when the number was fixed at 240. In 1978 the total was further reduced to 160, the present total.[2]

Election Dates: Senators were originally elected on the first Monday in April; the House held elections at least ten days before the last Wednesday in May. This unique election of different dates for the two houses ended in 1831 when both houses were elected on the second Monday in November. In 1855 this was changed to the present date of the first Tuesday after the first Monday in November.

Constitution: The state has had but one constitution, enacted in 1780. It is the oldest in effect in the U.S. today.

Affiliations	Senate D-R / F / oth	House D-R / F / oth
1797	1 / 29 / 10 ?	(199) 54 / 93 / 52 ?
1798	4 / 29 / 7 ?	(215) 54 / 139 / 22 ?
1799	3 / 35 / 2 ?	(213) 61 / 122 / 30 ?
1800	4 / 33 / 3 ?	(260) 81 / 166 / 13 ?
1801	16 / 23 / 1 ?	(289) 113 / 162 / 14 ?
1802	12 / 28	(234) 88 / 133 / 13 ?
1803	12 / 28	(258) 102 / 152 / 4 ?
1804	14 / 26	(281) 129 / 150 / 2 ?
1805	18 / 22	(347) 163 / 181 / 1 I, 2 ?
1806	21 / 19	(281) 263 / 215 / 3 ?
1807	21 / 19	(282) 250 / 130 / 2 ?
1808	17 / 23	(484) 231 / 253
1809	18 / 22	(594) 278 / 316
1810	20 / 20	(643) 335 / 308
1811	21 / 19	(660) 345 / 315
1812	29 / 11	(749) 320 / 429
1813	11 / 29	(636) 215 / 420 / 1 ?
1814	13 / 27	(514) 159 / 354 / 1 ?
1815	15 / 25	(452) 149 / 303
1816	18 / 22	(541) 214 / 324 / 3 ?
1817	13 / 27	(286) 92 / 189 / 5 ?
1818	14 / 26	(224) 82 / 132 / 10 ?
1819	18 / 22	(408) 161 / 231 / 16 ?

Affiliations	*Senate* *D-R / F / oth*	*House* *D-R / F / oth*		
1820	8 / 23	**(193)** 64 / 87 / 42 ?		
1821	7 / 24	**(246)** F majority		
1822	9 / 31	**(160)** 53 / 105 / 2 ?		
1823	24 / 16	**(298)** / / ?		
1824	28 / 12	**(203)** / / ?		
	(D)J / NR / oth	*D(J) / NR / oth*		
1829	1 / 37 / 2 ?	**(506)** ?		
1830	1 / 38 / 1 A-M	**(454)** ?		
1831[3]	2 / 29 / 6 A-M	**(481)** 68 / 320 / 87 A-M, 6 Wk		
1831[3]	1 / 36 / 3 A-M	**(528)** 92 / 313 / 119 A-M, 4 ?		
1832	0 / 37 / 3 A-M	**(573)** 73 / 372 / 117 A-M, 11 ?		
1833	0 / 32 / 8 A-M	**(570)** 116 / 314 / 131 A-M[4]		
	D / W / oth	*D / W / oth*		
1834	0 / 40	**(618)** 87 / 450 / 78 A-M, 3 Wk		
1835	10 / 22 / 8	**(624)** 174[5] / 397 / 53 A-M		
1836	16 / 24	**(635)** 262 / 373		
1837	0 / 40	**(480)** 114 / 363 / 3 ?		
1838	3 / 37	**(522)** 178 / 344		
1839	19 / 21	**(519)** 242 / 277		
1840	3 / 37	**(397)** 119 / 278		
1841	13 / 27	**(336)** 135 / 201		
1842	28 / 12	**(352)** 172 / 177 / 3 Lty		
1843	6 / 34	**(322)** 133 / 185 / 4 Lty		
1844	0 / 40	**(272)** 70 / 200 / 2 Lty		
1845	0 / 40	**(265)** 63 / 198 / 4 A		
1846	0 / 40	**(255)** 43 / 208 3Lty,1A		
1847	1 / 39	**(274)** 78 / 191 / 3 Lty, 1 I, 1 ?		
	Co[6] / W	*Co[6] / W / oth*		
1848	0 / 40	**(262)** 83 / 178 / 1 ?		
1849	13 / 27	**(298)** 129 / 168 / 1 ?		
1850	26 / 14	**(401)** 218 / 183		
1851	28 / 12	**(402)** 208 / 194		
1852	8 / 32	**(288)** 137 / 151		
1853	10 / 30	**(310)** 112 / 198		
	D / A / oth	*D / A / oth*		
1854	0 / 40	**(380)** 1 / 376 / 1 W, 1 R, 1 ?		
1855	2 / 29 / 9 R	**(329)** 34 / 168 / 58 W, 68 R, 1 Lib		
	D / R / A	*D / R / oth*		
1856	0 / 23 / 17[7]	**(355)** 8 / 314 / 27 A / 4 W, 2 ?		

Affiliations	*Senate* D / R / oth	*House* D / R / oth
1857	2 / 33 / 4 A, 1 W	**(240)** 41 / 169 / 29 A / 1 Cit
1858	3 / 37	29 / 197 / 10 A, 4 ?
1859	6 / 34	50 / 183 / 6 A, 1 ?
1860	4 / 28 / 8 U	15 / 223 / 2 NR
1861	6 / 31 / 3 U	24 / 156 / 45 U, 4 ?
1862	5 / 35	41 / 198 / 1 ?
1863	0 / 40	12 / 228
1864	0 / 40	6 / 234
1865	1 / 39	19 / 221
1866	0 / 40	11 / 229
1867	8 / 32	60 / 180
1868	2 / 38	16 / 224
1869	10 / 29 / 1 LR	58 / 160 / 22 LR
1870	5 / 34 / 1 LR	34 / 195 / 11 LR
1871	5 / 35	49 / 186 / 5 LR
1872	1 / 39	28 / 212
1873	11 / 25 / 4 I	70 / 168 / 2 I
1874	15 / 24 / 1 I	79 / 155 / 6 I
1875	9 / 31	58 / 182
1876	7 / 33	59 / 181
1877	5 / 35	69 / 171
1878	5 / 35	40 / 185 / 15 G
1879	8 / 32	52 / 185 / 3 G
1880	5 / 35	47 / 192 / 1 G
1881	4 / 36	55 / 181 / 4 I
1882	17 / 22 / 1 I	85 / 150 / 5 I
1883	14 / 25 / 1 I	92 / 137 / 3 G, 8 I
1884	5 / 34 / 1 IR	71 / 166 / 3I
1885	12 / 28	77 / 154 / 3 I, 3 IR, 2 GL, 1 ID
1886	15 / 25	82 / 158
1887	10 / 30	72 / 165 / 3 I
1888	7 / 33	58 / 181 / 1 I
1889	11 / 29	80 / 160
1890	20 / 20	98 / 141 / 1 P
1891	16 / 24	90 / 149 / 1 P
1892	10 / 30	74 / 166
1893	7 / 33	56 / 183 / 1 I
1894	4 / 36	46 / 194
1895	7 / 33	58 / 182
1896	5 / 35	38 / 198 / 4 I
1897	7 / 33	53 / 179 / 8 I
1898	7 / 33	65 / 164 / 1 P
1899	9 / 31	72 / 166 / 1 ICit, 1 CI
1900	9 / 31	58 / 180 / 2 SD
1901	7 / 33	72 / 166 / 2 SD
1902	9 / 31	84 / 153 / 3 S
1903	9 / 31	84 / 155 / 1 S
1904	6 / 34	69 / 170 / 1 I

Affiliations	Senate D / R / oth	House D / R / oth
1905	9 / 31	71 / 169
1906	11 / 28 / 1 I	62 / 174 / 5 IL
1907	8 / 32	61 / 174 / 5 IL
1908	6 / 34	56 / 180 / 3 IL, 1 ICit
1909	9 / 31	71 / 167 / 1 S, 1 ICit
1910	14 / 26	112 / 127 / 1 S
1911	13 / 27	97 / 140 / 1 ICit, IS,1 I
1912	14 / 25 / 1 Pg	96 / 134 / 8 Pg, 1 S, 1 I
1913	17 / 21 / 2 Pg	104 / 118 / 17 Pg, 1 S
1914	12 / 28	90 / 150
1915	6 / 34	73 / 166 / 1S
1916	6 / 34	64 / 174 / 1S,1I
1917	7 / 33	59 / 179 / 1 S, 1 ICit
1918	10 / 30	60 / 180
1919	7 / 33	62 / 177 / 1 I
1920	5 / 35	49 / 188 / 3 I
1922	7 / 33	75 / 164 / 1 I
1924	6 / 34	68 / 172
1926	5 / 35	54 / 155 / 31 NP
1928	9 / 31	80 / 160
1930	10 / 30	99 / 141
1932	14 / 26	92 / 148
1934	19 / 21	116 / 124
1936	14 / 26	104 / 136
1938	12 / 28	98 / 142
1940	15 / 25	99 / 141
1942	14 / 26	99 / 141
1944	17 / 23	103 / 137
1946	16 / 24	95 / 145
1948	20 / 20	122 / 118
1950	18 / 22	124 / 116
1952	15 / 25	116 / 124
1954	19 / 21	128 / 112
1956	18 / 22	132 / 108
1958	24 / 16	145 / 95
1960	26 / 14	156 / 84
1962	28 / 12	150 / 90
1964	28 / 12	169 / 71
1966	26 / 14	168 / 71 / 1 I
1968	27 / 13	173 / 67
1970	30 / 10	178 / 62
1972	33 / 7	181 / 57 / 2 I
1974	33 / 7	191 / 46 / 3 I
1976	33 / 7	194 / 43 / 3 I
1978	34 / 6	(160) 128 / 30 / 2 I
1980	32 / 7 / 1 I	128 / 31 / 1 I
1982	33 / 7	131 / 29
1984	32 / 8	126 / 34

Affiliations	*Senate* *D / R / oth*	*House* *D / R / oth*
1986	32 / 8	126 / 33 / 1 I
1988	31 / 9	127 / 33
1990	26 / 14	123 / 37
1992	31 / 9	124 / 35 / 1 I
1994	30 / 10	125 / 34 / 1 NP
1996	34 / 6	124 / 35 / 1 I
1998	33 / 7	131 / 28 / 1 I
2000	34 / 6	137 / 23
2002	34 / 6	136 / 23 / 1 I
2004	34 / 6	139 / 20 / 1 I
2006	35 / 5	141 / 19

SPECIAL BREAKDOWN

Listed below is a breakdown of the House totals between Massachusetts proper and the District of Maine for the elections of 1797–1819:

Affiliations	*Massachusetts* *D-R / F / ?*	*Maine* *D-R / F / ?*
1797	51 / 77 / 41	3 / 16 / 11
1798	43 / 115 / 21	11 / 24 / 1
1799	51 / 102 / 24	10 / 20 / 6
1800	69 / 129 / 13	12 / 37 / 0
1801	91 / 131 / 13	22 / 31 / 1
1802	77 / 115 / 9	19 / 69 / 4
1803	92 / 116 / 3	20 / 36 / 1
1804	104 / 123 / 2	25 / 27 / 0
1805	130 / 156 / 3	33 / 25 / 0
1806	192 / 178 / 1	71 / 37 / 2
1807	181 / 115 / 0	69 / 15 / 2
1808	188 / 210	65 / 43
1809	191 / 256	87 / 60
1810	226 / 259	109 / 49
1811	240 / 260	105 / 55
1812	205 / 330	115 / 99
1813	131 / 326	84 / 94 / 1
1814	102 / 291	57 / 63 / 1
1815	96 / 252	53 / 51
1816	137 / 273 / 1	77 / 54 / 2
1817	71 / 163 / 3	21 / 26 / 2
1818	55 / 101 / 5	27 / 31 / 5
1819	78 / 174 / 8	83 / 58 / 8

NOTES

1. Except for two years following the separation of Maine from Massachusetts, when the number was 31.

2. The House was the largest legislative body in U.S. history. During the 1812–1813 session, when Massachusetts still included what is now Maine, there were 749 members. The largest total after Maine separated was the 635 members who attended the 1837 session. The smallest number prior to 1857 was 255 in the 1847 session. See issues of the *Manual for the General Court* for annual totals.

3. Due to adoption of a constitutional amendment shifting the start of the political year to January, there were two elections in 1831. The first was held, as was past practice, in April–May for the term beginning the last Wednesday in May; the second was in November for the term beginning in January 1832.

4. 5 Wkm, 2 W, 2 ?

5. Democratic total includes 14 elected with Anti-Masonic support.

6. For the elections of 1848–1853 the Democrats and Free Soil parties ran the same candidates in almost all contests and were usually referred to as Coalition candidates (see issues of the *Whig Almanac* and the *Boston Atlas*). The Thomas manuscript identifies almost all these candidates by one or the other party as listed below:

	Senate	*House*
1848	—	30 D / 53 FS
1849	6 D / 7 FS	56 D / 41 FS / 32Co
1850	15 D / 11 FS	110 D / 98 FS / 10 Co
1851	15 D / 13 FS	118 D / 90 FS
1852	4 D / 4 FS	83 D / 54 FS
1853	6 D / 4 FS	64 D / 48 FS

Additionally for the elections of 1852 the *Atlas*, November 22, 1852 lists; Whigs-149, Coalition 121, Anti-Coalition Democrats 17 and 1853, December 5, 1853, Whigs-197, Coalition 101 and Democrats 11.

7. Includes 4 Americans elected with the support of the Republicans. The *Whig Almanac, 1858*, lists all members as Republicans.

SOURCES

Research was done at the State Archives and the Boston Public Library.

I am particularly indebted to Phil Lampi for his data prior to 1825 and to Edmund Thomas of Fitchburg, Massachusetts, who generously shared with me his definitive manuscript of individual members of each session of the legislature for the years 1797–1862. This formed the basis for the figures used here.

We relied primarily on *Manual for the General Court* for most of the years 1874–1892 and beginning in 1892 *Massachusetts Election Statistics*. The *Manual* was probably the first state publication to list party affiliation along with the returns.

Also: *Independent Chronicle*, November, December 24, 1832, January 8, 1833, January 4, December 27, 1834, January 10, November 14, 18, 1835, January 1836; *Boston Press*, January 4, 1834; *Worcester Spy*, November 14, 28, 1836; (Boston) *Atlas*, February 5, November 25, 1835, January 4, November 10, December 19, 1849, January 5, November 11, December 17, 1850, January 10, November 21, 29,

1851, January (dates unknown), November 9, 22, December 22, 1852, January 12, December 5, 21, 1853, January 9, 10, 1854; *Springfield Gazette*, January 8, 1834; Arthur B. Darling, *Political Changes in Massachusetts 1824–1848*, pp 251, 291–3; (Worcester) *National Aegis*, November 28, 1838, January 9, 1839; (Northampton) *Hampshire Gazette*, January 7, 1845, January, 20, 1846; *Niles Register*, January 4, 1840, November 20, 1841, January 27, 1844, November 30, 1844.

MICHIGAN

Statehood: Michigan began moving towards statehood before Congress passed an enabling act. Delegates to a constitutional convention were elected on April 4, 1835, and convened in Detroit on May 11. Forty-five days later they had written a constitution which was approved by the voters on October 5, 1835, by a vote of 6,752 to 1,374. On the same day the first legislature was chosen. The legislature convened on November 1 even though statehood had not been achieved. Indeed it would not be achieved until January 26, 1837, following a second convention. On July 24, 1836, this convention accepted additional terms from Congress concerning the boundary with Ohio. Detroit remained the capital until 1847 when it was moved to Lansing.

Term: Senators were originally elected for two years; terms overlapped, with one-half the body elected every year until 1852 when rules were changed so that all were elected at the same time. The term was increased to four years in 1966; again, all senators are elected at the same election. House members were elected annually until 1850 when the term was increased to two years. Members elected in 1850 carried over until 1852.

Districts/Elections: Initially the Senate was elected entirely from multi-member districts. In 1850 the Senate was elected from single-member districts, and that has been the practice ever since, but only counties entitled to two or more members could be divided. In 1952 a formula based on population and geography was added to the constitution. This provided for weighting population 80 percent and land 20 percent in determining representation. The House was apportioned among the counties, each existing county entitled to at least one member. Apparently counties entitled to more than one member elected all members county-wide. In 1850 counties entitled to two or members could be divided into districts, but no city or township entitled to more than one member could be divided. Counties with less than half a ratio were joined with like counties to form a district. In 1963 this was raised to ⁷⁄₁₀ of a ratio. In 1966 all districts in both houses were reapportioned in accordance with the one person, one vote standard.

Membership/Size: The Senate initially had 16 members. Membership increased to 22 in 1842 and was fixed at 32 in 1852. This figure remained unchanged until 1954 when the Senate was increased to 34; membership increased to 38 in 1964. The House had 49 members at its inception, increased to 63 members in 1842, 72 in 1852 and 100 in 1862. The only other change was an increase to 110 members in 1954.

Reapportionment/Redistricting: Enacted in 1838, 1841, 1846, 1851, 1855 (House), 1861, 1865, 1871, 1875, 1881, 1885, 1891, 1892, 1895, 1901, 1905, 1907 (House), 1913 (Senate), 1925, 1943 (House), 1952, 1964, 1972, 1982, 1992 and 2002. The reapportionment of 1963 was invalidated as part of the one person, one vote reapportionment decision of the U.S. Supreme Court.

Election Dates: Initially held on the first Monday and Tuesday in November; changed to the first Tuesday after the first Monday in November in 1850.

Constitutions: The current constitution, written in 1963, is the fourth in Michigan history. The other three were written in 1835, 1850 and 1908.

Affiliations	*Senate* *D / W / oth*	*House* *D / W / oth*
1835	**(16)** ?	**(49)** ?
1836	8 / 5 / 3 ?	23 / 24 / 2 ?[1]
1837	14 / 2	30 / 20
1838	**(17)** 11 / 6	**(52)** 31 / 21
1839	7 / 10	15 / 37
1840	5 / 12	20 / 31 / 1 tie[2]
1841	**(18)** 12 / 5 / 1 vac	**(53)** 47 / 6
1842	18 / 0	45 / 7
1843	18 / 0	47 / 6
1844	18 / 0	46 / 7
1845	20 / 1	50 / 16
1846	**(22)** 20 / 2	**(66)** 51 / 15
1847	21 / 1	51 / 15
1848	18 / 4	46 / 16 / 3 FS, 1 tie
1849	18 / 4	46 / 20
1850	16 / 5 / 1 FS-D	40 / 26
1852	**(32)** 25 / 7	**(72)** 52 / 19 / 1 ?

Affiliations	*Senate* D / R / oth	*House* D / R / oth
1854	7 / 25	24 / 48
1856	3 / 29	(80) 17 / 63
1858	8 / 24	(81) 25 / 56
1860	2 / 30	(83) 11 / 72
1862	14 / 18	(100) 39 / 60 / 1 ?
1864	11 / 21	27 / 73
1866	1 / 30 / 1 ?	21 / 79
1868	5 / 27	25 / 75
1870	5 / 27	29 / 71
1872	1 / 31	5 / 95
1874	15 / 17	46 / 54
1876	9 / 23	25 / 75
1878	9 / 23	35 / 65
1880	2 / 30	13 / 86 / 1 I
1882	13 / 19	38 / 62
1884	14 / 18	48 / 52
1886	10 / 22	37 / 63
1888	8 / 24	30 / 70
1890	17 / 15	66 / 34
1892	10 / 22	28 / 69 / 3 Pop
1894	0 / 32	1 / 99
1896	6 / 26	19 / 81
1898	5 / 27	8 / 92
1900	1 / 31	10 / 90
1902	1 / 31	10 / 90
1904	0 / 32	0 / 100
1906	0 / 32	5 / 95
1908	0 / 32	2 / 98
1910	4 / 28	12 / 88
1912	5 / 21 / 6 Pg	35 / 54 / 11 Pg
1914	3 / 29	5 / 95
1916	5 / 27	12 / 88
1918	0 / 32	2 / 98
1920	0 / 32	0 / 100
1922	0 / 32	5 / 95
1924	0 / 32	0 / 100
1926	0 / 32	2 / 98
1928	0 / 32	2 / 98
1930	1 / 31	2 / 98
1932	17 / 15	55 / 45
1934	11 / 21	49 / 51
1936	17 / 15	60 / 40
1938	9 / 23	27 / 73
1940	10 / 22	32 / 68
1942	7 / 25	26 / 74
1944	8 / 24	34 / 66
1946	4 / 28	5 / 95
1948	9 / 23	39 / 61

Affiliations	Senate D / R / oth	House D / R / oth
1950	7 / 25	34 / 66
1952	8 / 24	34 / 66
1954	(34) 11 / 23	(110) 51 / 59
1956	11 / 23	49 / 61
1958	12 / 22	55 / 55
1960	12 / 22	54 / 56
1962	11 / 23	52 / 58
1964	(38) 23 / 15	73 / 37
1966	18 / 20	54 / 56
1968	—	57 / 53
1970	19 / 19	58 / 52
1972	—	60 / 50
1974	24 / 14	66 / 44
1976	—	68 / 42
1978	25 / 13	70 / 40
1980	—	64 / 46
1982	20 / 18	63 / 47
1984	—	57 / 53
1986	18 / 20	64 / 46
1988	—	61 / 49
1990	18 / 20	61 / 49
1992	—	55 / 55
1994	16 / 22	54 / 56
1996	—	58 / 52
1998	15 / 23	52 / 58
2000	—	51 / 59
2002	16 / 22	47 / 63
2004	—	52 / 58
2006	17 / 21	58 / 52

NOTES

1. The *Free Press,* November 16, 1836, had the breakdown as 26 D / 10 W / 13?
2. There was dispute over the returns from Hamtramack township in Wayne County. The votes in the township were not included in the official returns based on the allegation they were tampered with, although they were counted for other officers elected at the same time. The *Detroit Daily Free Press* reported the debate over the disputed ballot on January 13, 1841. The House, according to the paper, by a party line vote seated the seven Whig candidates based on the exclusion of all votes from the township in question. The county canvass was published in the *Free Press* on November 25, 1840.

SOURCES

Newspapers were the main source for the earliest elections: *Detroit Free Press,* November 16, 1836, December 2, 1837, December 21, 1838, November 18, 1839, November 17, 25, 1840, January 13, 1841, December 5, 1843, November 25, 1844,

November 6, 18, 1847, November 27, December 4, 1848, November 17, 1849, November 20, 1850; *Springfield* (Massachusetts) *Gazette,* October 26, 1842; as well as *Niles Register,* December 12, 1836, November 11, 30, 1839, November 28, 1840, December 4, 1841, November 28, 1846, December 4, 1847. The 2002 edition of the *Michigan Manual* contains a compilation of party affiliation back to the election of 1854.

Also consulted George S. May and Willis F. *Dubnar, Michigan: A History of the Wolverine State* (Grand Rapids: William B. Eerdmans, 1980) and other issues of the *Michigan Manual.* For a history of reapportionment I used Karl A. Lamb, et al., *Apportionment and Representative Institutions: The Michigan Experience* (Washington, D.C.: The Institute For Social Science Research, 1963).

MINNESOTA

Statehood: An enabling act was signed by President Pierce on February 27, 1857. A constitutional convention was elected on June 1, 1857, and convened in St. Paul, the capital, on July 13. On October 18, 1857, the constitution was approved by the voters, 30,055 to 571. The initial election of the legislature took place on the same day. The legislature convened on December 2. Congress approved statehood on May 11, 1858.

Term: Senators were elected for a two-year term, with one-half the body elected annually, until 1880, when the term was increased to four years. House member were initially elected annually. In 1880 the term was increased to two years.

Districts/Elections: Members of both houses have always been elected from single-member districts. But House districts cannot be split between Senate districts.

Membership/Size: The original Senate consisted of 37 members, reduced to 21 members in 1860. The body reached its present size of 67 in 1914. It is the largest state senate in the nation. The House initially had 80 members, reduced to 42 in 1860. There have been eight changes since then, with the House reaching its present size of 134 in 1972.

Reapportionment/Redistricting: Enacted in 1860, 1866, 1871, 1883, 1890, 1898, 1914, 1962, 1966, 1972, 1982, 1992, 2002.

Election Dates: Initially the Tuesday after the first Monday in October; changed to the first Tuesday after the first Monday in November, commencing in 1862.

Constitutions: The original constitution of 1857 remains in effect today.

Addenda: From 1914 through 1972 candidates for the legislature ran on a non-partisan basis, with no party labels permitted. However, caucuses akin to the major parties regularly met during each session. One caucus adopted the name "Liberal" and was made up of Democrats; the other caucus called itself "Conservative" and was made up of Republicans. hence the party affiliations still existed, but unofficially. The data between 1950 and 1972 represents this process.

Since 1944 the Democratic Party has been officially listed on the ballot as the Democratic–Farmer Labor Party. The Republican was listed as the Independent Republican Party from 1974 to 1994.

Affiliations	*Senate* D / R	*House* D / R
1857	(37) 20 / 17	(80) 43 / 37
1858	19 / 18	31 / 49
1859	13 / 23 / 1 I	22 / 58
1860	(21) 2 / 19	(42) 2 / 40
1861	5 / 16	10 / 30 / 2 UD
1862	5 / 16	12 / 29 / 1 UD
1863	4 / 17	11 / 27 / 4 UD
1864	4 / 17	10 / 32
1865	5 / 16	13 / 29
1866	(22) 5 / 17	(47) 9 / 37 / 1 ?
1867	7 / 15	13 / 34
1868	6 / 16	9 / 38
1869	6 / 16	9 / 38
1870	8 / 14	20 / 27
1871	(41) 12 / 29	(106) 33 / 73
1872	10 / 31	27 / 79
1873	13 / 28	48 / 58
1874	18 / 21 / 2 I	48 / 54 / 4 I
1875	14 / 27	32 / 74
1876	15 / 26	29 / 77
1877	12 / 29	40 / 66
1878	16 / 23 / 2 G	30 / 73 / 3 G
1880	11 / 29 / 1 ?	15 / 87 / 1 ?
1882	(47) 10 / 36 / 1 I	(103) 28 / 72 / 2 I, 1 ?
1884	17 / 30	33 / 70
1886	16 / 30 / 1 FA	34 / 66 / 3 FA
1888	—	9 / 89 / 3 I, 2 FA
1890	(54) 16 / 25 / 13 Pop	(114) 52 / 43 / 19 FA
1892	—	41 / 71 / 2 Pop
1894	3 / 46 / 5 Pop	10 / 95 / 9 Pop
1896	—	11 / 90 / 13 Pop

Affiliations	Senate D / R	House D / R
1898	**(63)** 18 / 44 / 1 I	**(119)** 25 / 93 / 1 I
1900	—	17 / 96 / 6 Pop
1902	11 / 52	15 / 104
1904	—	10 / 109
1906	19 / 43 / 1 Pe	14 / 102 / 3 P
1908	—	22 / 94 / 3 P
1910	19 / 42 / 2 I	**(120)** 26 / 88 / 4 P, 1 IR, 1 PO
1912	—	20 / 98 / 1 P, 1 S
1914	**(67)** —	**(130)** —
1916	—	—
1918	—	—
1920	—	—
1922	—	—
1924	—	—
1926	—	—
1928	—	—
1930	—	—
1932	—	—
1934	—	—
1936	—	—
1938	—	—
1940	—	—
1942	—	—
1944	—	—
1946	—	—
1948	—	—
1950	16 / 51	44 / 87
1952	—	46 / 85
1954	19 / 48	66 / 65
1956	—	70 / 61
1958	24 / 43	72 / 59
1960	—	72 / 59
1962	24 / 43	**(135)** 54 / 80 / 1 oth
1964	—	56 / 78 / 1 oth
1966	22 / 45	42 / 93
1968	—	50 / 85
1970	33 / 34	65 / 70
1972	37 / 30	**(134)** 77 / 57
1974	—	104 / 30
1976	49 / 18	104 / 30
1978	—	67 / 67
1980	46 / 21	70 / 64
1982	42 / 24 / 1 I	77 / 57
1984	—	65 / 69
1986	47 / 20	83 / 51
1988	—	81 / 53
1990	45/ 22	83 / 51
1992	45 / 22	87 / 47

Affiliations	Senate D / R	House D / R
1994	—	71 / 63
1996	42 / 25	70 / 64
1998	—	63 / 70
2000	39 / 27 / 1 I	65 / 69
2002	35 / 31 / 1 In	52 / 82
2004	—	66 / 68
2006	44 / 23	85 / 49

SOURCES

(St. Paul) *Pioneer & Democrat*, January 7, 1862, November 10, 1877, *Minnesota Manual* 1901, 1903, 1907, 1911. Since 1950 all data was obtained from the Minnesota Legislative Reference Library.

MISSISSIPPI

Statehood: On March 1, 1817, an enabling act was signed into law authorizing the calling of a constitutional convention in the territory of Mississippi. The convention convened in Washington, Mississippi, on July 7, 1817, and finished its work on August 15, 1817. The first legislative elections were held on September 1 and 2, 1817. The state was formally admitted to the Union on December 10, 1817. Jackson became the capital in 1822.

Term: Senators were at first elected for three years, with one-third of the body elected each year. In 1832 the term was increased to four years, one-half the body every two years. Since 1890 all senators have been elected at the same time. House members were elected annually under the original constitution. The term was increased to two years in 1832 and four years in 1890.

Districts/Elections: Senators were initially elected from districts made up of one or more whole counties; no county could be divided in the formation of a district. This process remained largely unchanged until the constitution of 1890. The new constitution provided for single- and several multi-member districts as well as floterial districts. The House was apportioned by county and the cities of Natchez and Vicksburg, who were given separate representation.[1] Each county was guaranteed at least one member, and all members were elected on a countywide basis. This system was not significantly changed until the 1890 constitution. Under the 1890 constitution floterial districts were introduced and a county entitled to two or members could be divided into districts. Furthermore the House was divided into three large geographic areas, each to have an equal number of House members.

Single- and multi-member districts continued under one person, one vote reapportionment, but in all multi-member districts candidates ran for a specific post (seat). Some multi-member districts were also further divided into both single- and multi-member districts. Since the reapportionment of 1983 all members have been elected from single-member districts.

Membership/Size: The original legislature consisted of seven senators and 24 representatives. Under the constitution of 1832, four reapportionments increased the Senate to 32 and the House to 100. Under the 1861 reapportionment and subsequent documents the Senate was to be never less than one-fourth nor more than one-third the size of the House. The 1868 constitution determined that the House would have not less than 100 nor more than 120 members; this upper limit was reached in 1877. Additional increases as a result of constitutional amendments raised the House to 140 members.

Reapportionment/Redistricting: 1819, 1821, 1826, 1830, 1833, 1837, 1841, 1846, 1857, 1861, 1867, 1869, 1871, 1877, 1881, 1890, 1919, 1967, 1971, 1975, 1979, 1983, 1995, 2003.

Election Dates: Elections were held on the first Monday and Tuesday in August. In 1832 this was changed to the first Monday and Tuesday in November. In 1857 the date was changed to the first Monday in October and effective in 1869 to the first Tuesday after the first Monday in November.

Constitutions: There have been four constitutions, written in the years 1817, 1832, 1869 and 1890.

Affiliations	*Senate* D / W / oth		*House* D / W / oth	
1837	(30)	17 / 13	(91)	53 / 37 / 1 ?
1839		18 / 12		54 / 36 / 1 ?
1841	(32)	21 / 11	(96)	60 / 38
1843		20 / 12		66 / 32 / 1 ?
1845		23 / 9		70 / 29
1847		25 / 7	(99)	73 / 25 / 1 ?
1849		20 / 10 / 2 ?		62 / 36 / 1?
1851		/ / 21 SoR, 11 U		/ / 63 SoR, 35 U, 1 ?

Affiliations	Senate	House
	D / W / oth	*D / W / oth*
1853	20 / 10 / 1 UD, 1 vac	56 / 34 / 8 UD, 2 ?
1855	?	?
1857	**(31)** ?	**(100)** 85 / / 19 Opp[2]
1859	27 / / 4 Opp	86 / / 14 Opp
1865	13 / 17 / 1 ?	39 / 52 / 7 oth

Affiliations	Senate *D / R / oth*	House *D / R / oth*
1869	**(33)** 7 / 26	**(107)** 25 / 82
1871	**(37)** 14 / 23	**(115)** 50 / 65
1873	14 / 23	44 / 68 / 3 vac
1875	25 / 11 / 1 IR	97 / 19
1877	**(38)** 36 / 2	**(120)** 109 / 8 / 3 Fus
1879	35 / 1 / 2 G	101 / 5 / 14 G
1881	**(37)** 35 / 2	100 / 15 / 3 ID, 2 G
1883	33 / 3 / 1 I	100 / 13 / 4 G, 3 I
1885	**(40)** 39 / 1	**(130)** 119 / 9 / 2 I
1887	40 / 0	111 / 7 / 2 I
1889	40 / 0	113 / 7
1891	**(45)** 45 / 0	**(133)** 129 / 3 / 1 I
1895	45 / 0	131 / 2
1899	45 / 0	131 / 2
1903	45 / 0	133 / 0
1907	45 / 0	133 / 0
1911	45 / 0	133 / 0
1915	45 / 0	133 / 0
1919	**(49)** 49 / 0	**(140)** 140 / 0
1923	49 / 0	140 / 0
1927	49 / 0	140 / 0
1931	49 / 0	140 / 0
1935	49 / 0	140 / 0
1939	49 / 0	140 / 0
1943	49 / 0	140 / 0
1947	49 / 0	140 / 0
1951	49 / 0	140 / 0
1955	49 / 0	140 / 0
1959	49 / 0	140 / 0
1963	**(52)** 52 / 0	**(122)** 122 / 0
1967	52 / 0	122 / 0
1971	50 / 2	120 / 1 / 1 I
1975	50 / 2	119 / 2 / 1 I
1979	48 / 4	116 / 4 / 2 I
1983	49 / 3	117 / 5
1987	45 / 7	113 / 9
1991	39 / 13	93 / 27 / 2 I
1995	34 / 18	86 / 33 / 3 I
1999	34 / 18	86 / 33 / 3 I
2003	27 / 24 / 1 I	75 / 47

NOTES

1. This continued until the 1869 reapportionment.
2. *The Evening Journal Almanac, 1859,* gives this total. This exceeds the constitutional total of 100. No other information was located.

SOURCES

Melvin P. Lucas, *The Period of Political Alchemy: Party in the Mississippi Legislature 1835–1846* (M. A. Thesis, Cornell University, 1981). The data for 1865 was taken from William C. Harris, *Presidential Reconstruction in Mississippi* (Baton Rouge: Louisiana State University Press, 1967), p.113. James W. Garner, *Reconstruction in Mississippi* (New York: Columbia University Press, 1901; reprint edition, Gloucester: Peter Smith, 1964). Stephen Cresswell, *Multi-party Politics in Mississippi 1877–1902* (Jackson: University of Mississippi Press, 1995). (Vicksburg) *Daily Whig*, November 24, 1843, November 27, 1845, November 23, 1855; *The* (Jackson) *Mississippian*, December 3, 1847, November 30, 1849; (Jackson) *Mississippi State Gazette*, November 25, 1853; (Jackson) *Weekly Clarion*, November 14, December 5, 1877, March 10, 1880. *Niles Register*, January 20, 1838, December 21, 1839. Arthur C. Whittemore II, *An Analysis of the Problems of Legislative Reapportionment in Mississippi*, M. A. Thesis, State College, 1962. Edward H. Hobbs, *Apportionment in Mississippi* (Bureau of Public Administration, University of Mississippi, 1956).

MISSOURI

Statehood: President Monroe signed an enabling act on March 8, 1820. A constitutional convention held in St. Louis met from June 12 to July 19, 1820. The first election of the legislature took place on August 28, 1820, but statehood was not formally achieved until August 10, 1821. The capital was moved from St. Louis to St. Charles in 1821 and finally to Jefferson City in 1826.

Term: Senators since statehood have been elected for a term of four years; terms overlap so that half the body is elected every two years. House members have always been elected for a two-year term.

Districts/Elections: Senators were initially elected from both single- and multi-member districts made up of one or more whole counties. Since 1866 they have all been elected from single-member districts. The House members were elected by county, with every county entitled to at least one member; no county was to be divided into districts. Consequently all members were elected countywide. In 1866 counties entitled to more than one member were to be divided into districts, in essence providing the election of all members from single-member districts.

In 1848–49 a formula was introduced in determining representation that limited representation of the more populous counties. A county with six ratios of representation was entitled to five representatives. The 1945 constitution amended the formula to make it less representative. Thus a county with six ratios was entitled to four members and one additional representative for each additional two and one-half ratios. The advent of one person, one vote apportionment ended that formula in 1966.

Membership/Size: The Senate originally consisted of 14 members and reached the constitutional maximum of 33 by 1838. The number was increased to 34 in 1866 and has remained the same ever since. The House originally had 36 members and reached what was then the maximum of 100 by 1840. There have been several changes since 1848 when the number was increased to 128. In 1876 the number was increased to 143. It was decreased to 140 in 1884, then increased five more times, in 1962 reaching 163, the present total.

Reapportionment/Redistricting: Enacted in 1822, 1824, 1826, 1830, 1834, 1836, 1838, 1840, 1842, 1846, 1850, 1854, 1858, 1866 (Senate), 1868,[1] 1872, 1876, 1882, 1892, 1902, 1922, 1946, 1952, 1962, 1966, 1972, 1982, 1992 and 2002.

Election Dates: Originally the first Monday in August, changed to the first Tuesday after the first Monday in November beginning in 1864.

Constitutions: There have been four constitutions in state history, written in 1820, 1865, 1875 and 1945.

Affiliations	*Senate*		*House*	
	D / W / oth		*D / W / oth*	
1834	(24)	16 / 7 / 1 ?	(72)	47 / 22 / 3 ?
1836		20 / 4		60 / 17 / 3 ?
1838	(33)	20 / 13		58 / 39
1840		18 / 15	(100)	55 / 44 / 1 ?
1842		23 / 10		74 / 26
1844		24 / 9		56 / 44
1846		23 / 3 / 2 A, 5 ?		76 / 19 / 3 A, 2 ?
1848		24 / 2 / 2 A, 5 ?		65 / 24 / 11 ?
1850		21[2] / 12	(128)	75[3] / 53
1852		22 / 11		86 / 39 / 5 ?
1854		21[4] / 12		80[5] / 48 / 2 ?
1856		21[6] / 4 / 8 A		103[7] / 4 / 25 A, 1 vac

Affiliations	*Senate* D / W / oth	*House* D / W / oth
1858	24 / / 9 Opp	87 / / 46 Opp
1860	25 / / 8 CU	85 / / 47 CU

	D / R / oth	*D / R / oth*
1862	11 / 22	38 / 59[8]
1864	8 / 25	26 / 103 / 6 ?, 3 vac
1866	(34) 8 / 26	40 / 92 / 3 ?, 3 vac
1868	9 / 25	36 / 92 / 5 ?, 5 vac
1870	14 / 19 / 1 ?	78 / 23 / 37 oth[9]
1872	23 / 11	(131) 94 / 37
1874	28 / 6	91 / 40
1876	28 / 6	(143) 101 / 42
1878	27 / 5 / 2 G	105 / 11 / 26 G, 1 IR
1880	25 / 7 / 2 G	98 / 42 / 3 G
1882	28 / 6	110 / 25 / 6 G, 1 IR
1884	26 / 8	(140) 100 / 40
1886	24 / 8 / 2 GL	88 / 50 / 2 UL
1888	24 / 8 / 2 UL	78 / 51 / 11 Lab
1890	25 / 8 / 1 UL	106 / 23 / 11 oth[10]
1892	28 / 6	92 / 48
1894	19 / 15	58 / 80 / 2 Pop
1896	19 / 15	79 / 47 / 14 Pop
1898	25 / 9	80 / 58 / 2 Pop
1900	25 / 9	88 / 51 / 1 Pop
1902	26 / 8	(142) 82 / 60
1904	24 / 10	60 / 82
1906	23 / 11	84 / 58
1908	23 / 11	69 / 73
1910	22 / 12	82 / 60
1912	25 / 9	113 / 28 / 1 Pg
1914	26 / 8	76 / 65 / 1 Pg
1916	26 / 8	78 / 64
1918	22 / 12	67 / 75
1920	15 / 19	38 / 104
1922	19 / 15	(150) 83 / 67
1924	22 / 12	72 / 78
1926	21 / 13	71 / 79
1928	19 / 15	47 / 103
1930	19 / 15	86 / 64
1932	27 / 7	140 / 10
1934	32 / 2	102 / 48
1936	31 / 3	105 / 45
1938	31 / 3	98 / 52
1940	29 / 5	85 / 65
1942	17 / 17	55 / 95
1944	15 / 19	70 / 80
1946	15 / 19	(154) 54 / 100

Affiliations	Senate D / R / oth	House D / R / oth
1948	19 / 15	99 / 55
1950	21 / 13	85 / 69
1952	18 / 16	(157) 72 / 85
1954	19 / 15	97 / 60
1956	21 / 13	93 / 64
1958	26 / 8	112 / 45
1960	28 / 6	100 / 57
1962	23 / 11	(163) 101 / 62
1964	23 / 11	124 / 39
1966	23 / 11	107 / 56
1968	23 / 11	109 / 54
1970	25 / 9	112 / 51
1972	23 / 11	97 / 66
1974	23 / 11	113 / 50
1976	24 / 10	112 / 51
1978	23 / 11	116 / 47
1980	24 / 10	111 / 52
1982	22 / 12	110 / 53
1984	21 / 13	108 / 55
1986	21 / 13	111 / 52
1988	22 / 12	104 / 59
1990	23 / 11	98 / 65
1992	20 / 13 / 1 vac	100 / 62
1994	19 / 15	87 / 76
1996	19 / 15	88 / 75
1998	18 / 16	86 / 76 / 1 I
2000	17 / 17	87 / 76
2002	14 / 20	73 / 90
2004	11 / 23	66 / 97
2006	13 / 21	71 / 92

NOTES

1. Redistricting into single-member districts in counties entitled to two or more members, previously elected countywide.

2. 13 Benton Democrats, 8 Anti-Benton Democrats.

3. 48 Anti-Benton and 27 Benton Democrats.

4. 13 Anti-Benton, 8 Benton.

5. 46 Anti-Benton, 34 Benton.

6. 17 Anti-Benton, 4 Benton.

7. 71 Anti-Benton, 32 Benton.

8. The actual total elected is unclear. The journal of the Assembly lists 112 members. The Missouri Manual, 1935–6, lists 125 members plus 11 counties apparently not represented, for a potential total of 136. So at minimum the affiliation of 15 members is missing.

9. 20 Liberal, 16 Fusion, 1 Ind.

10. 8 Farmers Alliance, 1 Independent, 2 ?

SOURCES

The *Official Directory of Missouri* was used through 1970. Returns supplied by the state have been used since 1972. The 1935–36 edition contains a session-by-session list of members up to that time. Also consulted is the Secretary of State's website containing an alphabetical list of members from 1820 to present, including party affiliation for some members.

Newspapers: (Jefferson City) *Jefferson Republican*, August 23, 1834, *The* (Jefferson City) *Jeffersonian*, August 27, 1836, *Jefferson City Inquirer*, September 17, November 12, 1840, November 14, 1844, September 8, 1846, August 19, 1848, September 1, 1852, October 1, 1854, August 15, 27, 1856, *The* (St. Louis) *Republican*, September 15, 1856, November 12, 1868 *The* (Jefferson City) *Missouri State Times*, January 11, 1867, *The* (Jefferson City) *People's Tribune*, November 23, 1870.

Niles Register, December 3, 1842. *Journal of the Missouri House of Representatives*, 1863, 1865, 1867, 1869, 1871 (list of members).

William E. Parrish, *A History of Missouri Volume III 1860–1875* (Columbia: University of Missouri Press, 1973).

MONTANA

Statehood: An enabling act was signed by President Cleveland on February 22, 1889. A constitutional convention meeting in Helena convened on July 14, 1889, and submitted its work to the voters, who approved the constitution on October 1, 1889, by a vote of 26,950 to 2,274. On the same date elections were held for state's first legislature. Montana became a state on November 8, 1889. The first legislature convened on November 23, 1889. Helena has been the capital since territorial days.

Term: Senators have always been elected for a four-year term, one-half the body elected every two years. Representatives serve for two years.

Districts/Elections: Originally the Senate was apportioned one per county while House members were elected countywide regardless of the number of members apportioned to any county. Every county was entitled to at least one member. Since the U.S. Supreme Court's decision in *Reynolds v. Simms* all legislators have been elected from single-member districts except for the 1966 act which provided for a combination of both single- and multi-member districts in both houses without crossing county lines. Since 1974 each senatorial district has been divided into two representative districts.

Membership/Size: The Senate grew from 16 members to 56 members in 1924, as more counties were created. There have been two downward revisions, to 55 in 1966 and 50 in 1972.

The House originally had 55 members. There were numerous increases over the next 30 years as the House reached 108 members in 1920. Since then there have been both increases and decreases, with the present total of 100 members having been established by act in 1972.

Reapportionment/Redistricting: All reapportionments until 1966 were of the House only: 1894, 1896, 1912, 1914, 1922, 1942, 1952, 1962, 1966, 1972, 1974, 1982, 1992 and 2002.

Election Dates: Always the first Tuesday after the first Monday in November.

Constitutions: There have been two state constitutions: 1889 and 1972.

Affiliations	*Senate* D / R / oth	*House* D / R / oth
1889	(16) 8 / 8	(55) 25 / 25 / 5 ?[1]
1890	10 / 6	27 / 28
1892	9 / 7	26 / 26 / 3 Pop
1894	(21) 5 / 13 / 2 Pop, 1 Fus	(61) 3 / 44 / 14 Pop
1896	(23) 8 / 12 / 3 Pop	(68) 42 / 8 / 18 Pop
1898	(24) 17 / 6 / 1 Pop	(70) 57 / 9 / 4 SilR
1900	14 / 9 / 1 Pop	28 / 23 / 8 Lab, 6 Pop, 5 ID
1902	(26) 14 / 12	(72) 8 / 47 / 11 Lab, 6 Fus&A-TrD
1904	10 / 16	24 / 38 / 7 Lab, 3 Fus&A-TrD
1906	(27) 9 / 18	(73) 16 / 57
1908	10 / 17	(71) 38 / 33
1910	12 / 16	(74) 42 / 32
1912	(32) 17 / 13 / 2 Pg	(86) 49 / 20 / 16 Pg, 1 S
1914	(41) 16 / 19 5Pg,1I	(95) 55 / 36 3S,1I
1916	(40) 14 / 26	48 / 46
1918	(43) 12 / 31	(98) 33 / 65
1920	(54) 13 / 41	(108) 9 / 98 / 1 I
1922	16 / 38	(100) 44 / 56
1924	(56) 16 / 39 / 1 FL	(102) 34 / 66 / 2 FL
1926	15 / 40 / 1 FL	39 / 61 / 2 FL
1928	16 / 39 / 1 L	(102) 33 / 69
1930	15 / 41	43 / 59
1932	22 / 33 / 1 I	72 / 30
1934	28 / 27 / 1 I	69 / 33
1936	29 / 27	81 / 21
1938	31 / 25	58 / 44
1940	21 / 35	55 / 47
1942	19 / 37	(90) 39 / 51
1944	17 / 39	37 / 53

Affiliations	Senate D / R / oth	House D / R / oth
1946	15 / 41	31 / 58 / 1 ID
1948	23 / 31 / 2 I	54 / 36
1950	26 / 28 / 2 I	41 / 49
1952	20 / 36	(94) 32 / 62
1954	23 / 33	49 / 45
1956	31 / 25	59 / 35
1958	38 / 17 / 1 I	61 / 31 / 2 I
1960	38 / 17 / 1 I	40 / 54
1962	35 / 21	37 / 57
1964	32 / 24	56 / 38
1966	(55) 30 / 25	(104) 40 / 64
1968	30 / 25	46 / 58
1970	30 / 25	49 / 55
1972	(50) 27 / 23	(100) 54 / 46
1974	30 / 20	67 / 33
1976	25 / 25	57 / 43
1978	24 / 26	55 / 45
1980	22 / 28	43 / 57
1982	24 / 26	55 / 45
1984	28 / 22	50 / 50
1986	25 / 25	49 / 51
1988	23 / 27	52 / 48
1990	29 / 21	61 / 39
1992	30 / 20	47 / 53
1994	19 / 31	33 / 67
1996	16 / 34	35 / 65
1998	18 / 32	41 / 59
2000	19 / 31	43 / 57
2002	21 / 29	47 / 53
2004	27 / 23	50 / 50
2006	26 / 24	49 / 50 / 1 ct

NOTES

1. Five seats were in dispute in Silver Bow County. At stake was control of the House. The matter was never settled, and in fact Montana had two Houses during the entire first Legislature, one made up of Democrats and the other solely of Republicans. Each met separately, passed bills, and sent the bills to the Senate.

SOURCES

Ellis Waldron and Paul B. Wilson, *Atlas of Montana Elections 1889–1976* (Missoula: University of Montana, 1978).

Michael P. Malone and Richard B. Roeder, *Montana: A History of Two Centuries* (Seattle: University of Washington Press, 1976).

NEBRASKA

Statehood: An enabling act was signed by President Lincoln on April 19, 1864. Delegates to a constitutional convention were elected on June 6, 1864. On the day the convention convened, July 4, the members adjourned without writing a document. Eventually the territorial legislature, acting on its own, wrote a constitution which was approved by the voters on June 2, 1866 (3,983 to 3,838). On that day the first legislature was elected pending approval of statehood. Congress, over President Johnson's veto passed a second and conditional enabling act on February 9, 1867. The legislature accepted these conditions on February 21, 1867. Nebraska was formally admitted on March 1, 1867. The capital was moved to Lincoln in 1869, having been located in Omaha since territorial days.

Term: Members of both houses were elected for a term of two years. With the institution of the unicameral legislature in 1936, all members are elected for four years, with one-half the body elected every two years.

Districts/Elections: Both houses were elected from single- and multi-member districts made up of one or more counties. In addition floterial districts were provided for. Under the unicameral legislature members were also elected from single-member districts of one or more counties, but any county entitled to two or members could be divided into single-member districts. Under the one person, one vote apportionments all members are elected from single-member districts.

Membership/Size: The Senate originally had 13 members; two increases raised the membership to 33 in 1882, the last change in membership. Similarly the House grew from 39 members to 100 by 1882. The unicameral legislature originally had 43 members in 1936, increased to 49 in 1964.

Reapportionment/Redistricting: In 1874, 1882, 1922, 1936, 1962, 1972, 1982, 1992 and 2002.

Election Dates: Originally the second Tuesday in October, changed to the first Tuesday after the first Monday in November in 1876.

Constitutions: The first was written in 1866; this was followed by another in 1875.

Affiliations	*Senate* D / R / oth	*House* D / R / oth
1866	**(13)** 1 / 12	**(39)** 5 / 34
1868	3 / 10	8 / 31
1870	3 / 9 / 1 I	9 / 30
1872	4 / 9	10 / 29
1874	**(30)** 7 / 20 / 3 I	**(84)** 18 / 57 / 9 I
1876	5 / 19 / 6 G	12 / 56 / 16 G
1878	6 / 21 / 3 G	13 / 60 / 11 G
1880	3 / 27	6 / 78
1882	**(33)** 11 / 15 / 6 AMn, 1 G	**(100)** 26 / 55 / 16 AMn, 3 I
1884	8 / 25	18 / 82
1886	8 / 25	28 / 72
1888	6 / 27	22 / 76 / 2 I
1890	8 / 7 / 18 Pop	25 / 21 / 54 Pop
1892	5 / 14 / 14 Pop	13 / 47 / 40 Pop.
1894	1 / 25 / 7 Pop	23 / 73 / 4 Pop
1896	0 / 7 / 26 Fus	0 / 28 / 72 Fus
1898	0 / 20 / 11 Fus	0 / 55 / 45 Fus
1900	2 / 19 / 12 Fus	10 / 53 / 30 Fus, 7 Pop
1902	0 / 29 / 4 Fus	0 / 77 / 23 Fus
1904	0 / 31 / 2 Fus	0 / 91 / 9 Fus
1906	5 / 28	31 / 69
1908	20 / 13	69 / 31
1910	19 / 14	54 / 46
1912	15 / 18	55 / 45
1914	19 / 14	61 / 39
1916	22 / 11	62 / 38
1918	3 / 30	15 / 85
1920	0 / 33	4 / 96
1922	10 / 23	42 / 56 / 2 Pg
1924	6 / 27	38 / 60 / 2 Pg
1926	10 / 23	34 / 65 / 1 Pg
1928	9 / 24	26 / 74
1930	13 / 20	47 / 53
1932	31 / 2	83 / 17
1934	22 / 11	67 / 33
1936[1]	—	—

NOTES

1. Since 1936 Nebraska has had a unicameral legislature elected on a non-partisan basis.

NEVADA

Statehood: An enabling act was signed into law on March 21, 1864. A constitutional convention assembled in Carson City on July 4 and completed its work on July 28. The document was approved by the voters 11,393 to 2,262 on September 7. Nevada was formally admitted on October 31 and elected its first state legislature on November 8, 1864. The legislature convened for its first session on December 12, 1864. The capital has been Carson City since prior to statehood.

Term: Senators have been elected for a term of four years, with one-half the body elected every two years. Assemblymen serve a term of two years.

Districts/Elections: Senators were elected on a countywide basis, regardless of the number apportioned a county. With a few exceptions every county had at least one senator. Between 1892 and 1916 no county had more than two senators, and beginning with 1916 all counties had one member, an arrangement formally made part of the constitution in 1950. Assemblymen were apportioned among the counties based on population and elected countywide. With a single exception in the original apportionment, every county was allotted at least one member. This practice was made a matter of law in 1950. Under one person, one vote apportionment senators were elected from both single- and multi-member districts of one or more counties, with Clark and Washoe counties divided into both type of districts. In addition there was one floterial district for all of Washoe County. In all subsequent reapportionments members were elected from single-member districts except for a few multi-member districts in Clark County. The initial equal population apportionment (1966) of the Assembly was similar to the Senate. Assemblymen have been elected from single-member districts since 1972.

Membership/Size: There have been numerous changes in the size of both houses, with both increases and decreases occurring. The present totals were reached in 1982.

Reapportionment/Redistricting[1]: Have been enacted 1866, 1872 (affected one county), 1874, 1876, 1882, 1892, 1900, 1902, 1904 (affected one county), 1906 (affected one county), 1908, 1910, 1912, 1916, 1918, 1920, 1928, 1932, 1946, 1948, 1952, 1962, 1966, 1972, 1974, 1982, 1992 and 2002.

Election Dates: Since statehood, the first Tuesday after the first Monday in November.

Constitutions: The constitution of 1864 is the only one in Nevada's history.

Affiliations	Senate D / R / oth	Assembly D / R / oth
1864	**(18)** 1 / 17	**(35)** 1 / 34
1866	**(19)** 1 / 18	**(38)** 1 / 37
1868	**(20)** 5 / 15	**(39)** 5 / 34
1870	**(23)** 9 / 14	**(46)** 20 / 24 / 2 IR
1872	**(24)** 7 / 17	**(48)** 11 / 36 / 1 I
1874	**(25)** 8 / 17	**(50)** 18 / 32
1876	13 / 12	15 / 35
1878	7 / 17 / 1 Cit	8 / 39 / 3 Cit
1880	10 / 14 / 1 Cit	44 / 6
1882	**(20)** 12 / 8	**(40)** 11 / 29
1884	6 / 14	7 / 33
1886	6 / 14	8 / 32
1888	4 / 16	14 / 26
1890	2 / 18	5 / 35
1892	**(15)** 0 / 9 5 Sil, 1 P	**(30)** 5 / 2 / 15 Sil, 7 P, 1 I
1894	2 / 5 / 5 Sil, 2 I, 1 P	2 / 11 / 14 Sil, 3 P
1896	1 / 5 / 9 Sil, 1 I	4 / 2 / 20 Sil, 3 P, 1 I
1898	1 / 5 / 8 Sil, 1 I	1 / 10 / 18 Sil, 1 I
1900	1 / 3 / 9 Sil, 2 I	**(31)** 13 / 5 / 12 Sil, 1 I
1902	**(17)** 3 / 5 / 7 Sil, 2 I	**(37)** 16 / 5 / 12 Sil, 4 oth[2]
1904	3 / 7 / 6 Sil, 1 I	**(39)** 14 / 23 / 2 Sil
1906	7 / 7 / 2 Sil, 1 I	**(40)** 18 / 17 / 5 Sil
1908	**(19)** 12 / 6 / 1 I	**(48)** 34 / 14
1910	**(20)** 14 / 6	**(49)** 24 / 25
1912	**(22)** 14 / 6 / 1 S, 1 IR	**(53)** 30 / 18 / 5oth[3]
1914	9 / 9 / 4 oth[4]	23 / 26 / 3 I, 1 S
1916	**(17)** 5 / 9 / 3 I	**(37)** 20 / 14 / 3 I
1918	**(16)** 6 / 8 / 2 I	16 / 15 / 6 I
1920	**(17)** 7 / 6 / 4 I	7 / 28 / 2 I
1922	5 / 10 / 2 I	9 / 26 / 2 I
1924	8 / 9	13 / 23 / 1 I
1926	8 / 8 / 1 I	17 / 17 / 3 I
1928	4 / 12 / 1 I	14 / 21 / 2 I
1930	4 / 13	19 / 16 / 2 I
1932	7 / 9 / 1 I	**(40)** 25 / 12 / 3 I
1934	10 / 5 / 2 I	29 / 9 / 2 I
1936	11 / 3 / 3 I	30 / 10
1938	7 / 7 / 3 I	27 / 11 / 2 I
1940	6 / 10 / 1 I	26 / 13 / 1 I
1942	7 / 10	23 / 17
1944	8 / 9	27 / 13

Affiliations	Senate D / R / oth	Assembly D / R / oth
1946	7 / 10	(41) 22 / 18 / 1 I
1948	6 / 11	(43) 25 / 18
1950	6 / 11	23 / 20
1952	5 / 12	(47) 29 / 18
1954	4 / 13	30 / 17
1956	5 / 12	31 / 16
1958	7 / 10	33 / 14
1960	7 / 10	33 / 14
1962	7 / 10	32 / 15
1964	7 / 9 / 1 I	(37) 25 / 12
1966	(20) 11 / 9	(40) 21 / 19
1968	11 / 9	18 / 22
1970	13 / 7	19 / 21
1972	14 / 6	25 / 15
1974	17 / 3	31 / 9
1976	17 / 3	35 / 5
1978	15 / 5	26 / 14
1980	15 / 5	26 / 14
1982	(21) 17 / 4	(42) 22 / 20
1984	13 / 8	17 / 25
1986	9 / 12	29 / 13
1988	8 / 13	32 / 10
1990	11 / 10	22 / 20
1992	10 / 11	29 / 13
1994	8 / 13	21 / 21
1996	9 / 12	25 / 17
1998	9 / 12	28 / 14
2000	9 / 12	27 / 15
2002	9 / 12	23 / 19
2004	9 / 12	26 / 16
2006	10 / 11	27 / 15

NOTES

1. Reapportionments between 1916 and 1952 affected only the House.
2. 2 Fus, 2 I-Sil
3. 2 I, 1 IR, 1 Pg, 1 S
4. 2 I, 1 IR, 1 S

SOURCES

All data through 1996 was taken from John Koontz, Secretary of State (ed)., *Political History of Nevada 1997*, 10th ed.

NEW HAMPSHIRE

Constitutional Origins: The first constitution of New Hampshire was written between December 21, 1775, and January 5, 1776, and went into effect immediately. It was the first constitution in what would soon become the United States of America. The legislature met in various towns before selecting Concord as the permanent seat of government in 1809.

Term: Both houses were elected for a term of one year until 1877 when the present term of two years was established.

Districts/Elections: Members of the Senate, called the Council under the first constitution, were elected countywide until 1792 when the body was divided into single-member districts.

Single-member districts have been used exclusively ever since. The House was apportioned among the towns, places and city wards. House members have always been elected from either single- or multi-member districts. Both practices continue today. However, until 1978 no town, place or city ward could be divided into districts. Since that time they may be divided into two or more districts if by local referendum they make such a request.

Membership/Size: The Senate originally had 12 members and was increased in 1878 to 24, its present size. The size of the House until relatively recently varied from election to election.

Under the 1776 and 1784 constitutions separate representation was granted to every town, parish or place entitled to town privileges, having 150 rateable male polls of 21 years of age and upwards. Other provisions dealt with representation for larger communities as well as those with less than the minimum number. In 1877 the minimum number of rateable polls was increased to 600, as was the number for additional representation, producing an initial reduction in House size. Beginning in 1877 any town, place or city ward with less than a full ratio of inhabitants that could not be conveniently be classed with any other like unit "should send a representative to the general court [House] such proportionate part of the time as the number of inhabitants shall bear to six hundred." These provisions and the fact that communities did not always elect a member to serve in the House resulted in fluctuating House totals.

Since 1951 the House has consisted of not less than 375 nor more than 400. The present House is the largest such state body in the U.S. The first House in 1776 had 87 members, and the number fluctuated, reaching a low 63 in 1787. In 1942 the House reached a record number of 443 members, larger than the federal House of Representatives.

Reapportionment/Redistricting: Since 1878: 1881 (House), 1899 (Senate), 1901, 1911, 1915 (Senate), 1921 (House), 1931 (House), 1951 (House), 1961, 1965, 1971, 1981, 1991 and 2001.

Election Dates: Under the constitution of 1776 members were elected on November 1. The second constitution changed the election to the second Tuesday in March at town meetings. In 1877 this was changed to the present date, the first Tuesday after the first Monday in November.

Constitutions: The state has had two constitutions; 1776 and 1784. New Hampshire's present constitution is the second oldest still in effect in the United States. Only that of Massachusetts is older.

Affiliations	*Senate*	*House*
	D-R / F	*D-R / F*
1796	F majority	F majority
1797	F majority	F majority
1798	F majority	F majority
1799	F majority	F majority
1800	1 / 1	F majority
1801	1 / 11	F majority
1802	3 / 9	F majority[1]
1803	5 / 7	69 / 84
1804	6 / 6	87 / 75
1805	8 / 4	92 / 71
1806	10 / 2	108 / 52
1807	8 / 4	D-R majority
1808	9 / 3	99 / 63
1809	5 / 7	99 / 67
1810	7 / 5	91 / 81
1811	8 / 4	98 / 77
1812	7 / 5	104 / 79
1813	3 / 9	75 / 106
1814	4 / 8	89 / 98
1815	4 / 8	86 / 102
1816	8 / 4	105 / 84
1817	11 / 1	107 / 87
1818	10 / 2	119 / 75
1819	11 / 1	124 / 70

No calculations were made for the years 1820 / 1824.

	(J)D / NR	*(J)D / NR / oth*
1825	10 / 2	104 / 101 / 5 x
1826	8 / 4	(211) 91 / 98 / 18 ?, 4 x

Affiliations	*Senate* *(J)D / NR*	*House* *(J)D / NR / oth*
1827	11 / 1	(218) 84 / 89 / 40 ?, 5 x
1828	2 / 10	(206) 84 / 92 / 30 ?, 2 x
1829	8 / 4	99 / 82
1830	9 / 3	111 / 101
1831	10 / 2	140 / 73
1832	11 / 1	144 / 52 / 26 ?
1833	11 / 1	125 / 42
	D / W / oth	*D / W / oth*
1834	12 / 0	150 / 46
1835	11 / 1	150 / 58
1836	11 / 1	168 / 46
1837	11 / 1	(228) 177 / 51
1838	8 / 4	(245) 129 / 116
1839	10 / 2	(245) 154 / 91
1840	10 / 2	(240) 171 / 69
1841	10 / 2	(246) 161 / 85
1842	11 / 1	(230) 166 / 64
1843	10 / 2	(237) 139 / 98
1844	11 / 1	(234) 153 / 81
1845	12 / 0	(237) 156 / 74 / 7 Lty
1846	4 / 7 / 1 I	(242) 124 / 107 / 11 Lty, 16 I, 16 I
1847	11 / 1	(282) 146 / 136
1848	10 / 2	(280) 159 / 121
1849	11 / 1	(265) 158 / 107
1850	11 / 1	(275) 189 / 86
1851	10 / 2	(282) 114 / 114 / 54 FS, 10 x
1852	10 / 2	(279) 141 / 101 / 32 FS, 3 I, 1 NPty
1853	11 / 1	(304) 178 / 92 / 34 FS
1854	10 / 2	(311) 160 / 145 / 5 x, 1 ?[2]
1855	1 / / 11 A	(313) 79 / / 227 A, 5 x, 2 ?[3]
1856	4 / / 8 A	(314) 146 / / 168 A
	D / R / oth	*D / R / oth*
1857	4 / 8	(328) 128 / 196 / 4 vac
1858	3 / 9	(315) 119 / 196
1859	4 / 8	(325) 126 / 199
1860	2 / 10	(327) 121 / 206
1861	2 / 10	(321) 121 / 200
1862	3 / 9	(323) 120 / 203
1863	3 / 9	(331) 141 / 190
1864	3 / 9	(333) 123 / 210
1865	3 / 9	(328) 114 / 214
1866	3 / 9	(326) 118 / 208
1867	3 / 9	(330) 128 / 202
1868	3 / 9	(332) 138 / 194

Affiliations	Senate D / R / oth	House D / R / oth
1869	3 / 9	(334) 140 / 194
1870	1 / 11	(327) 126 / 201
1871	6 / 6	(329) 165 / 164
1872	4 / 8	(360) 150 / 210
1873	3 / 9	(348) 144 / 204
1874	8 / 4	(341) 177 / 164
1875	7 / 5	(373) 182 / 191
1876	3 / 9	(391) 180 / 211
1877	4 / 8	(379) 155 / 224
1878 (March)	4 / 8	(386) 170 / 216
(November)	(24) 4 / 20	(279) 100 / 168 / 11G
1880	8 / 16	(293) 114 / 179
1882	7 / 17	(314) 121 / 188 / 5 I
1884	8 / 16	(305) 122 / 183
1886	9 / 15	(307) 138 / 169
1888	6 / 18	(313) 144 / 169
1890	10 / 14	(355) 170 / 185
1892	9 / 15	(358) 149 / 209
1894	3 / 21	(363) 99 / 264
1896	2 / 22	(357) 66 / 291
1898	2 / 22	(360) 109 / 250 / 1 ID
1900	1 / 23	(397) 97 / 300
1902	4 / 20	(393) 136 / 257
1904	3 / 21	(391) 105 / 286
1906	6 / 18	(391) 128 / 162 / 1 I
1908	4 / 20	(387) 117 / 269 / 1 I
1910	8 / 16	(393) 173 / 220
1912	14 / 10	(402) 195 / 207
1914	4 / 19 / 1 Pg	(408) 153 / 250 / 5 Pg
1916	8 / 16	(404) 157 / 246 / 1 I
1918	5 / 19	(406) 160 / 244 / 1 I, 1 ID
1920	3 / 21	(404) 109 / 294 / 1 I
1922	8 / 16	(418) 220 / 196 / 2 I
1924	5 / 19	(421) 147 / 273 / 1 I
1926	4 / 20	(418) 131 / 286 / 1 I
1928	5 / 19	(421) 148 / 273
1930	5 / 19	(417) 163 / 254
1932	8 / 16	(418) 193 / 225
1934	9 / 15	(424) 208 / 213 / 1 I, 2 vac
1936	8 / 16	(418) 187 / 230 / 1 I
1938	6 / 18	(427) 158 / 269
1940	8 / 16	(423) 194 / 229
1942	7 / 17	(443) 167 / 276
1944	9 / 15	(400) 163 / 266 / 1 I
1946	5 / 19	126 / 273 1I
1948	6 / 18	(399) 145 / 254
1950	6 / 18	133 / 263 / 3 I
1952	6 / 18	(400) 122 / 276 / 1 I

Affiliations	*Senate*	*House*
	D / R / oth	*D / R / oth*
1954	6 / 18	(399) 135 / 264
1956	6 / 18	(397) 118 / 276 / 3 I
1958	6 / 18	(400) 136 / 264
1960	6 / 18	(399) 139 / 259 / 1I
1962	5 / 19	146 / 253
1964	10 / 14	183 / 215 / 1 vac
1966	10 / 14	(400) 155 / 245
1968	9 / 15	145 / 255
1970	9 / 15	148 / 252
1972	10 / 14	137 / 263
1974	12 / 12	167 / 233
1976	12 / 12	180 / 220
1978	12 / 12	175 / 225
1980	10 / 14	160 / 239 / 1 vac
1982	9 / 15	159 / 238 / 1 I, 1 IR
1984	6 / 18	103 / 296
1986	8 / 16	133 / 267
1988	8 / 16	119 / 281
1990	11 / 13	128 / 269 / 1 I, 1 w-I, 1 vac
1992	11 / 13	136 / 258 / 5Lbt, 1vac
1994	6 / 18	112 / 286 / 2Lbt
1996	9 / 15	143 / 255 / 2 I
1998	13 / 11	154 / 242 / 1 I, 3 vac
2000	11 / 13	140 / 256 / 1 I, 3 vac
2002	6 / 18	119 / 281
2004	8 / 16	148 / 252
2006	14 / 10	239 / 161

NOTES

1. The vote to fill Senatorial vacancies was 82 F / 67 D-R.

2. The (Concord) *Patriot & State Gazette* uses the term "opposition" to identify those elected besides Democrats (March 22, 1854). The (Concord) *New Hampshire Statesman* lists them as "Whigs & Free-Soil" (March 25, 1854). The two papers offer different totals. The *Patriot's* figures are listed above; the *Statesman's* figures are 150 D / 157 W&FS with two towns not reported. Based on the vote for Speaker, listed below, it seems the *Patriot's* figures are more accurate: 168 D / 109 W / 44 FS / 1 blank.

3. Referred to as the "opposition" by the *Patriot* (March 21, 1855) and listed as "all others" by the *Courier* (March 21,1855).The American Party was a coalition of Whigs, Free Soilers, anti-slavery Democrats and prohibitionists. Neither paper broke down these members' affiliation by any more specific label. It is not entirely clear if in fact all these individuals were in the American Party, but given the broad-based makeup of the party I have taken the liberty of assigning them this identification. Note that the vote for Speaker, listed below, closely parallels the above party breakdown: 218 A / 82 D / 4 oth.

SOURCES

Research was conducted at the State Archives, State Library and New Hampshire Historical Society, all located in Concord.

The material for the period through 1824 was largely supplied by Phil Lampi.

Concord papers were used for the years 1825–1842 and 1851–1855: *Patriot*, March 14, 21, 23, 1825, March 13, 20, 27, April 3, June 19, 1826, March 12, 19, 26, June 11, 1827, March 17, 24, 31, June 16, 1828, March 16, 23, 30, 1829, March 15, 22, 29, 1830, March 14, 21, 1831, March 19, 26, April 9, 1832, March 18, 25, 1833, March 24, 1834, March 23, 1835, March 14, 21, 1836, April 9, 1838, March 25, 1839, March 17, 1842; *New Hampshire Courier*, March 20, 1835, March 18, 1836, April 1836, April 20, 1838, March 20, 1840, March 19, 1841, March 11, 1842; *New Hampshire Statesman*, March 14, 21, 1851, March 25, 1854, March 24, 1855; *The Independent Democrat*, March 20, 1851, March 11, 18, 1852; *New Hampshire Patriot & State Gazette*, March 22, 1854, March 21, 1855. For the years between 1843 and 1863, several Concord and Portsmouth newspapers were consulted. From Concord: *Courier of New Hampshire, Herald & New Hampshire Intelligencer, New Hampshire Patriot* and the *Oracle of the Day*. From Portsmouth *New Hampshire Gazette, New Hampshire Spy* and *Portsmouth Oracle* as well as (Walpole) *The Farmer's Museum*.

Also, the *Tribune Almanac, Evening Journal* and the *American Almanacs* for the period 1856 and 1888. The primary source from 1863 to 1871 was the *New Hampshire Register*. Beginning with 1890 I relied primarily on the *Manual for the General Court* issued by the Department of State. Some additional data, particularly about the earliest years, was found in Lynn W. Turner, *The Ninth State* (Chapel Hill: University of North Carolina Press, 1983) and Leon W. Anderson, *To This Day* (Canaan NH: Phoenix Publishing, 1981).

NEW JERSEY

Constitutional Origins: The first constitution of the state was adopted by the Provincial Congress on July 2, 1776, having been written by a committee of the Congress in only three days. The body met in Burlington, one of two meeting places of the legislature. The first legislative elections took place in August 1776 and annually thereafter until 1947. The body was a typical two-house chamber, but the Council, although a legislative body, as a carryover from the colonial era was part of the executive as well. Burlington and Perth Amboy alternated as the meeting place of the legislature, a holdover from colonial days. This continued until 1790 when Trenton became the capital.

Term: Members of the Council, which later became the Senate,[1] were elected for a term of one year. In 1844 the state's second constitution provided for a three-year term, with overlap so that one-third of the body was elected annually. In 1947 the term was increased to four years, the present length. Assemblymen were elected for a one-year term until 1947 when the term was increased to its present length, two years. New Jersey was the last state to have a one-year legislative term.

Districts/Elections: The county was the basis for representation. Each county elected one Council (Senate) member and initially three assemblymen, also on a countywide basis. But from 1853 until 1894 the assemblymen were elected from single-member districts within each county. Countywide elections resumed after 1894 and continued until 1965 when as a result of the U.S. Supreme Court ruling on reapportionment the Senate was divided into 29 single-member districts of equal population. A year later the present format was introduced, creating 40 legislative districts of equal population crossing county lines; each district elects one senator and two assemblymen.

Membership: The Council and later the Senate's size was always the same as the number of counties. There were originally 13 councilors and the body grew as counties were created, reaching 21 in 1857 with the creation of Union County. That remained unchanged until 1965 when the number was increased to 29 and a year later to 40, its present size. The Assembly originally had 39 members but in part because of periodic reapportionments grew in size, to 40 in 1801 and through six additional increases to 60 in 1851.[2] That number that remained unchanged until 1967 when the membership was increased to 80, its present total.

Reapportionment/Redistricting: In the House only: 1797, 1815, 1818, 1830, 1851, 1853*, 1855*, 1857*, 1861, 1868*, 1869* , 1871, 1879*, 1880*, 1881, 1889, 1891, 1892*, 1901, 1911, 1922, 1931, 1941, 1961. (Those marked with an asterisk were redistricting only.) Both houses: 1965, 1967, 1971, 1981, 1991 and 2001.

Election Dates: Under the Constitution of 1776, elections were held for two days, commencing on the second Tuesday of October. This was changed to the first Tuesday after the first Monday in October, effective in 1842. The election was reduced to one day in 1846.

Constitutions: There have been three state constitutions: 1776, 1844 and 1947.

Affiliations	Council D-R / F	Assembly D-R / F / oth
1800	4 / 9	11 / 28
1801	6 / 7	(40) 24 / 16
1802	7 / 6	19 / 20 / 1 ?
1803	8 / 5	25 / 14 / 1 ?
1804	9 / 4	28 / 12
1805	8 / 5	25 / 14 / 1 Q/R[3]
1806	6 / 7	21 / 19
1807	9 / 4	25 / 15
1808	7 / 6	23 / 17
1809	8 / 5	24 / 16
1810	8 / 5	26 / 14
1811	9 / 4	30 / 10
1812	6 / 7	17 / 23
1813	7 / 6	23 / 17
1814	7 / 6	22 / 18
1815	7 / 6	(42) 27 / 15
1816	8 / 5	23 / 18
1817	8 / 5	26 / 16
1818	8 / 5	(43) 27 / 16
1819	9 / 4	31 / 12
1820	9 / 4	36 / 7
1821	9 / 4	30 / 13
1822	9 / 4	31 / 12
1823	8 / 5	29 / 14
1824	(14) ?	?

	Council (J)D / NR	Assembly (J)D / NR
1825	?	?
1826	?	?
1827	?	?
1828	5 / 9	18 / 25
1829	8 / 6	28 / 15
1830	10 / 4	(50) 37 / 13
1831	7 / 7	26 / 24
1832	6 / 8	17 / 33
1833	13 / 1	41 / 9

	Council D / W / oth	Assembly D / W / oth
1834	8 / 6	28 / 21 / 1 ?
1835	9 / 5	34 / 16
1836	7 / 7	31 / 19
1837	(16) 6 / 10	(53) 18 / 35
1838	(17) 7 / 10	20 / 33
1839	7 / 10	20 / 33
1840	(18) 5 / 13	12 / 41
1841	9 / 9	(58) 24 / 34

Affiliations	Council D / W / oth	Assembly D / W / oth
1842	8 / 10	26 / 32
1843	12 / 6	35 / 23
1844	(19) 6 / 13	18 / 40
1845	7 / 12	27 / 30 / 1 A
1846	7 / 12	18 / 40
1847	7 / 12	20 / 38
1848	7 / 12	19 / 39
1849	9 / 10	25 / 33
1850	(20) 10 / 10	30 / 28
1851	13 / 7	(60) 45 / 15
1852	13 / 7	39 / 21
1853	13 / 7	40 / 20
1854	10 / 9 / 1 A	29 / 25 / 6 A
1855	11 / 5 / 4 A	31 / 14 / 15 A
1856	11 / / 6 Opp, 3 A	38 / / 22 Opp
1857	(21) 15 / / 6 Opp	35 / / 25 Opp
1858	13 / / 8 Opp	24 / / 36 Opp

	D / R / oth	D / R / oth
1859	12 / 8 / 1 A	30 / 28 / 2 A
1860	10 / 11	32 / 28
1861	10 / 10 / 1 I	36 / 24
1862	13 / 8	45 / 15
1863	14 / 7	40 / 20
1864	13 / 8	30 / 30
1865	10 / 11	24 / 36
1866	8 / 13	27 / 33
1867	11 / 10	46 / 14
1868	12 / 9	32 / 28
1869	13 / 8	34 / 26
1870	9 / 12	26 / 34
1871	9 / 12	24 / 36
1872	7 / 14	16 / 44
1873	7 / 14	28 / 32
1874	8 / 13	41 / 19
1875	9 / 12	23 / 37
1876	11 / 10	30 / 30
1877	12 / 9	33 / 27
1878	9 / 11 / 1 I	27 / 33
1879	9 / 12	25 / 35
1880	5 / 15 / 1 I	26 / 34
1881	9 / 12	35 / 25
1882	9 / 12	35 / 25
1883	9 / 12	34 / 26
1884	10 / 11	26 / 34
1885	8 / 13	29 / 31
1886	9 / 12	28 / 32

Affiliations	_Senate_ _D / R / oth_	_Assembly_ _D / R / oth_
1887	9 / 12	23 / 37
1888	11 / 10	32 / 28
1889	10 / 11	37 / 23
1890	14 / 7	40 / 20
1891	16 / 5	42 / 18
1892	16 / 5	39 / 21
1893	10 / 11	21 / 39
1894	5 / 16	6 / 54
1895	3 / 18	7 / 53
1896	3 / 18	4 / 56
1897	7 / 14	23 / 37
1898	7 / 14	23 / 37
1899	7 / 14	17 / 43
1900	4 / 17	22 / 38
1901	4 / 17	14 / 46
1902	7 / 14	22 / 38
1903	7 / 14	22 / 38
1904	7 / 14	14 / 46
1905	4 / 17	3 / 57
1906	6 / 15	31 / 29
1907	7 / 14	20 / 40
1908	8 / 13	15 / 45
1909	6 / 15	19 / 41
1910	9 / 12	42 / 18
1911	10 / 11	23 / 37
1912	12 / 9	52 / 8
1913	11 / 10	37 / 23
1914	10 / 11	22 / 38
1915	8 / 13	20 / 40
1916	6 / 15	16 / 44
1917	6 / 15	14 / 46
1918	6 / 15	30 / 30
1919	6 / 15	27 / 33
1920	6 / 15	1 / 59
1921	5 / 16	15 / 45
1922	4 / 17	16 / 44
1923	4 / 17	18 / 42
1924	3 / 18	13 / 47
1925	3 / 18	14 / 46
1926	4 / 17	13 / 47
1927	3 / 18	14 / 46
1928	3 / 18	12 / 48
1929	4 / 17	14 / 46
1930	4 / 17	14 / 46
1931	6 / 15	34 / 26
1932	6 / 15	22 / 38
1933	6 / 15	27 / 33
1934	6 / 15	26 / 34

Affiliations	Senate D / R / oth	Assembly D / R / oth
1935	8 / 13	18 / 42
1936	10 / 11	39 / 21
1937	8 / 13	19 / 41
1938	5 / 16	15 / 45
1939	5 / 16	15 / 45
1940	4 / 17	16 / 44
1941	4 / 17	16 / 44
1942	3 / 18	16 / 44
1943	3 / 18	16 / 44
1944	4 / 17	18 / 42
1945	4 / 17	19 / 41
1946	5 / 16	12 / 48
1947	4 / 17	15 / 45
1948	6 / 15	16 / 44
1949	7 / 14	22 / 38
1951	5 / 16	17 / 43
1953	4 / 17	20 / 40
1955	7 / 14	20 / 40
1957	8 / 13	42 / 18
1959	10 / 11	34 / 26
1961	10 / 11	38 / 22
1963	6 / 15	27 / 33
1965	(29) 19 / 10	41 / 19
1967	(40) 9 / 31	(80) 22 / 58
1969	9 / 31	21 / 59
1971	16 / 24	40 / 39 / 1 I
1973	29 / 10 1 I	66 / 14
1975	—	49 / 31
1977	27 / 13	54 / 26
1979	—	45 / 35
1981	22 / 18	43 / 37
1983	23 / 17	44 / 36
1985	—	30 / 50
1987	25 / 15	39 / 41
1989	—	44 / 36
1991	13 / 27	22 / 58
1993	16 / 24	27 / 53
1995	—	30 / 50
1997	16 / 24	32 / 48
1999	—	35 / 45
2001	20 / 20	42 / 18
2003	22 / 18	47 / 33
2005	—	48 / 32

NOTES

1. Under the state's second constitution of 1847 the Council's name was changed to the Senate and its executive duties ended, no doubt because of the

direct election of the governor, who prior to that time was elected by the legislature.

2. The Assembly increased to 42 in 1815, 43 in 1818, 50 in 1830, 53 in 1837, 58 in 1841 and 60 in 1851.

3. Candidate was endorsed by two parties: Quid and Republican.

SOURCES

Research was done at the State Archives and Library in Trenton as well as the New Jersey Historical Society in Newark.

Phil Lampi's research is the basis for the pre–1825 data. From 1828 to 1874 two Trenton newspapers were used: the *True-American* and the *State Gazette*. Also consulted was the (Newark) *Sentinel of Freedom*. Beginning with the election 1874 the (New Jersey) *Manual* was used as was the (Secretary of State) *Results of the General Election* up to 2001.

Data on reapportionment and redistricting was obtained from Stanley H. Friedelbaum, "Apportionment Legislation in New Jersey," in *Proceedings of the New Jersey Historical Society* Vol. LXX (1952), pp. 262–277, and Richard McCormick, *The History of Voting in New Jersey* (New Brunswick: Rutgers University Press, 1953).

NEW MEXICO

Statehood: An enabling act was signed by President Taft on June 20, 1910. A constitutional convention met between October 8 and November 21, 1910. The document was revised to meet Congressional objections and approved by the voters on November 7, 1911 (31,742 to 13,309). New Mexico became a state on January 6, 1912. The initial election of the legislature occurred on November 7, 1911. The capital has always been Santa Fe.

Term: Senators since statehood have been elected for four years, all at the same time, except on two occasions when reapportionment required another election at the two-year mark. The extra elections were held in 1966 and 1976. Representatives since statehood have been elected for a term of two years.

Districts/Elections: Senators were originally chosen from single-member districts. By amendment in 1949 all counties but Los Alamos chose one member. By amendment in 1955 all counties had one member. The House was chosen from single- and multi-member districts, all members elected countywide. In 1955 counties entitled to more than one member continued to elect them at large but each member in such counties was elected separately by designated place. In 1964 an enlarged House was elected and cast weighted votes. Since 1966 all members of the legislature have been elected from single-member districts.

Membership/Size: The Senate had 24 members at statehood, increased three times, to 31 in 1952, to 32 in 1956 and to the present number of 42 in 1966. The House had 49 members at statehood, increased to 55 in 1950, 66 in 1956, and 77 in 1964, and decreased to 70 in 1966.

Reapportionment/Redistricting: Enacted in 1950 (House) and 1952 (Senate), 1956, 1964 (House), 1966, 1974, 1982, 1992 and 2002.

Election Date: Always the first Tuesday after the first Monday in November.

Constitutions: The constitution of 1911 is still in effect.

Affiliations	*Senate* D / R / oth	*House* D / R / oth
1911	(24) 7 / 16 / 1 P	(48) 16 / 29 / 3 P
1914	—	14 / 32 / 1 P, 1 S
1916	10 / 14	18 / 30
1918	—	15 / 34
1920	9 / 15	15 / 34
1922	—	31 / 18
1924	9 / 15	28 / 21
1926	—	21 / 28
1928	6 / 18	12 / 37
1930	—	28 / 21
1932	20 / 4	40 / 9
1934	—	37 / 12
1936	23 / 1	47 / 2
1938	—	42 / 7
1940	21 / 3	40 / 9
1942	—	33 / 16
1944	18 / 6	30 / 19
1946	—	30 / 19
1948	19 / 5	36 / 13
1950	—	(55) 46 / 9
1952	(31) 22 / 9	27 / 28
1954	—	51 / 4
1956	(32) 24 / 8	(66) 43 / 23
1958	—	60 / 6
1960	28 / 4	60 / 6
1962	—	55 / 11
1964	28 / 4	(77) 59 / 18
1966	(42) 25 / 17	(70) 45 / 25
1968	—	44 / 26
1970	28 / 14	48 / 22

Affiliations	Senate D / R / oth	House D / R / oth
1972	—	57 / 13
1974	29 / 13	51 / 19
1976	33 / 9	48 / 22
1978	—	41 / 29
1980	22 / 20	41 / 29
1982	—	45 / 25
1984	21 / 21	43 / 27
1986	—	47 / 23
1988	26 / 16	45 / 25
1990	—	49 / 21
1992	27 / 15	52 / 18
1994	—	46 / 24
1996	25 / 17	42 / 28
1998	—	40 / 30
2000	24 / 18	42 / 28
2002	—	42 / 28
2004	23 / 19	42 / 28
2006	—	42 / 28

NEW YORK

Constitutional Origins: The first constitution of New York was written in April 1777 and approved by the Fourth Provincial Congress on April 20, 1777. Elections for the first legislature took place in June 1777. The legislature first convened on September 1 of that year. They initially met in Kingston and then convened in different cities — Albany, New York and Poughkeepsie — until 1798 when Albany became the permanent capital.

Term: Senators were elected for a four-year term until 1847, when the present term of two years was initiated. The Assembly was elected annually until 1938 when the term was increased to two years, the present length of service. New York was the next to last state to elect their lower house for a term of one year. New Jersey continued to do so until 1947.

Districts/Elections: Senators were originally elected from four multi-member geographical named districts — Eastern, Southern, Middle and Western — until 1821 when the number of districts was doubled and districts were identified by number. Under the geographic district system the number of members per district had varied as a result of reapportionment but under the later system each of the eight districts always elected four members. District boundaries changed under periodic reapportionments under both methods. A quarter of the Senate was elected annually throughout this time period (1777–1846). As a result of the new constitution adopted in 1847 the Senate was elected solely from single-member districts and was elected in its entirety ever two years. With the constitution of 1894 Senate elections were switched to even-numbered years beginning in 1898.

Assemblymen were originally elected on a countywide basis regardless of the number of members given a county. There were a few multi-county Assembly districts prior to 1821. In that year the new constitution guaranteed all counties but Hamilton a minimum of one seat, regardless of population. When assemblymen were elected from single-member districts, beginning in 1847, the County Board of Supervisors was charged with drawing up the boundaries of such districts in any county entitled to two or more members. Under the 1894 constitution Assembly seats could no longer cross senatorial district boundaries and counties could not be divided in the formation of senatorial districts except to create districts wholly within a county. Since 1821 Assembly districts could not cross county lines — that is, until the impact of "one person, one vote," beginning in 1965.

Membership/Size: The Senate originally consisted of 24 members, a number based on a formula that automatically added to its total after each census and reapportionment. As a result of the formula the body grew from 24 to 43 members in 1796. The constitution was amended in 1801, eliminating the formula and fixing the number at 32. The number of senators remained unchanged until the constitution of 1894 increased it to 50 and established a new formula that has gradually increased the body to its present total of 62. There was a temporary increase to 65 in the 1965 election.

The Assembly initially had 70 members, and this was increased to 108 under a formula similar to that of the Senate in 1796. The body was reduced to 100 members by an amendment in 1801, which also provided for a more limited expansion that saw the Assembly increase to 126 members. The constitution of 1821 did away with automatic expansion and fixed the body's maximum size at 128. Under the constitution of 1894 the Assembly increased its numbers to 150. Except for a temporary increase to 165 (1965 election only), that number has remained the same ever since.

Reapportionment/Redistricting: Occurred in 1791, 1796, 1802, 1808, 1815, 1822, 1826, 1836, 1846, 1857, 1866, 1879, 1892, 1894, 1906, 1916, 1944, 1954, 1965, 1966, 1972, 1982, 1992 and 2002. Those of 1802, 1822, and 1894 were done by a constitutional convention. Those of 1965 and 1966 were court ordered to comply with the U.S. Supreme Court's ruling mandating equal population of districts (*Reynolds V. Sims*). The year refers to the first election under each act.

Election Dates: Originally three days beginning on the last Tuesday in April, changed in 1822 to the first Monday and Tuesday in November, changed in 1842 to the first Tuesday after the first Monday in November.

Constitutions: There have been four: 1777, 1821, 1847 and 1894.

Affiliations	*Senate* *af / f*	*Assembly* *af / f*
1788	(24) f majority	(70) 45 / 19 / 1 ?[1]
1789	f majority	23 / 38 / 4 ?
1790	?	?
	D-R / F	*D-R / F*
1791	?	?
1792	?	?
1793	?	?
1794	?	?
1795	F majority	F majority
1796	(43) 7 / 35 / 1 vac	(108) F majority
1797	5 / 36 / 2 vac	F majority
1798	11 / 32	F majority
1799	11 / 32	F majority[2]
1800	18 / 25	67 / 39 / 1 tie
1801	21 / 22	83 / 25
1802	(32) 21 / 11	(100) 73 / 32 / 3 ?
1803	27 / 5	82 / 18
1804	28 / 4	77 / 21 / 2 Bu
1805	32 / 0	76 / 19 / 5 Lew
1806	32 / 0	49 / 19 / 32 Lew
1807	24 / 8 &Lew[3]	65 / 23 / 11 Lew
1808	23 / 9	(112) 61 / 48 / 3 Lew, 1 IR
1809	20 / 12	48 / 64
1810	22 / 10	71 / 41
1811	25 / 7	69 / 43
1812	24 / 8	52 / 59 / 1 vac
1813	27 / 5	47 / 65
1814	26 / 6	71 / 41
1815	23 / 9	(126) 63 / 63
1816	25 / 7	90 / 36
1817	27 / 5	95 / 31
1818	28 / 4	95 / 30 / 1 ?
		Bk / Cl / F
1819	32 / 0	58 / 30 / 34

Affiliations	Senate	Assembly
	Bk / Cl	
1820	?	71 / 33 / 22
1821	13 / 18 / 1 ?	73 / 48 / 5
1822	32 / 0	(128) 112 / 26
1823	30 / 2	91 / 37
1824	21 / 11	42 / 86
1825	17 / 15	68 / 55 / 4 NP, 1 ?
1826	17 / 15	84 / 43 / 1 I
		J / Ad / A-M
1827	22 / 10	93 / 16 / 17
	J / Ad / A-M	
1828	20 / 9 / 3	82 / 16 / 30
1829	25 / 4 / 3	91 / 7 / 29
1830	25 / 2 / 5	93 / 4 / 31
1831	24 / 2 / 6	95 / 5 / 28
1832	26 / 0 / 6	100 / 3 / 25
1833	25 / 0 / 6	113 / 0 / 10 / 5 ID
	D / W / oth	D / W / oth
1834	28 / 4	91 / 36 / 1 vac
1835	28 / 4	111 / 16 / 1 A
1836	27 / 5	90 / 38
1837	22 / 10	28 / 100
1838	18 / 14	45 / 83
1839	12 / 20	58 / 70
1840	11 / 21	62 / 66
1841	17 / 15	96 / 32
1842	22 / 10	92 / 36
1843	26 / 6	92 / 36
1844	27 / 5	65 / 47 / 15 A, 1 D
1845	25 / 6	74 / 51 / 2 A-R, 1 ID
1846	21 / 10 / 1 ?	52 / 76
1847	8 / 24	36 / 91 / 1 I
1848	—	7 / 106 / 14 FS,1 A-R
1849	15 / 17	64 / 63 / 1 A-R
1850	—	44 / 82 / 1 FS, 1 I
1851	16 / 16	63 / 65
1852	—	88 / 40
1853	8 / 24	47 / 77 / 2 I, 1 FS, 1 AML
1854	—	38 / 75 / 9 A, 4 T, 2 R
	D / R / oth	D / R / oth
1855	7 / 14 / 11 A	46 / 39 / 37 A, 6 W

Affiliations	Senate D / R / oth	Assembly D / R / oth
1856	—	40 / 80 / 8 A
1857	14 / 15 / 2 A, 1 IR	56 / 61 / 11 A
1858	—	27 / 90 / 9 A, 1 ID
1859	9 / 23	37 / 90 / 1 vac
1860	—	35 / 93
1861	10 / 22	35 / 92 / 1 IR
1862	—	63 / 56 / 9 UD
1863	11 / 21	45 / 81 / 1 ID, 1 IU
1864	—	52 / 75 / 1 ID
1865	5 / 27	36 / 91
1866	—	45 / 83
1867	15 / 16 / 1 I	73 / 55
1868	—	52 / 74 / 2 ID
1869	18 / 14	56 / 72
1870	—	65 / 63
1871	7 / 25	31 / 97
1872	—	34 / 92 / 2 LR
1873	13 / 18 / 1 IR	54 / 72 / 2 LR
1874	—	74 / 53 / 1 ID
1875	12 / 20	57 / 71
1876	—	58 / 70
1877	12 / 19 / 1 ID	61 / 66 / 1 G
1878	—	27 / 98 / 3 G
1879	7 / 25	35 / 91 / 1 G, 1 ID
1880	—	47 / 80 / 1 ID
1881	17 / 15	67 / 60 1IR
1882	—	86 / 38 / 4 oth[4]
1883	13 / 19	56 / 72
1884	—	54 / 74
1885	12 / 20	49 / 77 / 1 IR, 1 ID
1886	—	54 / 74
1887	11 / 21	55 / 72 / 1 ID
1888	—	51 / 77
1889	13 / 19	57 / 71
1890	—	68 / 59 / 1 IR
1891	17 / 14 / 1 IR	67 / 61
1892	—	74 / 54
1893	12 / 19 / 1 ID	57 / 71
1894	—	23 / 105
1895	(50) 14 / 35 / 1 IR	(150) 47 / 103
1896	—	35 / 114 / 1 I
1897	—	69 / 77 / 3 CitU, 1 IR
1898	23 / 27	63 / 87
1899	—	59 / 92 / 1 vac
1900	15 / 35	45 / 105
1901	—	42 / 106 / 2 ID
1902	22 / 28	61 / 89
1903	—	52 / 97 / 1 ICit

Affiliations	*Senate* *D / R / oth*	*Assembly* *D / R / oth*
1904	14 / 36	46 / 104
1905	—	35 / 111 / 3 MOL, 1 ID
1906	(51) 20 / 31	51 / 98 / 1 IL
1907	—	54 / 96
1908	16 / 35	51 / 99
1909	—	56 / 94
1910	29 / 21 / 1 IL	87 / 63
1911	—	48 / 101 / 1 S
1912	33 / 16 / 2 Pg	104 / 42 / 4 Pg
1913	—	48 / 82 / 20 Pg
1914	17 / 34	50 / 100
1915	—	52 / 97 / 1 S
1916	15 / 36	48 / 100 / 2 S
1917	—	44 / 96 / 10 S
1918	22 / 29	54 / 94 / 2 S
1919	—	34 / 111 / 5 S
1920	11 / 39 / 1 S	28 / 119 / 3 S
1921	—	53 / 96 / 1 S
1922	26 / 25	69 / 81
1923	—	64 / 86
1924	22 / 29	54 / 96
1925	—	59 / 91
1926	24 / 27	66 / 84
1927	—	62 / 88
1928	24 / 27	61 / 89
1929	—	63 / 86 / 1 vac
1930	25 / 26	70 / 80
1931	—	70 / 80
1932	26 / 25	73 / 77
1933	—	65 / 85
1934	29 / 22	77 / 73
1935	—	67 / 82 / 1 vac
1936	29 / 22	74 / 76
1937	—	61 / 84 / 5 A-L
1938	24 / 27	64 / 85 / 1 A-L
1940	21 / 30	62 / 87 / 1 A-L
1942	20 / 31	58 / 90 / 1 A-L, 1 vac
1944	(56) 21 / 35	55 / 94 / 1 AL
1946	14 / 41 / 1 A-L	31 / 109
1948	25 / 32	63 / 87
1950	23 / 32 / 1 A-L	63 / 87
1952	19 / 37	52 / 98
1954	(58) 24 / 34	60 / 90
1956	20 / 38	54 / 96
1958	24 / 34	58 / 92
1960	25 / 33	66 / 84
1962	25 / 33	65 / 85
1964	33 / 25	88 / 62

Affiliations	Senate D / R / oth	Assembly D / R / oth
1965	(65) 28 / 37	(165) 90 / 75
1966	(57) 26 / 31	(150) 80 / 70
1968	24 / 33	72 / 76 / 2 C
1970	25 / 32	70 / 77 / 2 C / 1 UMAB
1972	(60) 23 / 37	66 / 83 / 1 C
1974	26 / 34	88 / 62
1976	25 / 35	90 / 60
1978	25 / 35	86 / 64
1980	25 / 35	85 / 64 / 1 L
1982	(61) 26 / 35	98 / 52
1984	26 / 35	92 / 56 / 2 L
1986	26 / 35	94 / 56
1988	27 / 34	92 / 58
1990	26 / 35	96 / 54
1992	26 / 35	101 / 49
1994	25 / 36	94 / 56
1996	26 / 35	96 / 54
1998	26 / 35	98 / 52
2000	25 / 36	99 / 51
2002	(62) 25 / 37	102 / 48
2004	27 / 35	104 / 46
2006	28 / 34	108 / 42

Notes

1. Five of the seats were apportioned to Cumberland (3) and Gloucester (2) counties which were claimed by the then unrecognized state of Vermont. Cumberland sent members to the Assembly only twice (1779 and 1783) and Gloucester never. So for all practical purposes the Assembly had a membership of 65.

2. Of those that could be identified there were 43 F, 34 D-R and 31 of unknown affiliation.

3. Lewisite party included in the Federalist total because Federalists were supported by the Lewisites in this election.

4. 1 CLU, 1 G, 1 ID, 1 IR

Sources

Research was done at the New York Historical Society, the New York Public Library, the State Library and many country libraries and historical societies.

Jabez D. Hammond, *The History of Political Parties in the State of New York*, 2 vols. (Albany: C. Van Benthuysen, 1842). Newspapers were almost the sole source of information prior to 1860. The most important were the *Albany Argus* 1813–, *The* (Albany) *Evening Journal* 1830–, and *The New York Tribune* 1841–. Other newspapers frequently consulted were *Albany Gazette*, (New York) *American Citizen, New York Columbian*, (New York) *Daily Advertiser, New York Journal Patriotic Register*. Many county newspapers were also used primarily prior to 1860. *The* (New York) *Legislative Manual* 1892–1989, (New York) *Red Book* 1892–.

It should be noted that several of the major political almanacs were published in New York State and gave extensive coverage to the legislative elections. Published in New York City were *Whig/Tribune Almanac* and the *World Almanac*. Published in Albany was the *Evening Journal Almanac*, the first to publish complete returns for the Assembly (1859), and the *Argus Almanac*.

NORTH CAROLINA

Constitutional Origins: A convention meeting at Halifax between November 12 and December 18, 1776, wrote the first state constitution. It was proclaimed in effect on December 18, 1776. The first legislature convened on April 7, 1777, at New Bern, then the capital. But after 1778 the legislature met in several different towns before a permanent site at Raleigh was selected in 1792.

Term: Both houses were elected annually until 1836 when the term was increased to two years, the present term.

Districts/Elections: The county was the unit of representation, and that representation exists on a modified basis today. Each county had one seat in the Senate in the original constitution. In 1835 that Senate was to be elected from 50 districts "in proportion to the public taxes paid into the Treasury of the State, by the citizens thereof" on an equal basis. No county could be divided in the formation of a district. Under the 1868 constitution the districts were based on equal population and only those counties entitled to two or members could be divided into districts. Initially in the House of Commons (changed in 1868 to House of Representatives) each county received two seats and six towns received one. Under the 1835 amendments the House was apportioned among the counties based on their federal population (all free persons + ⅗ of all slaves), but each county was guaranteed a minimum of one representative. Towns were no longer given separate representation. All members were elected countywide. With minor modifications this continued until the implementation of one person, one vote apportionment. Since that time both houses have been elected from single- and multi-member districts, but not until 1982 were counties divided into more than one district.

Beginning in 2002 all members of both houses were elected from single-member districts.

Membership/Size: The initial House had 88 members and grew as new counties were created, reaching a total of 137. In 1835 the number was fixed at 120 and that has remained the same ever since. The original Senate had 44 members and also grew as new counties were created. Today the state has 100 counties. The 1835 amendments fixed the Senate at 50 members. As with the House, the 1835 number has remained in place ever since.

Reapportionment/Redistricting: None enacted prior to 1836, 1844, 1852, 1868, 1872, 1882, 1892, 1902, 1912, 1922, 1942, 1962 (House), 1964, 1966, 1972, 1982, 1992, 2002 and 2004.

Election Dates: Initially the second Thursday in August (for three days), changed in 1856 to the first Thursday in August. In 1876 the date was changed to the first Tuesday after the first Monday in November.

Constitutions: The constitution of 1776 remained in effect until 1868 when a new constitution was adopted. The third and most recent constitution was adopted in 1970.

Affiliations	Senate D / W	House D / W
1835	33 / 30 / 2 ?	64 / 68 / 4 ?, 1 vac
1836	(50) 24 / 26	(120) 62 / 58
1838	23 / 27	54 / 66
1840	22 / 28	45 / 75
1842	20 / 30	67 / 53
1844	25 / 25	50 / 70
1846	23 / 27	55 / 65
1848	25 / 25	58 / 62
1850	27 / 23	65 / 55
1852	28 / 22	58 / 62
1854	30 / 20	63 / 57
1856	33 / 17 A&W[1]	80 / 40 A&W
1858	32 / / 18 Opp	82 / / 38 Opp
1860	31 / 19 W&Opp[2]	64 / 56 W&Opp
1865[3]	—	—
	C / R	**C / R / oth**
1866	10 / 40	54 / 66
1868	12 / 38	38 / 82
1870	36 / 14	75 / 42 / 3 I
	D / R / oth	**D / R / oth**
1872	32 / 18	65 / 54 / 1 I
1874	37 / 11 / 2 I	84 / 34 / 2 I
1876	40 / 10	84 / 36

Affiliations	Senate D / R / oth	House D / R / oth
1878	34 / 16	79 / 41
1880	38 / 12	83 / 37
1882	34 / 16	68 / 52
1884	43 / 7	97 / 23
1886	33 / 17	65 / 55
1888	37 / 13	85 / 35
1890	43 / 7	102 / 17 / 1 I
1892	46 / 1 / 3 Pop	92 / 19 / 9 Pop
1894	8 / 18 / 24 Pop	46 / 38 / 36 Pop
1896	9 / 17 / 24 Pop	36 / 49 / 35 Pop
1898	40 / 0 / 10 Pop	94 / 0 / 26 Pop
1900	39 / 8 / 3 Pop	101 / 17 / 2 Pop
1902	45 / 5	100 / 17 / 3 ID
1904	44 / 6	104 / 16
1906	46 / 4	99 / 21
1908	40 / 10	96 / 24
1910	43 / 7	99 / 21
1912	47 / 3	107 / 13
1914	43 / 7	98 / 20 / 2 I
1916	41 / 9	97 / 22 / 1 I
1918	40 / 10	93 / 27
1920	39 / 11	91 / 29
1922	47 / 3	110 / 10
1924	47 / 3	102 / 18
1926	47 / 3	104 / 16
1928	38 / 12	84 / 36
1930	48 / 2	115 / 5
1932	48 / 2	112 / 8
1934	48 / 2	108 / 12
1936	48 / 2	112 / 8
1938	48 / 2	114 / 6
1940	48 / 2	114 / 6
1942	48 / 2	108 / 12
1944	47 / 3	106 / 14
1946	48 / 2	108 / 12
1948	48 / 2	109 / 11
1950	48 / 2	111 / 9
1952	48 / 2	106 / 14
1954	49 / 1	110 / 10
1956	47 / 3	107 / 13
1958	49 / 1	116 / 4
1960	48 / 2	105 / 15
1962	48 / 2	99 / 21
1964	49 / 1	106 / 14
1966	43 / 7	94 / 26
1968	38 / 12	91 / 29
1970	43 / 7	97 / 23
1972	34 / 16	83 / 37

Affiliations	Senate D / R / oth	House D / R / oth
1974	49 / 1	111 / 9
1976	46 / 4	114 / 6
1978	45 / 5	106 / 14
1980	40 / 10	98 / 22
1982	44 / 6	102 / 18
1984	38 / 12	83 / 37
1986	41 / 9	5 / 85
1988	37 / 13	92 / 28
1990	37 / 13	74 / 46
1992	39 / 11	78 / 42
1994	26 / 24	52 / 68
1996	30 / 20	59 / 61
1998	35 / 15	66 / 54
2000	35 / 15	62 / 58
2002	28 / 22	59 / 61
2004	29 / 21	63 / 57
2006	31 / 19	68 / 52

NOTES

1. "A&W" signifies combined total, no breakdown indicated.
2. "W&Opp" signifies combined total, no breakdown indicated.
3. Election held on November 9. Most candidates ran without party affiliation; therefore no compilation was made for this election.

SOURCES

Research was done at the State Archives in Raleigh.

Raleigh Register, August 11, 18, 25, September 1, November 9, 1835.Some of the data of the pre–Civil War era was found in Marc W. Kruman, *Parties and Politics in North Carolina 1836–1865* (Baton Rouge: Louisiana State University Press, 1983). Also consulted: Hugh T. Lefler and Albert R. Newsome, *The History of a Southern State: North Carolina,* 3 ed. (Chapel Hill: University of North Carolina Press, 1973).

NORTH DAKOTA

Statehood: An enabling act was signed by President Harrison on November 2, 1889. A constitutional convention convened in Bismarck on

July 4, 1889. They finished their work on August 17. The voters approved the proposed constitution on October 1, 1889, by a vote of 27,440 to 8,107. On the same date the first legislature was elected. Statehood was achieved on November 2, 1889, and the legislature convened shortly thereafter. The capital has always been Bismarck.

Term: Senators have always been elected for a term of four years, with one-half the body elected every two years. The term for representatives was two years but effective in 1998 increased to four years, with one-half the body elected every two years.

Districts/Elections: Senators were elected from single-member districts of one or more counties. Counties entitled to more than one member could be divided into single-member districts. Representatives were elected from the same districts as senators, one to four representatives per district, elected district-wide. By a 1960 amendment the number of representatives within each senatorial district had to equal the number of counties in that district.

In 1966 in compliance with one person, one vote apportionment, single- and multi-member senatorial districts were created with twice as many representatives elected from these districts. This was carried over in the 1972 apportionment, but in 1976 all senators were elected from single-member districts. Two representatives were elected at large from these same districts.

Membership/Size: From an original membership of 31, the Senate quickly grew to 49 members by 1910. This total remained unchanged until 1972 when it was increased to 51. Three subsequent changes reduced membership back to 49 in 1992 and to 47 in 2002 The House started off with 62 members, and by 1914 membership reached 113. This remained unchanged until 1964 when the body was reduced to 109; in 1966 it was reduced to 98. Four subsequent changes produced a membership of 94 in 2002.

Reapportionment/Redistricting: 1902, 1908 (Senate), 1910, 1932, 1966, 1972, 1976, 1982, 1992 and 2002.

Election Dates: Always the first Tuesday after the first Monday in November.

Constitutions: The original constitution of 1889 is still in effect today.

Affiliations	Senate D / R / oth	House D / R / oth
1889	(31) 6 / 25	(62) 4 / 58
1890	6 / 23 / 2 FA	16 / 40 / 6 FA

Affiliations	*Senate* *D / R / oth*		*House* *D / R / oth*	
1892	7 / 19 / 4 Pop, 1 Fus[1]		16 / 33 / 13 Pop	
1894	2 / 25 / 4 Pop		4 / 52 / 6 Pop	
1896	3 / 24 / 4 Fus		0 / 44 / 18 Fus	
1898	0 / 22 / 9 Fus		2 / 55 / 5 Fus	
1900	0 / 24 / 7 Fus		0 / 56 / 5 Fus	
1902	(40) 7 / 30 / 3 Fus		(100) 11 / 86 / 2 Fus, 1 I	
1904	6 / 33 / 1 I		1 / 99	
1906	7 / 33		12 / 87 / 1 I	
1908	(47) 8 / 38 / 1 I		8 / 92	
1910	(49) 4 / 44 / 1 I		(103 12 / 90 / 1 S	
1912	6 / 43		(110) 8 / 102	
1914	5 / 44		(112) 6 / 106	
1916	6 / 43		16 / 97	
		(NP) *(IVA)*		*(NP)* *(IVA)[2]*
1918	6 / 43	(35)(14)	14 / 99	(81)(32)
1920		(25)(24)		(54)(59)
1922		(23)(26)		(56)(57)
1924	3 / 46	(24)(25)	7 / 106	(63)(50)
1926	0 / 49	(24)(25)	0 / 113	(53)(60)
1928	1 / 48	(26)(23)	1 / 112	(48)(65)
1930	2 / 47	(22)(27)	1 / 112	(55)(58)
1932	5 / 44		10 / 103	
1934	7 / 42		30 / 83	
1936	14 / 34 / 1 I		26 / 87	
1938	10 / 39		7 / 106	
1940	5 / 44		10 / 103	
1942	4 / 45		7 / 106	
1944	3 / 46		4 / 109	
1946	3 / 46		2 / 111	
1948	2 / 47		2 / 111	
1950	2 / 47		1 / 112	
1952	2 / 47		1 / 112	
1954	3 / 46		2 / 111	
1956	9 / 49		19 / 94	
1958	15 / 34		48 / 65	
1960	21 / 28		40 / 73	
1962	12 / 37		43 / 70	
1964	20 / 29		(109) 65 / 44	
1966	4 / 44 / 1 I		(98) 15 / 83	
1968	6 / 43		17 / 81	
1970	11 / 38		39 / 59	
1972	(51) 10 / 41		(102) 23 / 79	
1974	17 / 34		40 / 62	
1976	(50) 18 / 32		(100) 50 / 50	
1978	15 / 35		29 / 71	

Affiliations	*Senate* *D / R / oth*	*House* *D / R / oth*
1980	8 / 42	27 / 73
1982	(53) 21 / 32	(106) 55 / 51
1984	24 / 29	41 / 65
1986	26 / 27	44 / 62
1988	32 / 21	45 / 61
1990	27 / 26	47 / 59
1992	(49) 25 / 24	(98) 33 / 65
1994	20 / 29	23 / 75
1996	19 / 30	26 / 72
1998	18 / 31	34 / 64
2000	18 / 31	29 / 69
2002	(47) 16 / 31	(94) 28 / 66
2004	15 / 32	26 / 68
2006	21 / 26	33 / 61

NOTES

1. Throughout the data for North Dakota, "Fus" refers to a fusion of Democrats and Populists.

2. For the elections of 1918 through 1930 newspapers identified members of the legislature the as members of either the Non-Partisan League or the opposition Independent Voters Association. Most successful candidates, however, were listed on the ballot as Republicans.

The Non-Partisan and Independent Voter breakdown is listed here for two reasons. To begin with, for several of the above years the only affiliations reported were these parties and not the traditional party labels. (However, those named on the ballot as Republicans were numerical overwhelmingly in the majority throughout this period.)

Secondly, it is evident that these names were in fact the real difference between candidates. Even after 1930, when traditional affiliations were again listed, the Non-Partisan and Independent Voters identification was frequently mentioned. It is interesting to note the *Blue Book* does not list the affiliation of members of the legislature for the elections of 1914 through 1940, which roughly corresponds to the years in which the Non-Partisan and Independent Voters were most prominent.

SOURCES

North Dakota Blue Book, 1981, for the years from statehood through 1912 and 1942 through 1972. The *Blue Book* does not list party affiliation for the intervening years. *Bismarck Tribune,* December 10, 1918, November 5, 1920; *Fargo Forum* November 5, December 9, 1920, November 1922, November 7, 1924, November 15, 1926, November 23, 1928, November 6, 1930; *Bismarck Tribune,* December 9, 1936, November 11, 1938, November 8, 1940. Robert L. Morlan, *Political Prairie Fire: The Nonpartisan League 1915–1922*, pp. 89, 302, for 1918, 1920.*Book of the States* 1939, 1941.

OHIO

Statehood: On October 12, 1802, the voters of Ohio elected 35 delegates to a convention to write a constitution. The delegates met in Chillicothe, the territorial capital, between November 1 and November 25, 1802, and then declared the document in effect.

On January 11, 1803, the first legislature was elected, and the body convened on March 1, 1803. Chillicothe remained the meeting place of the legislature until 1809, when they met in Zanesville. The legislature again met in Chillicothe 1812–1815. Columbus became the permanent capital the following year.

Term: Senators were originally elected for two years; one-half the body was elected annually. Beginning in 1851 all Senators were elected at the same election. A 1956 amendment increased the term to four years, with one-half elected every two years. The House was initially elected for a one-year term, which was increased to two years by the 1850 constitution. All legislators selected in 1905 served a three-year term to permit future elections to be held in even-numbered years.

Districts/Elections: Senators were elected from single- and multi-member districts. Counties entitled to more than one senator elected them countywide. Since 1966 all members have been elected from single-member districts. Like to the Senate, the House was originally elected from both single- and multi-member districts, no county being divided into districts. In 1902 an amendment was added guaranteeing each county at least one seat in the House. Under the 1850 constitution and until 1966, partial representation was used in both houses. Since 1966 all members have been elected from single-member districts, districts that cross county lines or take in part of a county.

Membership/Size: The Senate initially consisted of 14 members. Total membership was tied to the size of the House: The Senate had to be not less than ⅓ nor more than ½ the size of the House. By the time the 1850 constitution was written the Senate had 36 members, a number first reached in 1824. As a result of the introduction of partial representation[1] in 1851 the size of the Senate varied from election to election, with as few as 31 members and as many as 38. In 1966 the total was fixed at 33. The first House of Representatives had 30 members; the House grew so rapidly that by 1827 it totaled 72 members. The number remained unchanged until the 1850 constitution was written. The House size varied under the new constitution also due to the use of partial representation. Between 1851 and 1903 the membership varied from a low of 94 to a high of 114. Between 1905 and 1964 it fluctuated between 117 and 138 (see individual elections for details). In 1966 the membership was fixed at 99, when partial representation was eliminated.

Reapportionment/Redistricting: 1804 (House), 1806 (House), 1808, 1812, 1817 (House), 1822 (Senate), 1825 (House), 1827 (Senate), 1831 (House), 1832 (Senate), 1836, 1837 (Senate), 1840 (House), 1841, 1842 (Senate), 1845 (House), 1847 (House), 1849 (Senate), 1851, 1861, 1871, 1881, 1891, 1901, 1903 (House), 1911, 1921, 1931, 1941, 1951, 1961, 1966, 1972, 1982, 1992, 2002.

Election Dates: Until 1887 elections were held on the second Tuesday in October. Since 1887 they have been held on the first Tuesday after the first Monday in November.

Constitutions: There have been but two constitutions in 1802 and 1851.

Affiliations	Senate J / NR	House J / NR / oth
1827	13 / 22	(72) 28 / 44
1828	17 / 19	34 / 38
1829	21 / 15	37 / 32 / 3 ?[2]
	D / NR	D / NR / oth
1830	18 / 18	29 / 38 / 5 A Cu
1831	16 / 20	30 / 42
1832	19 / 17	39 / 31 / 2 ?[3]
1833	22 / 14	46 / 26
	D / W	D / W
1834	19 / 17	29 / 42 / 1 ?[4]
1835	20 / 16	46 / 26
1836	16 / 20	37 / 35
1837	16 / 20	32 / 40
1838	19 / 17	38 / 34
1839	25 / 11	48 / 24
1840	22 / 14	21 / 51
1841	19 / 17	37 / 35
1842	22 / 14	39 / 33
1843	20 / 16	34 / 38
1844	14 / 22	31 / 41

Affiliations	Senate D / W	House D / W
1845	15 / 21	28 / 44
1846	18 / 18	32 / 39 / 1 I
1847	17 / 19	32 / 40
1848	18 / 18	35 / 37
1849	16 / 16 / 4 FS	29 / 36 / 7 FS
1850	16 / 17 / 3FS	32 / 34 / 6 FS
1851	(34) 24 / 9 / 1 FS	(94) 65 / 28 / 1 FS
1853	(35) 26 / 7	(96) 70 / 17 / 9 FS

	D / R / oth	D / R / oth
1855	6 / 29	(112) 34 / 78
1857	(33) 20 / 13	(107) 62 / 44 / 1 I
1859	(35) 10 / 25	(105) 46 / 58 / 1 I
1861	(34) 8 / 26	(97) —⁵
1863	4 / 30	21 / 76
1865	(37) 12 / 25	(105) 34 / 71
1867	19 / 18	56 / 49
1869	18 / 19	(111) 54 / 57
1871	(36) 18 / 18	(105) 48 / 57
1873	22 / 14	58 / 44 / 3 I
1875	(37) 17 / 20	(111) 46 / 65
1877	(35) 25 / 10	(109) 68 / 38 / 3 G
1879	(37) 14 / 23	(114) 45 / 69
1881	(33) 11 / 22	(105) 35 / 70
1883	22 / 11	60 / 45
1885	(37) 20 / 17	(110) 42 / 68
1887	(36) 11 / 25	45 / 65
1889	19 / 17	(114) 60 / 54
1891	(31) 10 / 21	(107) 35 / 72
1893	5 / 26	22 / 85
1895	(37) 6 / 30 / 1 Pop	(112) 25 / 87
1897	(36) 18 / 17 / 1 IR	(109) 47 / 62
1899	(31) 19 / 11 / 1 IR	(110) 45 / 62 / 3 IR
1901	(33) 12 / 21	42 / 68
1903	4 / 29	22 / 88
1905	(37) 18 / 18 / 1 I	(121) 57 / 62 / 2 I
1908	(34) 14 / 20	(117) 45 / 71 / 1 I
1910	19 / 15	(119) 70 / 49
1912	(33) 26 / 7	(123) 87 / 33 / 3 Pg
1914	13 / 20	50 / 72 / 1 Pg
1916	(36) 25 / 11	(128) 72 / 56
1918	(33) 12 / 21	(124) 47 / 77
1920	(37) 1 / 36	(125) 12 / 113
1922	(35) 4 / 31	(130) 27 / 103
1924	2 / 33	20 / 110
1926	(37) 2 / 35	(136) 33 / 103
1928	(31) 0 / 31	(133) 11 / 122

Affiliations	Senate D / R / oth	House D / R / oth
1930	(32) 14 / 18	(128) 58 / 70
1932	16 / 16	(135) 84 / 51
1934	19 / 13	67 / 68
1936	(36) 31 / 5	(138) 105 / 33
1938	(35) 8 / 27	(136) 36 / 100
1940	(36) 17 / 19	(138) 60 / 78
1942	(33) 5 / 28	(136) 25 / 111
1944	13 / 20	47 / 89
1946	(36) 4 / 32	(139) 16 / 123
1948	(33) 19 / 14	(135) 69 / 66
1950	7 / 26	36 / 98 / 1 I
1952	10 / 23	(136) 34 / 102
1954	12 / 21	47 / 89
1956	(34) 12 / 22	(139) 42 / 97
1958	(33) 20 / 13	78 / 61
1960	(38) 18 / 20	55 / 84
1962	(33) 13 / 20	(137) 49 / 88
1964	(32) 16 / 16	62 / 75
1966	(33) 10 / 23	(99) 37 / 62
1968	12 / 21	35 / 64
1970	13 / 20	45 / 54
1972	16 / 17	57 / 42
1974	21 / 12	59 / 40
1976	21 / 12	62 / 37
1978	18 / 15	63 / 36
1980	15 / 18	56 / 43
1982	17 / 16	62 / 37
1984	15 / 18	59 / 40
1986	15 / 18	60 / 39
1988	14 / 19	59 / 40
1990	12 / 21	61 / 38
1992	13 / 20	53 / 46
1994	13 / 20	43 / 56
1996	12 / 21	39 / 60
1998	12 / 21	40 / 59
2000	12 / 21	39 / 60
2002	11 / 22	37 / 62
2004	11 / 22	40 / 59
2006	12 / 21	46 / 53

NOTES

1. The formula provided for additional representation for from one to four sessions out of every five based on the fractional remainder per county.

2. *Niles Register* gives the following: Senate, 21 J / 15 NR; House, 32 J / 40 NR.

3. *Niles Register* lists the House as 38 J / 34 NR.

4. *Niles* lists the House as 31 D / 41 W.

5. There is disagreement here on the party totals. *The* (Columbus) *Crisis* lists the totals as 44 Republicans plus 29 Union Democrats for a total of 73 under the heading Union along with 24 Democrats. *The* (Columbus) *Ohio Statesman* lists 57 Republicans, 18 Fusionists (Union) and 22 Democrats. *The Tribune Almanac, 1862* lists 39 Republicans, 32 Union Democrats and 26 Democrats. Smith's *History* has 74 Republicans and 23 Democrats.

SOURCES

Research was done at the Ohio Historical Center (Archives) in Columbus.

For the years prior to 1850 newspapers were the primary source. *The* (Columbus) *Ohio State Journal* was the most consistently used paper. Also consulted was *Niles Register* from 1828 until it ceased publication in 1849. Joseph P. Smith, *A History of the Republican Party in Ohio* (Chicago: Lewis, 1898), and the *Whig/Tribune Almanac* were the primary sources from 1850 through 1895. Smith's volume gives party affiliation from 1855 through 1895 while the *Almanac,* with interruptions in the 1840s, starts in 1843. At least two sources were used for each election. However, once the state began to publish party affiliation with its returns in 1895, I relied solely on this source. This material was originally published in *Ohio General Statistics* but in 1928 the election material was separated into a volume called *Ohio Election Statistics*, the title in use today.

OKLAHOMA

Statehood: An enabling act was signed by President Theodore Roosevelt on June 16, 1906. A constitutional convention elected from the territories of the Indian Territory and Oklahoma met at Guthrie from November 20, 1906, to July 16, 1907. The constitution was approved on September 17, 1907, by a vote of 180,330 to 73,059. Oklahoma became a state on November 16, 1907. The initial election of the legislature occurred on September 17, 1907. The legislature convened for its first session on December 2, 1907. The capital, originally at Guthrie, was moved to Oklahoma City in 1910.

Term: Senators, since statehood, have been elected for four years; one-half the body is up for election every two years. Representatives have been elected for a two-year term since statehood.

Districts/Elections: The Senate initially was elected from single- and two-member districts. If a county was entitled to three or members, this would be added to the overall total. No county ever had more two members prior to 1964. A county could not be divided into districts except to create two or more districts within the same county. The House was apportioned into districts; a county had to have at minimum a half a ratio to be entitled to separate representation. On the other hand, to achieve a second seat, a county had to have 1¾ ratios and a full ratio for all additional members. In no event could a county have more than seven members. Only counties entitled to two or members could be divided into districts. Floterial districts providing for part-time representation were used through 1910. Beginning in 1932 all counties were given at least one seat. Since the implementation of one person, one vote apportionment all members of the legislature have been elected from single-member districts with several districts crossing county lines.

Membership/Size: Membership of the Senate has been increased only once since statehood, from 44 to 48 in 1964. The total of the House has fluctuated several times; starting at 110 members, three successive decreases reduced the body to 92 in 1920. Five changes by 1962 produced a House of 120 members. This was reduced to a total of 99 in 1964 and raised to 101 members in 1972.

Reapportionment/Redistricting: Enacted in 1912, 1920, 1922, 1938, 1940, 1952, 1964,[1] 1972, 1982, 1992 and 2002.

Election Date: Always the first Tuesday after the first Monday in November.

Constitutions: The constitution of 1907 is still in effect today.

Affiliations	*Senate*		*House*		
	D R		*D R*		
1907	(44) 39 / 5		(110) 93 / 17		
1908	36 / 8		(109) 72 / 37		
1910	29 / 15		76 / 33		
1912	36 / 8		90 / 19		
1914	38 / 5 / 1 S		87 / 17 / 5 S		
1916	38 / 5 / 1 S		83 / 26		
1918	34 / 10		(104) 74 / 30		
1920	27 / 17		(92) 37 / 55		
1922	32 / 12		(109) 96 / 13		
1924	37 / 7		(108) 81 / 27		
1926	35 / 9		87 / 21		
1928	32 / 12		59 / 49		
1930	32 / 12		99 / 9		
1932	39 / 5		(118) 112 / 6		
1934	43 / 1		111 / 7		

Affiliations	Senate DR	House DR
1936	43 / 1	110 / 8
1938	43 / 1	106 / 12
1940	42 / 2	111 / 7
1942	40 / 4	94 / 24
1944	38 / 6	96 / 22
1946	37 / 7	95 / 23
1948	39 / 5	105 / 13
1950	40 / 4	99 / 19
1952	38 / 6	(121) 100 / 21
1954	39 / 5	102 / 19
1956	39 / 5	101 / 20
1958	41 / 3	111 / 10
1960	40 / 4	107 / 14
1962	38 / 6	(120) 95 / 25
1964	(48) 41 / 7	(99) 78 / 21
1966	38 / 10	74 / 25
1968	38 / 10	76 / 23
1970	39 / 9	78 / 21
1972	38 / 10	(101) 76 / 25
1974	39 / 9	76 / 25
1976	39 / 9	81 / 20
1978	39 / 9	75 / 26
1980	38 / 10	76 / 25
1982	34 / 14	76 / 25
1984	34 / 14	69 / 32
1986	31 / 17	70 / 31
1988	33 / 15	70 / 31
1990	37 / 11	69 / 32
1992	37 / 11	69 / 32
1994	35 / 13	65 / 36
1996	33 / 15	65 / 36
1998	33 / 15	61 / 40
2000	30 / 18	53 / 48
2002	28 / 20	53 / 48
2004	26 / 22	44 / 57
2006	24 / 24	44 / 57

NOTES

1. The 1963 reapportionment was held to be invalid and a court-ordered reapportionment was put into effect. See *Reynolds v. State Election Board*, 233 F. Supp. 323, 329, 332–68 (W.D. Okla. 1964).

SOURCES

Lee Slater, Secretary of State (compiler), *Directory of Oklahoma 1973* (Oklahoma City: State Election Board, 1973) was used for data through 1972.

OREGON

Statehood: A constitutional convention convened in Salem on August 17, 1857, wrote a proposed state constitution, and completed its work on September 18, 1857. The voters approved the document on November 9, 1857, by a vote of 7,195 to 3,215. The first legislative elections were held on June 27, 1858, and the legislature convened on July 5, 1858.[1] Statehood was granted on February 14, 1859. The capital has been located at Salem since statehood.

Term: Senators have always been elected for a term of four years, with one-half the body up for election every two years. Representatives have always been elected for a term of two years.

Districts/Elections: Members were elected from both single- and multi-member districts made up of one or more counties. Counties in multi-county districts could not be divided. In addition floterial districts were included. Since one person, one vote apportionment, districts cross county lines, and each senatorial district is divided into two representative districts. All members therefore are elected from single-member districts.

Membership/Size: Both houses reached their present size — 30 senators and 60 representatives — in 1874 after several increases from the original apportionment of 16 senators and 34 representatives.

Reapportionment/Redistricting: Enacted in 1862, 1874, 1888, 1900, 1908, 1954, 1962, 1972, 1982, 1992 and 2002.

Election Dates: Originally the first Monday in June, changed in 1910 to the first Tuesday after the first Monday in November.

Constitutions: The original constitution written in 1857 is in effect today.

Affiliations	*Senate*	*House*
	D / R / oth	*D / R / oth*
1858	(16) 14 / 2	(34) 30 / 4
1860	13 / 3	24 / 10
1862	5 / 10 / 1 I	1 / 33
1864	(18) 3 / 15	(38) 5 / 33
1866	(25) 7 / 17 / 1 I	(47) 23 / 24
1868	(22) 12 / 10	(43) 25 / 18
1870	13 / 9	(47) 28 / 19

Affiliations	*Senate* D / R / oth	*House* D / R / oth
1872	9 / 13	(49) 17 / 32
1874	(30) 13 / 11 / 6 I	(60) 20 / 17 / 23 I
1876	18 / 11 / 1 I	27 / 30 / 3 I
1878	18 / 10 / 2 I	30 / 28 / 2 I
1880	14 / 16	20 / 40
1882	14 / 16	21 / 37 / 2 I
1884	13 / 17	25 / 35
1886	11 / 19	26 / 34
1888	9 / 21	9 / 51
1890	7 / 23	17 / 43
1892	13 / 16 / 1 Pop	19 / 38 / 3 Pop
1894	8 / 19 / 3 Pop	0 / 53 / 7 Pop
1896	3 / 24 / 3 Pop	4 / 39 / 17 Pop
1898	3 / 24 / 3 Pop	1 / 42 / 17 Pop
1900	1 / 21 / 8 oth[2]	7 / 35 / 18 oth[3]
1902	3 / 21 / 6 oth[4]	11 / 48 / 1 Cit
1904	5 / 25	10 / 50
1906	6 / 24	1 / 59
1908	6 / 24	7 / 53
1910	3 / 27	2 / 58
1912	2 / 28	5 / 48 / 7 Pg
1914	2 / 28	4 / 56
1916	5 / 24 / 1 I	4 / 55 / 1 I
1918	3 / 24 / 3 I	6 / 54
1920	1 / 27 / 2 I	2 / 58
1922	4 / 26	9 / 51
1924	4 / 26	3 / 57
1926	3 / 27	4 / 56
1928	2 / 28	2 / 58
1930	1 / 29	7 / 53
1932	8 / 22	17 / 43
1934	13 / 17	38 / 22
1936	12 / 18	39 / 21
1938	8 / 22	13 / 47
1940	5 / 25	22 / 38
1942	3 / 27	9 / 51
1944	5 / 25	10 / 50
1946	5 / 25	2 / 58
1948	10 / 20	9 / 51
1950	9 / 21	9 / 51
1952	4 / 26	11 / 49
1954	6 / 24	25 / 35
1956	15 / 15	37 / 23
1958	19 / 11	33 / 27
1960	20 / 10	31 / 29
1962	21 / 9	31 / 29
1964	19 / 11	28 / 32
1966	19 / 11	22 / 38

Affiliations	Senate D / R / oth	House D / R / oth
1968	16 / 14	22 / 38
1970	16 / 14	26 / 34
1972	16 / 14	33 / 27
1974	22 / 7 / 1 I	38 / 22
1976	24 / 6	36 / 24
1978	23 / 7	34 / 26
1980	21 / 9	33 / 27
1982	20 / 10	36 / 24
1984	18 / 12	34 / 26
1986	17 / 13	31 / 29
1988	19 / 11	32 / 28
1990	20 / 10	28 / 32
1992	16 / 14	28 / 32
1994	11 / 19	26 / 34
1996	10 / 20	29 / 31
1998	12 / 18	25 / 34 / 1 I
2000	14 / 16	27 / 33
2002	15 / 15	25 / 35
2004	18 / 12	27 / 33
2006	17 / 11 / 2 I	31 / 29

NOTES

1. This session and one that convened on September 18 are not listed in the official enumeration of state legislative sessions, since they occurred before statehood was granted. The official first session after statehood began on September 10, 1860.

2. 4 Cit, 3 P, 1 U

3. 13 Cit, 3 U, 1 Pe, 1 vac

4. 3 Cit, 2 U, 1 P

SOURCES

The State Archives provided data for the years from statehood to 1872 and 1900 and 1902.

PENNSYLVANIA

Constitutional Origins: The first Constitution of the Commonwealth of Pennsylvania was written between July and September, 1776, and was proclaimed by that body the supreme law of the state of Pennsylvania on September 26, 1776. The first elections were held in November and the first legislature convened later that month. Philadelphia, as in colonial times, was the capital. In 1799 the capital was moved to Lancaster and in 1812 to its present location, Harrisburg.

Term: The 1776 constitution created a unicameral legislature called a House of Representatives. The term was one year: in 1874 it was increased to its present length, two years. Meanwhile, in 1790 a second constitution created the Senate. Members of this body were elected for four years. The term was reduced to three years by the constitutional convention of 1837. The four-year term was restored in 1874 by another convention and this has been the term ever since.

District/Elections: Senators were elected from both single- and multi-member districts made up of one or more whole counties with a maximum of three members from any one district. The 1838 constitution limited any one county to four seats. Single-member districts were mandated by the constitution of 1874 but only whole counties could be joined in creating multi-county districts. The maximum number of seats any county could have was increased to eight. One-quarter of the Senate was elected annually until 1838 when it was changed to one-third per year. In 1874 when the four-year term was restored, half the Senate was elected every two years. Originally House members were elected countywide regardless of the number apportioned any county or multi-county district. The 1874 constitution provided that any city entitled to one or more members had to be set off and to be a separate district(s) from the rest of the county. Any county with a population of 100,000 or more or any city entitled to four or more members had to be divided into districts. Single- and multi-member districts continued to be used and each county was guaranteed at least one seat. In 1966 the House was divided into all single-member districts as a result of the U.S. Supreme Court's decision in *Reynolds v. Sims* (one person, one vote).

Membership/Size: The Senate originally consisted of 18 members and in three reapportionments was increased to 33 members in 1822. In 1874 the number was increased to 50, its present size. The House was originally a 72-member body but through five increases reached its constitutional maximum of 100 in 1822. Not until 1874 was the body increased again, when its number was more than doubled to 201. The House gradually reached 210 members in 1954, under the formula then in the constitution. Largely as a result of the impact of *Reynolds v. Sims* litigation and collateral state cases the House membership was fixed at 203 beginning in 1966.

   Reapportionment/Redistricting: 1790 (Senate created), 1794, 1801, 1808, 1815, 1822, 1829, 1836, 1843, 1850, 1857, 1864, 1871, 1874, 1888 (House only) 1906, 1922 (House only), 1954 (House only), 1964, 1966, 1972, 1982, 1992, and 2002.

   Election Dates: Second Tuesday in October until 1874, when the date was changed to the first Tuesday after the first Monday in November.

   Constitution: There have been five constitutions in Pennsylvania history: 1776, 1790, 1838, 1874 and 1968.

Affiliations	Senate D-R / F / oth	House D-R / F / oth
1797	F majority	F majority
1798	F majority	F majority
1799	8 / 16	41 / 37
1800	11 / 13	55 / 23
1801	(25) 17 / 8	(86) 71 / 15
1802	21 / 4	77 / 9
1803	24 / 1	81 / 5
1804	25 / 0	78 / 8
1805	—[1]	33 / 0 / 53 Csts
1806	—	46 / 0 / 40 Csts
1807	14 / 4 / 7 Q	43 / 23 / 20 Q
1808	(31) 19 / 5 / 7 Q	(95) 74 / 21
1809	22 / 6 / 3 Q	73 / 15 / 7 Q
1810	21 / 7 / 1 Q, 2 OSR	72 / 17 / 6 Q
1811	26 / 5	84 / 11
1812	26 / 5	77 / 18
1813	25 / 6	85 / 10
1814	21 / 10	71 / 24
1815	19 / 12	(97) 71 / 26
1816	19 / 12	57 / 30 10OSR
1817	19 / 0 / 12 IR	55 / 0 / 42 IR[2]
1818	20 / 0 / 11 IR	64 / 0 / 33 IR
1819	23 / 6 / 20 OSR	67 / 24 / 6 OSR
	D-R / IR / oth	D-R / IR
1820	20 / 11	45 / 52
1821	17 / 14	67 / 30
1822	(33) 23 / 10	(100) 71 / 29
1823	21 / 11 / 1 ?	77 / 23
1824	26 / 7	79 / 21
1825	27 / 6	77 / 23
1826	27 / 6	74 / 26

Affiliations	Senate	House
	D / Ad	D / Ad / oth
1827	26 / 7	76 / 22 / 2 vac
1828	26 / 7	89 / 11
	D / A-M / oth	D / A-M / oth
1829	26 / 1 / 6 NR	87 / 13
1830	25 / 4 / 5 NR	72 / 28
1831	23 / 6 / 4 NR	74 / 22 / 4 NR
1832	22 / 9 / 2 NR	61 / 33 / 5 NR, 1 ?
1833	24 / 7 / 2 NR	64 / 25 / 11 NR
1834	25 / 6 / 2 W	62 / 27 / 11 W
1835	23 / 9 / 1 W	28 / 72 A-M&W[3]
	D / W / oth	D / W / oth
1836	15 / 12 / 6 A-M	72 / 7 / 21 A-M
1837	14 / 19	56 / 44
1838	15 / 18	56 / 44
1839	17 / 16	69 / 31
1840	13 / 20	45 / 55
1841	16 / 17	64 / 34 / 2 Wk
1842	19 / 14	57 / 40 / 2 Wk, 1 I
1843	22 / 11	58 / 42
1844	21 / 11 / 1 A	51 / 41 / 8 A
1845	14 / 18 / 1 A	67 / 33
1846	14 / 18 / 1 A	44 / 56
1847	14 / 19	64 / 36
1848	12 / 21	50 / 45 / 5 A
1849	17 / 16	59 / 41
1850	16 / 16 / 1 I	60 / 36 / 2 ID, 1 IW, 1 vac
1851	16 / 17	58 / 37 / 5 A
1852	15 / 17 / 1 A	62 / 38
1853	18 / 14 / 1A	70 / 26 / 4 A
1854	17 / 15 / 1 A	—[4]
	D / R / oth	D / R / oth
1855	17 / / 16 Fus	66 / / 34 Fus
1856	15 / / 18 Fus	53 / / 47 Fus
1857	21 / 12	68 / 30 / 2 I
1858	17 / 16	33 / 67
1859	12 / 21	34 / 66
1860	6 / 27	29 / 71
1861	10 / 23	51 / 49
1862	12 / 21	55 / 45
1863	16 / 17	48 / 52
1864	13 / 20	36 / 64

Affiliations	Senate D / R / oth	House D / R / oth
1865	12 / 21	33 / 67
1866	12 / 21	38 / 62
1867	14 / 19	46 / 54
1868	15 / 18	38 / 62
1869	15 / 18	40 / 60
1870	17 / 16	45 / 55
1871	16 / 17	36 / 63 1 I
1872	14 / 18 / 1 LR	39 / 60 / 1 I
1873	12 / 20 1LR	43 / 57
1874	(50) 20 / 30	(201) 110 / 89 / 1 I, 1 P
1875	21 / 29	—
1876	19 / 31	81 / 119 / 1 ID
1878	17 / 32 / 1 G	77 / 107 / 17 G
1880	17 / 32 / 1 G	78 / 121 / 1 G, 1 FusD
1882	20 / 30	113 / 88
1884	19 / 31	60 / 140 / 1 G-R
1886	16 / 34	69 / 131 / 1 GL
1888	16 / 34	(204) 60 / 144
1890	19 / 31	79 / 122 / 3 Fus
1892	17 / 33	69 / 135
1894	6 / 44	29 / 175
1896	6 / 44	32 / 172
1898	13 / 37	71 / 127 / 6 Fus
1900	12 / 38	48 / 156
1902	10 / 40	44 / 160
1904	10 / 40	17 / 187
1906	10 / 40	(207) 50 / 157
1908	11 / 39	34 / 173
1910	12 / 38	44 / 162 / 1 S
1912	13 / 34 / 3 Fus	57 / 127 / 14 Pg, 9 K
1914	11 / 38 / 1 Pg	41 / 164 / 1 S
1916	10 / 39 / 1 Pg	37 / 169 / 1 S, 1 Pg
1918	6 / 44	23 / 184
1920	3 / 47	14 / 193
1922	7 / 43	(208) 41 / 167
1924	8 / 42	14 / 194
1926	5 / 45	17 / 191
1928	6 / 44	16 / 192
1930	4 / 46	22 / 184 / 2 S
1932	7 / 43	65 / 140 / 2 I, 1 S
1934	19 / 31	117 / 89 / 2 S
1936	34 / 16	154 / 54
1938	22 / 27 / 1 vac	79 / 129
1940	18 / 32	126 / 82
1942	18 / 32	76 / 132
1944	18 / 32	99 / 109
1946	16 / 34	38 / 170
1948	15 / 35	91 / 117

Affiliations	Senate D / R / oth	House D / R / oth
1950	20 / 30	88 / 120
1952	18 / 32	98 / 110
1954	24 / 26	(210) 112 / 98
1956	23 / 27	84 / 126
1958	22 / 28	108 / 102
1960	25 / 25	109 / 100 / 1 vac
1962	23 / 27	102 / 108
1964	22 / 28	(209) 116 / 93
1966	23 / 27	(203) 99 / 104
1968	23 / 27	107 / 96
1970	26 / 24	113 / 90
1972	26 / 24	96 / 107
1974	30 / 20	113 / 90
1976	31 / 19	118 / 85
1978	28 / 22	101 / 102
1980	24 / 26	100 / 103
1982	23 / 27	103 / 100
1984	23 / 27	103 / 100
1986	24 / 26	102 / 101
1988	23 / 27	104 / 99
1990	24 / 26	107 / 96
1992	25 / 25	105 / 98
1994	21 / 29	101 / 102
1996	20 / 30	99 / 104
1998	20 / 30	100 / 103
2000	20 / 30	99 / 104
2002	21 / 29	94 / 109
2004	20 / 30	93 / 110
2006	21 / 29	102 / 101

NOTES

1. The split in the Democratic-Republican Party over the calling of a constitutional convention also meant that several senators did not have to run for election in 1805 or 1806. Few papers gave the party affiliation for the Senate, even though they listed affiliation for the House, where all were elected. Those listings that exist differ widely, even as to who was the majority party. It appears that in 1805 the Constitutionalists had a majority but their number varied from source to source. The Dem.-Rep. totals ranged from as few as 9 to a high of 17 out of 25. For 1806 Higginbotham (see Sources) discuss the differences found in the various papers regarding the House members. Three newspapers give the Dem.-Rep. as few as 42 seats and a high of 51. He favors the middle figure of 46 Dem.-Rep. and 40 Constitutionalists.

2. The second split within the Dem.-Rep. gave rise to the Independent Republicans. This new group often attracted members of the dying Federalist Party. Some papers, depending upon their political affiliation, listed all opponents of the Dem.-Rep. as Federalists; others separated the Independents and the Federalists,

while others called all opponents Independent-Republicans. This party seemed to have encompassed all opponents of the regular Dem.-Rep, but from election to election some candidates ran as Federalists while in 1820 all opponents to the Dem.-Rep. were listed as Independent Republicans. The papers of this time period listed party totals more frequently than those of the earlier period and differences between them were less common.

3. The Anti-Masons and the Whigs often supported the same candidate between 1834 and 1838, after which the parties merged or perhaps the former were absorbed by the latter. While most papers did not distinguish between the two, often simply listing candidates as Whigs and Anti-Masons or the opposition, a few did make the distinction. Where this information was available it was used in preference to the above.

4. The confusion over party affiliation in this election was due to the breakup of the Whig Party and the rise of the American (Know-Nothing), Free Soil and Temperance parties. It seems there was no majority party in the House. Sources listing party membership suggested that some members had a dual allegiance: a Democrat elected with American support, a Whig elected with Temperance support. Listed below are various sources and their totals of party members:

Whig Almanac, 1855	Whigs 46, Democrats 32, Americans 22
Coleman (see Sources) citing the *Pittsburgh Gazette*	Whigs 49, including 17 as Whig-Americans and 2 as Temperance Whigs; Democrats 42, including 11 as Democrats-Americans, 3 as Independent Democrats, one Temperance Democrat, two Independent and American Democrats; 36 listed as Americans of all kinds; three others listed as Free Soil
(Philadelphia) *Evening Bulletin*	Whigs 53, Democrats 42, Americans 5 — but 29 Democrats and Whigs are listed as also being American.
Cox (see Sources) *Wilkes Election Statistics*	Whig and Whig-American 47, Democrat and Democrat-American 33, Independent American 20, based on three sources: (Harrisburg) *Morning Herald*, October 24, 1854, *Pittsburgh Gazette*, October 23, 1854, (Philadelphia) *Public Ledger* October 10, 14, 1854.

The Speaker of the House was Henry K. Strong, who is listed as a Whig-American by Cox.

Sources

Research was conducted at the State Library in Harrisburg (which houses the largest collection of Pennsylvania newspapers), the State Archives also in Harrisburg, the Philadelphia Public Library, and the Carnegie Library in Pittsburgh.

The data for many of the years through 1850 is often based on limited sources, sometimes even a single source. Newspapers were the predominant source for this period. In several instances one paper differed from another, although usually by a matter of one or two members per party. In some cases because there was no consensus I arbitrarily chose one set of totals over another. Where substantial differences were found they are discussed in the notes.

For this period a variety of newspapers were used. From Philadelphia: *American Daily Advertiser, Aurora, American Sentinel* and the *Democratic Press*. From Lancaster: *Lancaster Intelligencer and Journal.* From Harrisburg: *Harrisburg Chronicle, Pennsylvania Reporter, Pennsylvania Intelligencer.* Also the (Greensburgh) *Farmers Register* and (Crawford) *Messenger.*

Several volumes dealing with the state's political history were rich sources for legislative results, although in most instances they cited newspapers: Sanford W. Higginbotham, *The Keystone in the Democratic Arch: Pennsylvania Politics 1800–1816* (1952), and Charles M. Snyder, *The Jacksonian Heritage: Pennsylvania Politics 1833–1848* (1958). Both volumes were published by the Pennsylvania Historical and Museum Commission, Harrisburg.

From the 1840s through 1870 I relied on various editions of the *Whig/Tribune Almanac and the Evening Journal Almanac* and on John F. Coleman, *The Disruption of the Pennsylvania Democracy 1848–1860* (Harrisburg: Pennsylvania Historical and Museum Commission, 1975), and Henry R. Mueller, *The Whig Party in Pennsylvania* (New York: Columbia University Press, 1922).

Beginning in 1874 the *Pennsylvania Manual,* initially called *Smull's Manual,* contained the official legislative returns with party affiliation. This source was used along with the above mentioned almanacs. The *Manual* was used for all elections through the 1970s. At that point I used *America Votes* Volumes 1–8, and election returns supplied by the Secretary of the Commonwealth.

Sometime after all of the above research was completed I came across a website at Wilkes University (Wilkes-Barre, Pennsylvania). This comprehensive source of Pennsylvania election returns, a project that as of this writing is still in progress, contains among other data the affiliation by session and member of both houses of the legislature. I checked this against my initial findings and made changes accordingly. The complete citation is *The Wilkes University Election Statistics Project,* Dr. Harold E. Cox, Director, http://wilkes-fs1.wilkes.edu-hcox/

RHODE ISLAND

Constitutional Origins: Rhode Island had been governed since 1663 by a royal charter and remained so even after statehood was declared on July 18, 1776. The legislature held at least two sessions a year and met in Providence and Newport as well as several other towns until 1843. In that year the new constitution, which replaced the royal charter, designated the above two cities as the places where they legislature would meet. In 1900 Providence was designated as the sole meeting place.

Term: House members were elected for a term of six months until 1843 when the term was increased to one year. The term reached its present length of two years in 1912. Members of the Senate, known until 1799 as the Assistants, were elected annually until 1912 when the term was increased to two years.

Districts/Elections: The Assistants (senators) were elected statewide until 1843, when each town and city was given one member. A change in 1928 provided for additional representation by allowing any town with more than 25,000 qualified electors to have one additional senator for every 25,000 additional electors and major fraction thereof. Such towns or cities were divided into single-member districts. The maximum number of senators allowed any one city or town was six. The House's apportionment was fixed in the charter for existing towns and expansion was provided for by allowing each new town or city two members. In 1843 all cities and towns were guaranteed a minimum of one member and additional representation was provided for. However maximum representation was fixed at one-sixth of the total membership, increased to one-fourth in 1910. All members were elected at large from the town or city until 1910, when single-member districts were mandated throughout the state.

Until 1894 a majority vote was necessary for election to both houses, with additional election(s) required until a candidate received a majority of the vote.

Membership/Size: There were 10 Assistants under the charter. Under the constitution of 1843 the Senate had 31 members. The body automatically increased when a new town or city was created. There were several increases under this system in addition to those brought about by the above-mentioned 1928 amendment.[1] The Senate reached 50 members in 1966 and was reduced to 38 effective with the election of 2002. In 1776 the House had 68 members and also automatically increased.[2] A maximum of 72 was established by the constitution in 1843 and reached in 1851. Since 1851 there has been only one additional increase, to a total of 100, beginning in 1910. Effective with the election of 2002 the House was reduced to 75 members.

Reapportionment/Redistricting: There was no reapportionment prior to 1843 and none of the Senate until 1928. We could not ascertain House reapportionments between 1851 and 1910. Other reapportionments:

1851 (House), 1910, 1930 (House), 1940 (Senate), 1966, 1974, 1982–3, 1992 and 2002.

Election Dates: Voters went to polls twice a year, on the first Wednesday in April and the last Tuesday in August. Under the 1843 constitution annual elections were established and the August elections eliminated. In 1901 the date was changed to the first Tuesday after the first Monday in November.

Constitutions: There have been two basic governing documents in addition to the charter, which was replaced by a constitution in 1843. In 1986 another constitution was enacted, the newest in the nation.

Affiliations	Senate D-R / F	House D-R / F
1801 (April)	10 / 0	48 / 22
(August)	—	—
1802 (April)	?	?
(August)	—	?
1803 (April)	?	50 / 20
(August)	—	?
1804 (April)	10 / 0	54 / 16
(August)	—	?
1805 (April)	10 / 0	48 / 22
(August)	—	?
1806 (April)	?	54 / 16
(August)	—	46 / 24
1807 (April)	?	?
(August)	—	?
1808 (April)	?	34 / 38
(August)	—	32 / 40
1809 (April)	2 / 8	25 / 47
(August)	—	34 / 38
1810 (April)	?	38 / 34
(August)	—	34 / 38
1811 (April)	0 / 10	32 / 40
(August)	—	?
1812 (April)	0 / 10	32 / 40
(August)	—	32 / 40
1813 (April)	?	?
(August)	—	?
1814 (April)	—	23 / 49
(August)	—	?
1815 (April)	0 / 10	25 / 47
(August)	—	?
1816 (April)	0 / 10	24 / 48
(August)	—	?
1817 (April)	10 / 0	23 / 49
(August)	—	33 / 39

Affiliations	*Senate* *D-R / F*	*House* *D-R / F*
1818 (April)	10 / 0	37 / 35
(August)	—	?
1819 (April)	10 / 0	40 / 32
(August)	—	?
1820 (April)	?	48 / 24
(August)	—	?
1821 (April)	?	?
(August)	—	?
1822 (April)	?	36 / 36
(August)	—	?
1823 (April)	?	?
(August)	—	?
1824 (April)	?	?

	(J)D / NR / oth	*(J)D / NR / oth*
1831 (April)	0 / 10	26 / 44 / 2 ?
(August)	—	?
1832 (April)	0 / 6 / 4 vac	?
(August)	—	?
1833 (April)	8 / 2	?

	D / W / oth	*D / W / oth*
1834 (April)	8 / 1 / 1 vac	28 / 39 / 1 A-M, 4 ?
(August)	—	20 / 39 / 5 A-M, 8 ?
1835 (April)	4 / 4 / 2 vac	35 / 37
(August)	—	?
1836 (April)	10 / 0	31 / 33 / 8 ?
(August)	—	40 / 32
1837 (April)	10 / 0	?
(August)	—	?
1838 (April)	0 / 10	28 / 44
(August)	—	27 / 45
1839 (April)	0 / 10	32 / 40
(August)	—	26 / 45 / 1 ?
1840 (April)	0 / 10	20 / 52
(August)	—	24 / 48
1841 (April)	0 / 10	17 / 55
(August)	—	?
1842 (April)	0 / / 10 L&O	10 / / 62 L&O
(August)	—	?
1843	(31) 7 / / 24 L&O	(69) 19 / 50
1844	7 / 24	13 / 56
1845	10 / 21	27 / 42
1846	(Lr) 11 / 20	(Lr) 25 / 44
1847	7 / 22 / 2 x	20 / 48 / 1 ?
1848	11 / 20	26 / 43

Affiliations	Senate		House	
	D / W / oth		D / W / oth	
1849	11 / 19 / 1 FS		23 / 43 / 1 FS, 2 vac	
1850	12 / 19		24 / 45	
1851	17 / 14	(72)	35 / 37	
1852	14 / 17		32 / 40	
1853	17 / 14		46 / 26	
1854	13 / 18		31 / 41	
1855	2 / / 29 A		3 / / 69 A	
	D / R		D / R / oth	
1856	8 / 23		17 / 55	
1857	(32) 3 / 29		7 / 65	
1858	2 / 30		4 / 67 / 1 ?	
1859	5 / 27		9 / 62 / 1 ?	
	U / R / oth		U / R / oth	
1860	15 / 17		42 / 29 / 1 ?	
1861	18 / 14		47 / 25	
1862	(33) 19 / 12 / 1 ?		47 / 25	
1863	11 / 22		50 / 22	
	D / R / oth		D / R / oth	
1864	12 / 21		18 / 54	
1865	9 / 23 / 1 ?		18 / 54	
1866	5 / 28		7 / 65	
1867	(34) 6 / 28		7 / 65	
1868	5 / 29		7 / 65	
1869	6 / 27 / 1 ?		11 / 61	
1870	9 / 25		18 / 54	
1871	(36) 9 / 27		17 / 55	
1872	10 / 26		16 / 56	
1873	11 / 25		16 / 56	
1874	8 / 28		17 / 55	
1875	10 / 26		13 / 59	
1876	10 / 26		10 / 62	
1877	8 / 28		18 / 54	
1878	11 / 25		17 / 55	
1879	8 / 28		18 / 54	
1880	9 / 27		12 / 60	
1881	8 / 28		8 / 64	
1882	7 / 29		7 / 65	
1883	7 / 29		17 / 55	
1884	8 / 28		15 / 57	
1885	7 / 29		7 / 64 / 1 P	
1886	6 / 29 / 1 I		6 / 65 / 1 P	
1887	16 / 20		40 / 30 / 2 P	

Affiliations	Senate D / R / oth	House D / R / oth
1888	5 / 31	11 / 60 / 1 P
1889	11 / 25	39 / 33
1890	13 / 23	43 / 29
1891	9 / 27	21 / 51
1892	9 / 27	29 / 43
1893	14 / 22	40 / 32
1894	2 / 34	3 / 69
1895	(37) 3 / 34	6 / 66
1896	2 / 35	4 / 68
1897	4 / 33	19 / 53
1898	4 / 33	7 / 65
1899	6 / 31	13 / 58 / 1 P
1900	3 / 34	12 / 60
1901	(38) 8 / 30	18 / 53 / 1 I
1902	11 / 27	35 / 37
1903	10 / 26 / 1 I	32 / 39 / 1 I
1904	7 / 30 / 1 I	8 / 62 / 2 I
1905	5 / 33	12 / 60
1906	8 / 29 / 1 Cit	34 / 37 / 1 I
1907	11 / 26 / 1 Cit	29 / 42 / 1 Cit
1908	6 / 31 / 1 Cit	6 / 64 / 1 Cit, P
1909	6 / 29 / 3 Cit	6 / 64 / 2 Cit
1910	13 / 25	(100) 38 / 62
1911	5 / 33	28 / 71 / 1 S
1912	10 / 28	45 / 54 / 1 Pg
1914	(39) 3 / 35 / 1 I	29 / 70 / 1 Pg
1916	13 / 25 / 1 I	34 / 65 / 1 Pg
1918	8 / 31	33 / 67
1920	6 / 32 / 1 Cit	23 / 75 / 1 I, 1 ?
1922	16 / 20 / 3 I	48 / 50 / 2 DI
1924	6 / 33	33 / 67
1926	5 / 34	25 / 75
1928	10 / 29	39 / 61
1930	(42) 11 / 31	38 / 62
1932	15 / 27	49 / 51
1934	22 / 20	57 / 43
1936	15 / 27	54 / 46
1938	(44) 10 / 34	39 / 61
1940	19 / 25	59 / 41
1942	18 / 26	58 / 42
1944	20 / 24	67 / 33
1946	16 / 28	56 / 44
1948	22 / 22	64 / 36
1950	21 / 23	67 / 33
1952	18 / 26	58 / 42
1954	22 / 22	67 / 33
1956	19 / 25	64 / 36
1958	23 / 21	71 / 29

Affiliations	Senate D / R / oth	House D / R / oth
1960	28 / 16	80 / 20
1962	(46) 27 / 19	74 / 26
1964	30 / 15 / 1 I	76 / 24
1966	(50) 35 / 15	67 / 33
1968	37 / 13	76 / 24
1970	41 / 9	75 / 24 / 1 I
1972	37 / 13	75 / 25
1974	46 / 4	86 / 14
1976	45 / 5	83 / 17
1978	45 / 5	84 / 16
1980	43 / 7	82 / 18
1982	—	86 / 14
1983[3]	29 / 21	—
1984	36 / 14	76 / 23 / 1 I
1986	38 / 12	80 / 20
1988	41 / 9	86 / 14
1990	45 / 5	89 / 11
1992	39 / 11	85 / 15
1994	40 / 10	84 / 16
1996	41 / 9	84 / 16
1998	42 / 8	86 / 13 / 1 I
2000	44 / 6	85 / 15
2002	(38) 32 / 6	(75) 63 / 11 / 1 I
2004	33 / 5	59 / 16
2006	33 / 5	60 / 15

NOTES

1. The Senate under this formula reached a total of 46 members. Providence elected five members; three towns elected two; and the remaining cities and towns each elected one.

2. Two towns were created between 1776 and 1806, when the House reached 72 members.

3. As a result of legal action concerning reapportionment, Senate elections were delayed until June 21, 1983.

SOURCES

Research was done at the State Archives, the Rhode Island Historical Society and the Providence Public Library.

For the pre–1825 data I am indebted to Philip Lampi, who provided me with the returns for those years, largely taken from Providence and Newport newspapers. For the period between 1825 and 1860, I relied largely on the *Providence Journal,* (see below) as well as the *Whig/Tribune Almanac, Evening Journal Almanac* and *Niles Register.* The first two titles were used through the 1880s. Thereafter I used the *Rhode Island Manual* beginning in 1885. Since 1972 I have used returns furnished by the State Elections Board, which publishes returns in a volume called

The Official Count. Also, Chilton Williamson, "Rhode Island Suffrage Since the Dorr War," in the *New England Quarterly* March 1955; Elmer E. Cornwell et al., *The Rhode Island General Assembly* (Washington, D.C.: American Political Science Association, 1970), p. 136. The Rhode Island Archives provided a list of Assistants/Senators for the years 1790–1851.

Providence Journal, April 13, May 5, 1832, March 25, May 3, 1833, March 30, May 7, 1835, August 31, 1838, September 1, 1840, April 29, 1841. Also *Niles Register,* April 30, 1831, September 6, 1834, April 25, May 16, 1835,September 10, 1836, September 2, 1837, October 6, 1838, May 11, 1839, May 9, 1840.

SOUTH CAROLINA

Constitutional Origins: The first two constitutions of the state of South Carolina were written by the sitting state legislature. The first, of 1776, went into effect immediately. The second document was written in 1777; time was set aside for public comment and the constitution was proclaimed in effect in March 1778.The capital was originally Charleston but in 1790 was moved to Columbia.

Term: Members of the Senate — under the short-lived 1776 constitution called the Legislative Council — were elected by and from the General Assembly for two years. The Senate created by the constitution of 1778 was elected for a term of two years. The term was increased to four years, one-half the body elected every two years, beginning in 1868. This is the term today, but since 1972 all Senators have been elected at the same time.

The General Assembly, the name of the lower house under the original constitution, was elected for two years. Beginning in 1778, The House of Representatives was elected for one year. The present term of two years became effective in 1868.

Districts/Elections: The Senate, until one person, one vote reapportionment, was chosen from the districts and parishes and then the counties (1865), one per district except that Charleston (St. Michael's and St. Phillips' parishes) was entitled to two. Charleston lost its extra seat in 1895. The House of Representatives (General Assembly) as early as the first constitution, was apportioned among the parishes and (judicial) districts, 30 seats going to Charleston while the other 27 districts and parishes elected from 6 to 10, all elected on a district- or parish-wide basis. When the county became the unit of representation in 1865, all counties entitled to two or more members elected them on a countywide (at large) basis. The 1868 constitutional convention continued the county as the unit of representation, guaranteeing each a minimum of one seat with population determining additional representation.

Equal districting apportionment went into effect in 1966, creating a series of multi-county Senate districts, each electing two or more members. However, while election was district-wide, each seat was individually contested. This was continued in the 1980s, but beginning in the 1990s the Senate was elected as the House had been since 1966, from single-member districts.

Membership/Size: The Legislative Council consisted of 13 members, the original Senate 29. That body increased to 37 in 1790 but was reduced to 32 by the constitution of 1865, when parish representation was eliminated. The Senate increased as the number of counties increased, reaching 46 in 1918. There was a temporary increase to 50 members in 1966, but the number reverted back to 46 in 1970.

The General Assembly and the first House of Representatives had a membership of 202. This was reduced to 124 in 1790 and the total has remained unchanged ever since.

Reapportionment/Redistricting: 1778, 1790, 1808, 1822, 1832, 1852, 1862, 1865, 1868, 1895, 1902, 1912, 1922, 1932, 1942, 1952, 1962, 1966, 1970, 1972, 1982, 1992, 1996 and 2002. Those of 1778, 1790, 1865, 1868, and 1895 were by constitutional convention.

Election Dates: Originally the last Monday in October, changed in 1778 to the last Monday in November. In 1790 the date changed to the second Monday and Tuesday in October. In 1870 this became the third Wednesday in October. Finally, effective in 1874, the date was moved to the first Tuesday after the first Monday in November.

Constitutions: There have been seven in the state's history: 1776, 1778, 1790, 1861, 1865, 1868 and 1895.

Affiliations	Senate D / R / oth	House D / R / oth
1868[1]	(31) 6 / 25	14 / 110
1870	5 / 26	24 / 100
1872	(33) 8 / 25	23 / 101
1874	7 / 26	33 / 91
1876[2]	15 / 18	65 / 59

Affiliations	*Senate* D / R / oth	*House* D / R / oth
1878	28 / 5	121 / 3
1880	(35) 33 / 2	120 / 4
1882	33 / 2	118 / 6
1884	32 / 3	119 / 5
1886	33 / 2	120 / 4
1888	35 / 0	121 / 3
1890	32 / 3	115 / 9
1892	(36) 36 / 0	120 / 4
1894	29 / 0 / 7 ID	104 / 3 / 17 ID
1896	36 / 0	123 / 1
1898	(41) 41 / 0	123 / 1
1900	41 / 0	123 / 1
1902	41 / 0	123 / 1
1904	41 / 0	124 / 0
1906	41 / 0	124 / 0
1908	41 / 0	124 / 0
1910	(44) 44 / 0	124 / 0
1912	44 / 0	124 / 0
1914	44 / 0	124 / 0
1916	44 / 0	124 / 0
1918	(46) 46 / 0	124 / 0
1920	46 / 0	124 / 0
1922	46 / 0	124 / 0
1924	46 / 0	124 / 0
1926	46 / 0	124 / 0
1928	46 / 0	124 / 0
1930	46 / 0	124 / 0
1932	46 / 0	124 / 0
1934	46 / 0	124 / 0
1936	46 / 0	124 / 0
1938	46 / 0	124 / 0
1940	46 / 0	124 / 0
1942	46 / 0	124 / 0
1944	46 / 0	124 / 0
1946	46 / 0	124 / 0
1948	46 / 0	124 / 0
1950	46 / 0	124 / 0
1952	46 / 0	124 / 0
1954	46 / 0	124 / 0
1956	46 / 0	124 / 0
1958	46 / 0	124 / 0
1960	46 / 0	124 / 0
1962	46 / 0	124 / 0
1964	46 / 0	124 / 0
1966	(50) 44 / 6	107 / 17
1968	47 / 3	119 / 5
1970	(46) 44 / 2	113 / 11
1972	43 / 3	103 / 21

Affiliations	Senate	House
	D / R / oth	D / R / oth
1974	—	108 / 16
1976	42 / 4	112 / 12
1978	—	108 / 16
1980	41 / 5	108 / 16
1982	—	105 / 19
1984	36 / 10	96 / 27 / 1 vac
1986	—	91 / 32 / 1 vac
1988	36 / 10	88 / 36
1990	—	83 / 40 / 1 I
1992	30 / 16	73 / 50 / 1 I
1994	—	58 / 62 / 4 I
1996	26 / 20	53 / 70 / 1 I
1998	—	59 / 64 / 1 vac
2000	22 / 24	54 / 70
2002	—	51 / 73
2004	19 / 27	50 / 74
2006	—	51 / 73

NOTES

1. The compilation does not begin until 1868 because South Carolina lacked traditional party contests, except in the early part of the Federalist/Democratic-Republican era, and for this period there is insufficient data available to list party totals.

2. The returns for many members of both houses were disputed in the 1876 election. Both parties initially organized in separate bodies. Eventually this was resolved by a decision of the State Supreme Court giving the Democrats the right to organize the House and ordering the Senate to convene as one body. The figures used here are the original figures, notwithstanding contested elections. Shortly after each house met, several Republicans resigned or were expelled, substantially reducing their number, as apparently all were replaced by Democrats. Cooper estimates that when all the replacements were seated the Democrats controlled the Senate 28–5 and the House 87–37. See Cooper (see Sources), *Conservative Regime*, pp. 24–25.

SOURCES

William J. Cooper, Jr., *The Conservative Regime: South Carolina, 1877–1890* (Baltimore: Johns Hopkins University Press, 1968); Walter Edgar, *South Carolina: A History* (Columbia: University of South Carolina Press, 1998); William A. Schaper, *Sectionalism and Representation in South Carolina* (New York: Da Capo Press, 1968); George B. Tindall, *South Carolina Negroes 1877–1900* (Baton Rouge: Louisiana State University Press, 1952, 1966).

SOUTH DAKOTA

Statehood: An enabling act was signed by President Harrison February 22, 1889. A constitutional convention convened at Sioux Falls on July 4, and a constitution was approved by the voters on October 1 (16,411 to 3,247). The initial election of the legislature was held on October 1; they took office October 19, 1889. The capital since statehood has been Pierre.

Term: Members of both houses have always served a two-year term.

Districts/Elections: The senate initially had 45 members elected from 41 districts, made up of one or more whole counties. Single- and multi-member districts, primarily single-member districts, continued until 1982; since that year all members have been elected from single-member districts. The House was chosen by countywide elections of one or more members. In 1972 House members were elected from senatorial districts, a minimum of two per district. Since 1984 House members have been elected two per Senate district at large except for one district, which under the 1992 and 2002 act was divided into two single-member districts.

Membership/Size: The senate initially had 45 members, reduced to 43 in 1892 and increased to 45 in 1898. Since 1938 the total membership has been 35. The House had 124 members at the outset, reduced to 84 in 1892. There were four changes through 1914 when the House totaled 103 members. The number was reduced to 75 in 1938 and 70 in 1972.

Reapportionment/Redistricting: Enacted in 1898, 1904, 1908, 1912, 1918, 1938, 1952, 1962, 1966, 1972, 1984, 1992 and 2002.

Election Date: Since statehood the first Tuesday after the first Monday in November.

Constitutions: Written in 1889 and still in effect today.

Affiliations	*Senate* D / R / oth	*House* D / R / oth
1889	(45) 4 / 37 / 4 I	(124) 13 / 106 / 2 Pop, 1 Fus,[1] 1 I, 1 NP
1890	8 / 22 / 10 I, 3 Pop, 2 ?	(122) 58 / 20 / 33 I,[2] 10 Pop, 1 Fus
1892	(43) 4 / 35 / 3 I, 1 Pop	(83) 4 / 69 / 8 I, 2 Pop
1894	3 / 35 / 3 Pop, 3 Fus, 1 I	(84) 2 / 69 / 11 Pop, 2 I
1896	2 / 20 / 15 Fus, 6 Pop	9 / 39 / 18 Fus, 17 Pop, 1 NP
1898	(45) 4 / 31 / 6 Fus, 4 Pop	(87) 9 / 61 / 15 Fus, 2 P
1900	1 / 41 / 2 Fus, 1 Pop	7 / 79 / 1 Fus
1902	3 / 40 / 1 Fus	8 / 77 / 2 Fus

Affiliations	*Senate* *D / R / oth*	*House* *D / R / oth*
1904	1 / 42 / 2 Pop	2 / 86 / 1 Fus
1906	8 / 35 / 1 Fus, 1 Pop	9 / 80
1908	6 / 38 / 1 Pop	(103) 9 / 92 / 1 Pop, 1 NP
1910	11 / 32 / 1 NP, 1 Pop	(104) 5 / 97 / 1 Pop, 1 NP
1912	11 / 34	(103) 13 / 89 / 1 NP
1914	11 / 34	19 / 84
1916	10 / 35	14 / 89
1918	2 / 43	11 / 88 / 2 I, 1 NP, 1 ?
1920	1 / 44	4 / 95 / 2 I, 2 NP
1922	9 / 34 / 2 NP	12 / 84 / 5 NP, 1 Fus
1924	9 / 35 / 1 FL	15 / 85 / 1 Fus, 1 I, 1 NP
1926	16 / 29	25 / 77 / 1 ?
1928	12 / 33	21 / 82
1930	14 / 31	24 / 79
1932	30 / 15	69 / 34
1934	32 / 13	63 / 40
1936	22 / 23	37 / 66
1938	(30) 5 / 30	(75) 13 / 62
1940	4 / 31	10 / 65
1942	4 / 31	6 / 69
1944	0 / 35	3 / 72
1946	0 / 35	4 / 71
1948	8 / 27	11 / 64
1950	6 / 29	9 / 66
1952	0 / 35	2 / 73
1954	6 / 29	18 / 57
1956	17 / 18	27 / 48
1958	20 / 15	32 / 43
1960	12 / 23	18 / 57
1962	9 / 26	17 / 58
1964	15 / 19 / 1 I	30 / 45
1966	6 / 29	11 / 64
1968	8 / 27	16 / 59
1970	11 / 24	30 / 45
1972	18 / 17	(70) 35 / 35
1974	19 / 16	33 / 37
1976	11 / 24	22 / 48
1978	11 / 24	22 / 48
1980	10 / 25	21 / 49
1982	9 / 26	18 / 52
1984	10 / 25	13 / 57
1986	11 / 24	22 / 48
1988	15 / 20	24 / 46
1990	17 / 18	25 / 45
1992	20 / 15	29 / 41
1994	16 / 19	24 / 45 / 1 I
1996	13 / 22	23 / 47
1998	13 / 22	18 / 52

Affiliations	Senate	House
	D / R / oth	D / R / oth
2000	12 / 23	20 / 50
2002	10 / 25	21 / 49
2004	10 / 25	19 / 51
2006	15 / 20	20 / 50

NOTES

1. Throughout the data for South Dakota, "Fus" refers to a fusion of Democrats and Populists.

2. Farmers' Alliance ran as Independents.

SOURCES

South Dakota Political Almanac, p. 26 (lists party affiliation from statehood through the election of 1968). Legislative Research Council website giving historical listing of legislative members, 1890–1932.

TENNESSEE

Statehood: The process of creating a state government preceded statehood. On December 18 and 19, 1795, delegates were elected to a constitutional convention. This body met in Knoxville between January 11 and February 6, 1796, and proclaimed that the constitution they had written was in effect. The first state legislative elections were held on March 10, 1796. Tennessee became the sixteenth state on June 1, 1796. The legislature met in Knoxville, which served as the capital until 1812, when the legislature met at Nashville. The legislature continued to meet there until 1817, when they again met in Knoxville. The next year they met in Murfreesboro and continued to meet in that city until again meeting in Nashville in 1826. They legislature has met in Nashville ever since.

Term: Senators were originally elected for a two-year term, increased to four years in 1870; one-half of the members are up for election every two years. Members of the House have always been elected for a two-year term.

Districts/Elections: Senators were elected from single- and multi-member districts under the 1796 constitution. No district could elect more than three members. The constitution of 1834 provided for only single-member districts and this has been the method ever since. The House was also elected from both single- and multi-member districts and this continued until 1966, when all members were elected from single-member districts, as is the case today. In 1834 floterial districts were introduced and remained in existence until 1966.

Membership/Size: The Senate originally had 11 members and by 1834 had 25 members, a figure that remained unchanged until 1882, when the present total of 33 was established. The House initially had 23 members, with the provision that it could be increased to 40 when the taxable population reached 40,000. The constitution of 1834 increased the size to 75 and provided for an increase to 99 when the population reached 1,500,000. There was a brief increase to 83 in 1865–1869, and then the number was reduced to 75 in 1870. The present total of 99 was reached in 1882 after the 1880 census showed the state's population had reached 1,500,000.

Reapportionment/Redistricting: 1797 (House),1799 (Senate), 1801 (Senate), 1803, 1805, 1807, 1809 (House), 1813, 1821, 1829 (Senate), 1833 (House), 1835 (Senate), 1843, 1853, 1865 (House), 1867 (House), 1872, 1882, 1892, 1901, 1964, 1968, 1972, 1980, 1982, 1992, 1994, 2000 and 2002.

Election Dates: Initially the first Thursday in August (two days). The second day was eliminated in 1834. In 1870 the present date was established: the first Tuesday after the first Monday in November.

Constitutions: There have been three constitutions, written in 1796, 1834 and 1870.

Affiliations	Senate D / W / oth	House D / W / oth
1835[1]	(25) A-J majority	(75) A-J majority
1837	7 / 18	25 / 46 / 4 ?
1839	14 / 11	42 / 33
1841	13 / 12	36 / 39
1843	11 / 14	35 / 40
1845	13 / 12	39 / 36
1847	12 / 13	34 / 41
1849	14 / 11	39 / 36
1851	9 / 16	36 / 39
1853	13 / 12	31 / 44
1855	11 / 14	37 / / 38 A[2]
1857	18 / / 7 A	42 / / 33 A
1859	14 / /11 Opp	41 / / 34 Opp

Affiliations	*Senate*	*House*
	C / R	*C / R*
1865	0 / 25	(83) 4 / 79
1867	0 / 25	0 / 83
	D / R / oth	*D / R / oth*
1869	20 / 5	66 / 17
1870	22 / 3	(75) 63 / 12
1872	18 / 7	49 / 26
1874	23 / 2	70 / 5
1876	20 / 5	59 / 16
1878	22 / 3	61 / 14
1880	15 / 10	37 / 37 / 1 G
1882	(33) 27 / 6	(99) 71 / 28
1884	22 / 11	81 / 18
1886	21 / 12	63 / 36
1888	23 / 10	69 / 30
1890	25 / 8	79 / 20
1892	26 / 6 / 1 Pop	68 / 26 / 5 Pop
1894	20 / 10 / 3 Pop	60 / 32 / 7 Pop
1896	25 / 8	63 / 32 / 4 Pop
1898	28 / 5	77 / 22
1900	28 / 5	76 / 23
1902	28 / 5	83 / 16
1904	28 / 5	80 / 19
1906	27 / 6	78 / 21
1908	28 / 5	77 / 22
1910	25 / 8	74 / 25
1912	18 / 6 / 9 I	52 / 27 / 20 I
1914	26 / 7	72 / 27
1916	27 / 6	72 / 27
1918	26 / 7	72 / 27
1920	24 / 9	67 / 32 / 1 I
1922	28 / 5	76 / 23
1924	29 / 4	76 / 23
1926	28 / 5	80 / 19
1928	25 / 8	72 / 27
1930	28 / 5	83 / 16
1932	29 / 4	81 / 18
1934	28 / 5	81 / 18
1936	29 / 4	81 / 18
1938	29 / 4	83 / 16
1940	29 / 4	83 / 16
1942	28 / 5	80 / 19
1944	28 / 5	75 / 24
1946	29 / 4	81 / 18
1948	29 / 4	80 / 19
1950	29 / 4	80 / 19
1952	28 / 5	81 / 18

Affiliations	Senate D / R / oth	House D / R / oth
1954	28 / 5	80 / 19
1956	27 / 6	78 / 21
1958	28 / 5	82 / 17
1960	27 / 6	80 / 19
1962	27 / 6	78 / 21
1964	25 / 8	75 / 24
1966	25 / 8	58 / 41
1968	20 / 13	49 / 49 / 1 I
1970	19 / 13 / 1 I	56 / 43
1972	19 / 13 / 1 I	51 / 48
1974	20 / 12 / 1 A	63 / 35 / 1 I
1976	23 / 9 / 1 I	66 / 32 / 1 I
1978	20 / 12 / 1 I	66 / 32 / 1 I
1980	20 / 13	60 / 39
1982	22 / 11	61 / 37 / 1 I
1984	23 / 10	64 / 35
1986	23 / 10	61 / 38
1988	22 / 11	60 / 39
1990	20 / 13	57 / 42
1992	19 / 14	63 / 36
1994	18 / 15	59 / 40
1996	18 / 15	61 / 38
1998	18 / 15	59 / 40
2000	18 / 15	57 / 42
2002	18 / 15	54 / 45
2004	16 / 17	53 / 46
2006	16 / 17	53 / 46

NOTES

1. The general use of party labels for legislative candidates does not become common until the mid–1830s, making earlier compilations impossible. See Richard P. McCormack, *The Second American Party System* (Chapel Hill: University of North Carolina Press, 1966), pp.199–208, and Atkins (see Sources), Chapter 3.

2. The (Nashville) *Republican Banner* indicates that the affiliations of three members were questionable. One was Colburn of Blount, listed as an American. The other two were Kinney of Greene, Hawkins, Hancock and Jefferson, and Cloud of Claiborne, both listed as Democrats but claimed by other sources as Americans. The vote for Speaker through many ballots was 36 for the American candidate, 35 for the Democratic candidate, one other and two not cast. The (Nashville) *Daily Union & American*, August 25, 1855, gives the House breakdown as 38 Democrats and 37 Americans, listing Colburn of Blount as a Democrat, accounting for the Democratic majority in their listings. The Speaker vote seems to support an American majority, and that is why the *Banner's* totals are used here.

SOURCES

Research was done at the State Archives and Library in Nashville.

The *Tennessee Pocket Manual*, published under different titles back to 1890, provided data from that point on. Some secondary titles also added to the data; Richard E. Corlew et al., *Tennessee: A Short History* (Knoxville: University of Tennessee Press), 1969, Jonathan M. Atkins, *Parties, Politics and the Sectional Conflict in Tennessee 1832–1861* (Knoxville: University of Tennessee Press, 1997), Roger L. Hart, *Redeemers Bourbons and Populists: Tennessee 1870–1896*, (Baton Rouge: Louisiana State University Press, 1975), and Charles G. Sellers, *James K. Polk: Jacksonian, 1795–1843* (Princeton: Princeton University Press, 1957).

Providence (Rhode Island) *Journal*, August 30, 1837, *Niles Register* August 18, 1843, September 28, 1847, (Nashville) *Republican Banner*, August 15, October 6, 1845, August 17, 1855, (Nashville) *Daily Union*, September 28, 1849, August 25, 1855.

TEXAS

Statehood: Texas had been an independent nation for nine years when the U.S. Congress on March 1, 1845, proposed terms by which it would become a state. The Texas legislature approved the terms of admission on July 4, 1845. The legislature set up a committee to draft a state constitution. Its work was submitted to the voters on October 13, 1845, and was overwhelmingly approved. The first election of the state legislature took place on December 15, 1845. Two weeks later on December 29, 1845, President Polk signed the bill formally making Texas the twenty-seventh state. The first legislature convened on February 16, 1846. Washington-on-the Brazos had been the capital during independence, but Austin has served as the capital since statehood.

Terms: With the exception of 1869–75, Senators have been elected for a term of four years, with one-half the body elected every two years. Between 1869 and 1875 they were elected for six years, one-third every two years. House members have always been elected for two years.

Districts/Elections: Senators were originally elected from single-member and a few multi-member districts. In 1851 only single-member districts were used, and that has been the basis for Senate elections ever since. House members were apportioned among the counties, with each county entitled to at least one, a standard repealed by the 1875 constitution. All members were elected countywide. In 1869 House members were elected from Senate districts, for the most part three per district, all members running district-wide. The 1875 constitution divided the state into single- and multi-county districts and provided for the division of any county entitled to two or more members into districts. A 1936 amendment capped representation at seven for any one county, but did allow for one additional representative for each additional 100,000 people. With the advent of one person, one vote apportionment the state was divided into single- and multi-member districts. But initially through 1974 candidates in multi-member districts (single counties) ran for a specific post rather than the typical all at-large procedure. Since 1976 all House members have been elected from single-member districts.

Membership/Size: The Senate had 21 members at statehood, increasing in three of the next four elections to 33 by 1853. It was reduced to 30 in 1869 and reached its present size of 31 in 1876. The House started off with 66 members and totaled 90 members by 1853. There have been several increases since, with the House reaching its present membership of 150 in 1922.

Reapportionment/Redistricting: In 1848, 1850, 1853, 1860, 1869, 1873, 1875, 1881, 1891, 1901, 1911, 1921, 1952, 1962, 1966 (House), 1972, 1974 (House), 1982, 1992, 1996 and 2002.

Election Dates: Originally the first Monday in November, changed to the first Monday in August, 1849. In 1866 the election was held on October 15; in 1869, on November 30–December 4; in 1872, on November 5; in 1873, on December 2, in 1876, on February 15. Beginning in 1878, the first Tuesday after the first Monday in November.

Constitutions: There have been five constitutions in state history, written in 1845, 1861, 1866, 1869 and 1875. Under the Republic of Texas there was also a constitution written in 1836.

Affiliations	*Senate*		*House*	
	D / W		*D / W*	
1845[1]	(21) ?		(66) ?	
1847	?		?	
1849	(22) ?		(48) ?	
1851	(26) ?		(68) ?	
1853	(33) ?		(90) ?	
	D / A / oth		*D / A*	
1855	20 / 9 / 4 ?		60 / 30	
1857	27 / 6		81 / 9	

Affiliations	*Senate*	*House*
	D / A / oth	*D / A*
1859	?	?
1866[2]	—	—
	D / R / oth	*D / R / oth*
1869[3]	(30) 11 / 19	(90) 36 / 54
1872	17 / 13	72 / 16 / 2 ?
1873	26 / 4	79 / 11
1876	(31) 27 / 3 / 1 I	(93) 81 / 6 / 6 I
1878	25 / 4 / 2 G	74 / 9 / 10 G
1880	29 / 1 / 1 G	82 / 8 / 3 G
1882	30 / 0 / 1 I	(106) 96 / 3 / 7 I
1884	28 / 0 / 3 I	103 / 3
1886	31 / 0	103 / 5 / 1 P[4]
1888	31 / 0	105 / 7[4]
1890	31 / 0	104 / 2
1892	29 / 0 / 1 I, 1 Pop	(128) 119 / 1 / 8 Pop
1894	29 / 0 / 2 Pop	103 / 3 / 22 Pop
1896	28 / 1 / 2 Pop	120 / 2 / 6 Pop
1898	30 / 1	118 / 1 / 9 Pop
1900	31 / 0	126 / 0 / 1 Pop, 1 IR
1902	31 / 0	(133) 131 / 1 / 1 Pop, 1 IR
1904	31 / 0	131 / 2
1906	31 / 0	132 / 1
1908	30 / 1	131 / 2
1910	30 / 1	132 / 1
1912	30 / 1	(142) 141 / 1
1914	31 / 0	140 / 1 / 1 NPty
1916	31 / 0	142 / 0
1918	31 / 0	141 / 1
1920	30 / 1	137 / 1 / 4 A
1922	30 / 1	(150) 149 / 1
1924	30 / 1	149 / 1
1926	30 / 1	149 / 1
1928	31 / 0	149 / 1
1930	31 / 0	150 / 0
1932	31 / 0	148 / 0 / 2 I
1934	31 / 0	149 / 0 / 1 I
1936	31 / 0	149 / 0 / 1 I
1938	31 / 0	150 / 0
1940	31 / 0	150 / 0
1942	31 / 0	150 / 0
1944	31 / 0	150 / 0
1946	31 / 0	150 / 0
1948	31 / 0	150 / 0
1950	31 / 0	149 / 1
1952	31 / 0	150 / 0
1954	31 / 0	150 / 0

Affiliations	Senate D / R / oth	House D / R / oth
1956	31 / 0	150 / 0
1958	31 / 0	150 / 0
1960	31 / 0	150 / 0
1962	31 / 0	143 / 7
1964	31 / 0	149 / 1
1966	30 / 1	147 / 3
1968	29 / 2	142 / 8
1970	29 / 2	140 / 10
1972	29 / 2	133 / 17
1974	29 / 2	134 / 16
1976	29 / 2	135 / 15
1978	28 / 3	128 / 22
1980	23 / 8	114 / 36
1982	26 / 5	114 / 36
1984	25 / 6	97 / 53
1986	25 / 6	94 / 56
1988	23 / 8	94 / 56
1990	24 / 7	93 / 57
1992	18 / 13	91 / 58 1 vac
1994	17 / 14	89 / 61
1996	15 / 16	82 / 68
1998	15 / 16	79 / 71
2000	15 / 16	78 / 72
2002	12 / 19	62 / 88
2004	12 / 19	63 / 87
2006	11 / 20	69 / 81

NOTES

1. Fifty-five of 86 members were D.
2. Largely conducted without party labels, no affiliation determined.
3. As a consequence of Reconstruction, civilian government was suspended in 1867 and the general elections originally scheduled for 1870 and 1871 were successively postponed until 1872. The election of 1876 was held in February simultaneously with a vote on the new constitution, which was approved.
4. These are the only figures found. Both the 1886 and 1888 totals exceed the actual number elected, 106. Since I did not find a member-by-member list that included affiliation, there was no way of reconciling the figures with the total elected.

SOURCES

For the period up to 1888 I relied on five sources: Alwyn Barr, *Reconstruction to Reform Texas Politics 1876–1906* (Dallas: Southern Methodist University press, 1971, 2000), Overdyke, W. Darrell, *The Know-Nothing Party in the South* (Baton Rouge: Louisiana State University Press, 1950), p. 117, Carl H. Moneyhon, *Republicanism in Reconstruction Texas* (Austin: University of Texas Press, 1980), Charles

W. Ramsdell, *Reconstruction in Texas* (Gloucester: Peter Smith, reprint ed., 1964), and Patsy McDonald Spaw, *The Texas Senate*, Volume I, 1836–1861, and II, 1861–1889 (College Station: Texas A&M University Press, 1990, 1999).

Also the *Texas Legislative Manual*, 1882–3, the (Austin) *Weekly Statesman*, December 24, 1872, *and the Galveston Daily News*, November 12, 1884.

The State Archives provided a two-page document entitled "Republican Members of the Texas Legislature 1867–1899" and another entitled "Republicans and Other Non-Democrats in the Texas Legislature." This covered the years 1901–1961.

UTAH

Statehood: An enabling act was signed by President Cleveland on July 16, 1894. Constitutional convention delegates were elected on November 6, 1894. They met in Salt Lake City from March 4 to May 8, 1895. The voters approved the constitution on November 5, 1895, by a vote of 31,305 to 7,687. Utah became a state on January 4, 1896. The first election of the legislature occurred on November 5, 1895; they took office in January 1896. The capital has always been located in Salt Lake City.

Term: Senators are Elected for a term of four years, with one-half the body elected every two years. Representatives are elected for a term of two years.

Districts/Elections: Senators were elected from single- and multi-member districts. No county could be divided unless entitled to two or more members; no parts of counties could join with any other county in the formation of a district. Representatives were apportioned among the counties, each county entitled to at least one member. All members were elected countywide. In the 1964 apportionment any county entitled to more than one member of either house was divided into single-member districts, but no representative district could be in more than one senatorial district. The initial one person, one vote apportionment did not cross county lines, but all subsequent apportionments did in a few instances. Since 1972 all members of both houses have been elected from single-member districts.

Membership/Size: The Senate originally had 18 members, increased by 1932 to 23 members and in 1956 to 25. Three subsequent increases between 1964 and 1972 raised the total to its present figure of 29. The House initially had 45 members, increased three times by 1932 to 60 members and to 1956 to 64. Two later increases in 1964 and 1972 raised the total to 75, the present figure.

Reapportionment/Redistricting: 1922, 1932, 1956, 1964, 1966, 1972, 1982, 1992 and 2002.

Election Date: Always the first Tuesday after the first Monday in November.

Constitutions: The original constitution of 1895 is still in effect today.

Affiliations	Senate D / R / oth	House D / R / oth
1895	(18) 6 / 12	(45) 14 / 31
1896	0 / 17 / 1 Pop	2 / 40 / 3 Pop
1898	14 / 2 / 2 I	26 / 15 / 4 I
1900	10 / 8	17 / 28
1902	6 / 12	7 / 38
1904	3 / 15	4 / 41
1906	0 / 18	7 / 38
1908	0 / 18	2 / 43
1910	2 / 16	7 / 38
1912	1 / 17	15 / 30
1914	6 / 12	8 / 23 / 10 DPg, 3 Pg, 1 S
1916	14 / 4	44 / 0 / 1 S
1918	18 / 0	(45) 37 / 8
1920	7 / 11	(47) 1 / 46
1922	(20) 1 / 19	(55) 10 / 45
1924	1 / 19	9 / 46
1926	1 / 19	6 / 49
1928	9 / 11	26 / 29
1930	9 / 11	14 / 41
1932	(23) 13 / 10	(60) 51 / 9
1934	19 / 4	56 / 4
1936	22 / 1	56 / 4
1938	21 / 2	45 / 15
1940	19 / 4	44 / 16
1942	17 / 6	39 / 21
1944	18 / 5	45 / 15
1946	12 / 11	21 / 39
1948	12 / 11	41 / 19
1950	16 / 7	30 / 30
1952	8 / 15	21 / 39
1954	7 / 16	27 / 33
1956	(25) 10 / 15	(64) 24 / 39 / 1 I
1958	12 / 13	42 / 22
1960	14 / 11	36 / 28
1962	12 / 13	30 / 34
1964	(27) 15 / 12	(69) 39 / 30
1966	(28) 5 / 23	10 / 59
1968	8 / 20	21 / 48

Affiliations	Senate D / R / oth	House D / R / oth
1970	12 / 16	40 / 29
1972	(29) 13 / 16	(75) 31 / 44
1974	15 / 14	40 / 35
1976	17 / 12	35 / 40
1978	10 / 19	24 / 51
1980	7 / 22	17 / 58
1982	5 / 24	16 / 59
1984	6 / 23	13 / 62
1986	8 / 21	27 / 48
1988	7 / 22	28 / 47
1990	10 / 19	31 / 44
1992	11 / 18	26 / 49
1994	10 / 19	20 / 55
1996	9 / 20	20 / 55
1998	11 / 18	21 / 54
2000	9 / 20	24 / 51
2002	7 / 22	19 / 56
2004	8 / 21	19 / 56
2006	8 / 21	20 / 55

Sources

Data through 1976 was taken from Richard D. Poll et al., *Utah's History* (Provo, Utah: Brigham Young University Press, 1978). (Salt Lake City) *Deseret Evening News,* January 9, 1915, January, 13, 1919.

VERMONT

Constitutional Origins/Statehood: A constitutional convention met in Windsor from July 2 to 8, 1777. Upon completion of its work the body proclaimed the constitution in effect. But until 1791 Vermont's status was that of an independent but unrecognized state. When New York, last of two states, gave up her claim to Vermont's territory (the other was New Hampshire), the most significant obstacle to statehood was removed. On January 9, 1791, Vermont requested admission when a convention, authorized by the legislature, voted 105–3 to seek statehood. On February 18, 1791, Congress voted for the admission of Vermont, effective March 4, 1791. The legislature met in no fewer than 15 different locations before settling on a permanent capital, Montpelier, in 1808.

Term: The legislature was unicameral until 1836, when a Senate was created. The term was set at one year, increased to two years in 1870. The House was elected annually and also was increased to two-year terms in 1870.

Districts/Elections: In the House each town and city was entitled to one member. This system was in effect for the entire period prior to one person, one vote apportionment. The county served as the unit of election for the Senate. Each county was entitled to at least one member, and the remaining seats were apportioned among the counties based on population. All members were elected countywide. The county, with modifications, remains the unit of election in the Senate. Senators are still elected from countywide districts, but county lines have been crossed to equalize population. The number of members elected per district ranges from one to six. In the House under the acts of 1965 and 1974 there were single- and multi-member districts that elected as many as four members. Since the 1982 act, multi-member districts have elected only two members. Districts largely follow town and city lines, but in the more populous communities cities and towns are divided into districts.

Membership/Size: The Senate since its inception has been made up of 30 members. The House expanded as each new town was created. There were 115 towns in 1777; by 1922 the House had a total of 248 members. The body was reduced to its present size of 150 in 1965, the year one person, one vote apportionment took effect.

Reapportionment/Redistricting: Until 1965 all reapportionments were of the Senate; in 1852, 1862, 1872, 1902, 1912, 1922, 1932 and the last in 1941. Both houses were reapportioned in 1965, 1974, 1982, 1992 and 2002.

Election Dates: The first election under the constitution took place on March 3, 1778. Thereafter elections were held on the first Tuesday of September. Effective in 1914 the date was changed to the first Tuesday after the first Monday in November.

Constitutions: There have been three constitutions in Vermont's history: 1777, 1786 and 1793.

Affiliations	House
	D / F
1798	34 / 130
1799	52 / 112
1800	75 / 99
1801	96 / 82
1802	102 / 81
1803	?

Affiliations			*House*
			D / F
1804			?
1805			111 / 80
1806			?
1807			?
1808			108 / 91
1809			122 / 78
1810			125 / 65
1811			129 / 77
1812			124 / 85
1813			104 / 108
1814			94 / 117
1815			114 / 101
1816			119 / 93
1817			148 / 67
1818			?
1819			?
1820			?
			(J)D / NR / A-M
1826			?
1827			?
1828			?
1829			45 / 136 / 33
1830			28 / 121 / 76
1831			33 / 79 / 83[1]
1832			40 / 68 / 87[2]
1833			—[3]
1834			59 / 87 / 86
1835			75 / 35 / 110
		Senate	
		D / W / oth	*D / W / oth*
1836	**(30)**	12 / 18	100 / 118 / 2 ?
1837		10 / 20	88 / 128[4]
1838		10 / 20	70 / 156 / 3 C
1839		12 / 18	112 / 118
1840		2 / 28	56 / 178
1841		9 / 21	74 / 127 / 4 ?
1842		14 / 16	99 / 132 / 7 ?
1843		9 / 21	93 / 117 / 7 Lty
1844		10 / 20	65 / 129 / 8 Lty, 33 x
1845		7 / 23	67 / 116 / 12 Lty, 40 x
1846		7 / 23	68 / 116 / 10 Lty, 39 x
1847		9 / 21	78 / 104 / 18Lty, 37 x
1848		7 / 21 / 2 FS	49 / 102 / 65 FS, 20 x
1849		1 / 22 / 7 FS	10 / 120 / 84 FS, 22 x

Affiliations	*Senate* *D / W / oth*	*House* *D / W / oth*
1850	3 / 20 / 7 FS	19 / 132 / 72 FS, 17 x
1851	1 / 21 / 8 FS	30 / 112 / 69 FS, 29 x
1852	8 / 20 / 2 FS	59 / 98 / 34 FS, 47 x
1853	11 / 17 / 2 FS	82 / 95 / 37 FS, 27 x
1854	1 / 29	46 / 133 / 31 FS, 5 ?, 15 x

	D / R / oth	*D / R / oth*
1855	1 / 29	28 / 157 / 30 A, 12 x
1856	0 / 30	8 / 227 / 4 x
1857	0 / 30	30 / 200 / 2 oth, 7 x
1858	1 / 29	38 / 190 / 1W, 1 Ab, 9 x
1859	0 / 30	32 / 199 / 2 I, 1 W,1 NPty, 4 x
1860	1 / 29	25 / 210 / 2 I, 3 x
1861	0 / 30	17 / 200 / 5 x
1862	0 / 30	R majority
1863	0 / 30	14 / 224 / 1 x
1864	0 / 30	19 / 212 / 2 x
1865	0 / 30	11 / 213 / 4 x
1866	0 / 30	**(240)** 13 / 224 / 3 x
1867	0 / 29 / 1 C	**(241)** 25 / 213 / 3 x
1868	0 / 30	15 / 224 / 2 x
1869	0 / 30	24 / 210 / 1 C, 5 x, 1 ?
1870	2 / 28	25 / 208 / 1 C, 1 ?, 6 x
1872	0 / 30	16 / 216 / 7 LR, 2 x
1874	1 / 29	50 / 174 / 8 LR, 4 I, 5 x
1876	0 / 30	31 / 205 / 5 x
1878	1 / 29	45 / 175 / 6 G, 5 I, 1 vac, 9 x
1880	0 / 30	19 / 217/ 1 G, 1 I, 3 x
1882	2 / 28	47 / 183 / 3 ID, 2 G, 1 I, 1 vac, 4 x
1884	3 / 27	35 / 195 / 4 G, 3 I, 1 IR, 1 P,1 vac, 1 x
1886	1 / 29	29 / 206 / 1 I, 1 IR, 1 PR, 1 ID, 2 x
1888	0 / 30	**(244)** 19 / 219 / 1 ID, 1 I, 1 vac, 3 x
1890	1 / 29	**(242)** 62 / 172 / 2 I, 2 Pop, 1 ID, 3 x
1892	0 / 30	**(243)** 40 / 200 / 1 P, 2 x
1894	0 / 30	**(245)** 11 / 228 / 1 I, 1 Pop, 3 x
1896	0 / 30	**(246)** 19 / 224 / 1 I, 1 Pop, 1 vac
1898	0 / 30	41 / 203 / 1 P, 1 NPty
1900	0 / 30	48 / 196 / 1 ID, 1 vac
1902	5 / 25	48 / 192 / 1 ID, 1 Lab, 1 vac, 3 x
1904	0 / 30	33 / 206 / 3 I, 2 ID, 1 Cit
1906	0 / 30	35 / 199 / 6 I, 2 Fus, 1 ID, 1 P, 1 Pop, 1 x
1908	2 / 28	39 / 201 / 3 I, 1 IR, 1 vac, 1 x
1910	0 / 30	47 / 194 / 2 I, 1 ID, 1 IR, 1 Rs
1912	3 / 27	56 / 147 / 22 Pg, 7 PgR,3 IR, 2 IPg, 1 PgD, 1 ID, 1 P, 1 I, 1 Lab, 1 NPty, 3 x
1914	0 / 30	32 / 175 / 24 Pg, 4 PgR, 3 I, 2 ID, 2 IR, 2 LabR, 1 IPg, 1 NPty

Affiliations	*Senate* D / R / oth	*House* D / R / oth
1916	0 / 30	42 / 195 / 3 I, 2 I, 2 NPty, 1 S, 1 vac
1918	1 / 29	(247) 25 / 212 / 4 IR, 4 NPty, 1 I, 1 vac
1920	1 / 29	22 / 216 / 4 I, 2 IR, 1 ID, 1 NPty
1922	0 / 30	(248) 37 / 203 / 3 I, 2 NPty, 1 IR, 1 ID, 1 vac
1924	0 / 30	29 / 214 / 4 NPty, 1 I
1926	0 / 30	29 / 217 / 1 ID, 1 NPty
1928	1 / 29	19 / 224 / 3 NPty, 1 ID, 1 NPty
1930	3 / 27	34 / 210 / 3 I, 1 ID
1932	4 / 26	38 / 200 / 4 I, 4 NPty, 2 IR
1934	7 / 23	48 / 193 / 3 I, 3 IR, 1 NPty
1936	8 / 22	39 / 203 / 3 I, 2 IR, 1 NPty
1938	5 / 25	(246) 31 / 204 / 5 I, 4 NPty, 1 IR, 1 ID
1940	8 / 22	37 / 197 / 5 NPty, 4 I, 3 IR,
1942	2 / 28	28 / 206 / 5 I, 4 IR, 3 NPty
1944	7 / 23	23 / 213 / 5 NPty, 4 I, 1 IR
1946	3 / 27	28 / 209 / 4 IR, 3 I, 2 NPty
1948	6 / 24	33 / 208 / 3 I, 1 IR, 1 NPty
1950	1 / 29	22 / 216 / 3 I, 3 IR, 2 NPty
1952	3 / 27	18 / 223 / 3 I, 2 NPty
1954	7 / 23	25 / 221
1956	6 / 24	33 / 212 / 1 NPty
1958	8 / 22	46 / 200
1960	7 / 23	50 / 190 / 6 I
1962	9 / 21	45 / 193/ 3 I, 2 IR, 2 NPty, 1 ID
1964	13 / 17	50 / 195 / 1 I
1965[5]	6 / 24	(150) 15 / 135
1966	8 / 22	55 / 93 / 2 I
1968	8 / 22	50 / 100
1970	8 / 22	54 / 96
1972	7 / 23	57 / 91 / 1 ID, 1 I
1974	12 / 18	68 / 78/ 2 ID, 2 I
1976	9 / 21	73 / 75 / 1 ID, 1 I
1978	10 / 20	69 / 79 / 2 I
1980	14 / 16	63 / 84/ 2 I, 1 ?
1982	13 / 17	65 / 84 / 1 I
1984	18 / 12	72 / 77 / 1 I
1986	18 / 12	75 / 74 / 1 I
1988	16 / 14	76 / 74
1990	15 / 15	73 / 75 / 2 Pg
1992	14 / 16	87 / 57 / 4 I, 2 Pg
1994	12 / 18	86 / 61 / 2 PgCo, 1 I
1996	17 / 13	88 / 58 / 3 Pg, 1 I
1998	17 / 13	77 / 66 / 4 Pg, 2 I, 1 Lbt
2000	16 / 14	62 / 83 / 4 PgCo, 1 I
2002	19 / 11	70 / 73 / 4 Pg, 3 I
2004	21 / 9	83 / 60 / 6 Pg, 1 I
2006	23 / 7	93 / 49 / 6 Pg, 2 I

NOTES

1. 7 party not given, 7 missing, 12 towns did not send.
2. *Niles Register*, September 22, 1832 lists these figures as estimates.
3. In the absence of the actual party breakdown, the vote for Speaker was A-M 114, D/NR-105,5 others.
4. Five seats undecided.
5. Election held by court order to implement reapportionment.

SOURCES

Research was done at the State Archives and the State Library in Montpelier. Phil Lampi kindly shared his manuscript with me for the years prior to 1825.

The 1831 totals were obtained from the (Burlington) *Press*, September 16, 1831, and the vote for Speaker in 1833 from the same source on October 18, 1833.

House party affiliation for most of the 19th century was taken from *The Vermont Almanac and Statistical Register* published originally by Hosea Doton in Woodstock. The first edition appeared in 1843 and was frequently referred to as *Doton's Almanac*. This title contained a complete list of House members with party affiliation from its first edition on, with a few exceptions. Also used was *Vermont Register and Almanac* published by E. P. & G. S. Walton in Montpelier beginning in 1818. Unfortunately party affiliations did not appear in this title until after the publication of Doton's work. A third source was *Deming's Statistical View of the Legislature of Vermont,* also published in Montpelier, starting in 1850.

The Vermont Legislative Directory and State Manual was the primary source of data beginning in 1900. Since 1986 information has been obtained from the election returns supplied by the Secretary of State. Vermont was the last state to publish its returns for the legislature, not doing so until 1986.

No totals are listed for 1862. None of the above titles published party affiliations, nor were they found in Vermont newspapers of that year.

Until the election of 1914 many Vermont towns simply did not wish to undertake the expense of sending a member to the House. Consequently virtually every session until 1914 contained less than the full membership allowed by the constitution. All three of the above sources regularly listed the towns that did not send a member to the House.

VIRGINIA

Constitutional Origins: The first constitution of Virginia was drawn up by a convention that met from May 6 to June 29, 1776, in Williamsburg. The constitution was then declared in effect and the first legislature elected. Richmond became the capital in 1780.

Term: Senators have always been elected for a term of four years; initially one-fourth of the body was elected annually. Beginning in 1851 one-half of the Senate was chosen every second year. Since 1903 all Senators have been elected at the same time. The House of Delegates was originally elected for a one-year term, increased to two years in 1851. This is the current term.

Districts/Elections: Senators were originally elected from single-member districts, made up of two or more counties. Floterial districts were instituted as a method of equalizing representation in 1851. Until one person, one vote reapportionment went into effect in 1967, districts did not cross county lines, but the 1902 constitution no longer specified the type of districts to be created and some multi-member districts were created. In 1967 only single-member districts were created, and that has been the case since. Since 1967, districts cross county lines.

The county was the unit of representation in the House of Delegates and all members were elected countywide, thus providing for multi-member districts, until 1983. Initially each county was entitled to two members. The number of seats apportioned each district was fixed in the constitution of 1830. Floterial districts were introduced in 1851 and the number of members per county was fixed at a minimum of one and a maximum of three. Virginians elected House members from single-member districts for the first time in 1983 and continues to do so.

Membership/Size: The Senate initially had 24 members, increased to 32 in 1831 and to 50 in 1851. The present total of 40 has been in effect since 1879. The House originally had 126 members and was increased by two every time a new county was created. The 1830 constitution fixed the number at 134, raised to 152 by the constitution of 1851. Since 1879 the number of House members has been 100.

Reapportionment/Redistricting: 1830, 1851, 1869, 1871, 1879, 1891, 1903, 1913, 1923, 1933, 1943, 1953, 1959, 1963, 1965, 1971, 1983, 1993 and 2003.

Election Dates: Elections were held on the third Monday in March as far back as 1793. They were changed to the fourth Wednesday in April beginning in 1799. In 1803 they were changed to the "respective court days" in April. Court days differed from county to county and therefore the elections took place over a four- to-five week period. This meant that the election of senators who were elected from multi-county districts occurred on different dates. This practice ended in 1837 when elections were moved to the fourth Thursday in April. Beginning in 1851 they were held on the fourth Thursday in May. The election of 1865 was held on October 12, that of 1869 on July 6; the date changed to the first Tuesday after the first Monday in November in 1871.

Constitutions: The state has had six constitutions: 1776, 1830, 1851, 1869, 1902 and 1970.

Addendum: Virginia included the present state of Kentucky until 1792 and West Virginia until 1863.

Affiliations	Senate	House
	D / W / oth	D / W / oth
1830	(32) ?	(134) ?
1831	?	?
1832	?	?
1833	?	?
1834	20 / 12	61 / 73
1835	18 / 14	74 / 60
1836	21 / 12	77 / 55 / 2 ?
1837	20 / 12	85 / 47 / 2 ?
1838	19 / 10 / 3 C	51 / 72 / 11 C
1839	17 / 12 / 3 C	56 / 68 / 10 C
1840	17 / 15	63 / 71
1841	15 / 17	66 / 68
1842	20 / 12	82 / 52
1843	20 / 12	75 / 59
1844	21 / 11	61 / 73
1845	21 / 11	79 / 55
1846	20 / 12	72 / 60 / 2 ?
1847	21 / 11	71 / 63
1848	D majority	75 / 60
1849	21 / 11	80 / 55
1850	21 / 11	76 / 59
1851	(50) 34 / 16	(152) 89 / 61 / 2 ?
1853	—	—
	D / A	D / A
1855	?	96 / 56
1857	?	?
1859	?	?
	C / R	C / R / oth
1865[1]	—	—
1869	(43) 30 / 13	(138) 97 / 41
1871	33 / 10	(132) 99 / 33
1873	34 / 9	99 / 32 1I

Affiliations	*Senate* *D / R / oth*	*House* *D / R / oth*
1875	37 / 6	101 / 251I
1877	38 / 4 / 1 I	102 / 9 / 21 I
1879	**(40)** 31 / 9	**(100)** 83 / 17
1881	17 / 0 / 23 Rdj	42 / 0 / 58 Rdj
1883	25 / 0 / 12 Rdj, 3 vac	63 / 0 / 37 Rdj
1885	30 / 10	70 / 30
1887	26 / 14	61 / 38 / 1 I
1889	30 / 10	86 / 14
1891	39 / 1	97 / 3
1893	38 / 2	90 / 10
1895	34 / 3 / 3 oth[2]	68 / 17 / 12 Pop, 3 I
1897	35 / 4 / 1 Pop	95 / 4 / 1 I
1899	38 / 2	93 / 7
1901	38 / 2	93 / 7
1903	35 / 5	86 / 14
1905	—	86 / 14
1907	35 / 5	86 / 14
1909	—	86 / 14
1911	35 / 5	90 / 10
1913	—	92 / 8
1915	36 / 4	88 / 12
1917	—	88 / 12
1919	34 / 6	88 / 12
1921	—	95 / 5
1923	39 / 1	97 / 3
1925	—	95 / 5
1927	38 / 2	93 / 7
1929	—	95 / 5
1931	38 / 2	95 / 5
1933	—	93 / 7
1935	38 / 2	93 / 7
1937	—	93 / 7
1939	38 / 2	97 / 3
1941	—	97 / 3
1943	37 / 3	94 / 6
1945	—	93 / 7
1947	38 / 2	93 / 7
1949	—	94 / 6
1951	37 / 3	94 / 6
1953	—	94 / 6
1955	37 / 3	94 / 6
1957	—	94 / 6
1959	38 / 2	96 / 4
1961	—	94 / 5 / 1 I
1963	37 / 3	89 / 11
1965	—	87 / 12 / 1 I
1967	34 / 6	86 / 14
1969	—	85 / 15

Affiliations	Senate D / R / oth	House D / R / oth
1971	33 / 7	74 / 22 / 4 I
1973	—	65 / 20 / 15 I
1975	35 / 5	77 / 18 / 5 I
1977	—	79 / 18 / 3 I
1979	34 / 6	75 / 24 / 1 I
1981	—	67 / 31 / 2 I
1983	32 / 8	65 / 34 / 1 I
1985	—	65 / 33 / 2 I
1987	30 / 10	64 / 35 / 1 I
1989	—	62 / 37 / 1 I
1991	22 / 18	58 / 41 / 1 I
1993	—	52 / 47 / 1 I
1995	20 / 20	52 / 47 / 1 I
1997	—	50 / 49 / 1 I
1999	19 / 21	47 / 52 / 1 I
2001	—	31 / 67 / 2 I
2003	16 / 24	37 / 61 / 2 I
2005	—	39 / 58 / 3 I

NOTES

1. The 1865 election was largely contested without party consideration. No new legislative elections were held until 1869 because of Congressional Reconstruction.
2. 1 Cit / 1 Fus / 1 Opp

SOURCES

Research was done at the State Archives and Library in Richmond.

Most of the pre–Civil War data was taken from William G. Shade, *Democratizing the Old Dominion: Virginia And The Second Party System, 1824–1861* (Charlottesville: University Press of Virginia, 1995), and Jack P. Maddex, Jr., *The Virginia Conservatives 1867–1879* (Chapel Hill: University of North Carolina Press, 1970). The *Whig/Tribune Almanac* was used for the election of 1855.

Niles Register, May 14, 21, 1842, May 24, 1845; *Richmond Whig*, May 12, September 15, 1843, May 11, 1847; *Richmond Dispatch*, November 25, 1883, November 1895.

WASHINGTON

Statehood: An enabling act was signed by President Cleveland on February 22, 1889. A constitutional convention was held at Olympia between July 4 and August 22, 1889. The constitution was approved on

October 1 by a vote of 40,152 to 11,787. The initial election of the legislature occurred on October 1, 1889, and the legislators assumed office on November 18. Washington became a state on November 11, 1889. The capital has always been Olympia.

Term: Senators have always served a four year term, with one-half the body elected every two years. Representatives since statehood have been elected for a two-year term.

Districts/Elections: The Senate was initially elected from single- and multi-member districts as well as floterial districts. Ever since 1966 all senators have been elected from single-member districts. Representatives were originally apportioned among the counties, one to eight members, all elected countywide (at large). In 1890 and again in 1901 every county had at least one member. In 1932 House districts were placed entirely within single Senate districts, with at least two representatives elected from each district. In 1966 each Senate district contained from one to three representatives. Since 1972 each Senate district has two Representative elected by the entire district but elected for a separate seat (post).

Membership/Size: The Senate grew from 32 members at statehood to 34 in 1890, 42 in 1902, 46 in 1932 and 49 since 1958. The House originally had 70 members; four increases by 1910 raised the total to 97. Membership was increased to 99 in 1932 and reduced to 98 in 1972.

Reapportionment/Redistricting: 1890, 1901, 1930,[1] 1956–7,[2] 1966, 1972, 1982, 1992 and 2002.

Election Date: Since statehood, the first Tuesday after the first Monday in November.

Constitutions: The only constitution in state history was written in 1889.

Affiliations	*Senate* D / R / oth	*House* D / R / oth
1889	(31) 1 / 31	(70) 6 / 64
1890	(34) 4 / 30	(78) 17 / 61
1892	9 / 25	20 / 50 / 8 Pop
1894	5 / 26 / 3 Pop	4 / 54 / 20 Pop
1896	5 / 16 / 13 Pop	10 / 24 / 43 Pop
1898	6 / 15 / 13 Pop	0 / 68 / 9 Pop, 1 Cit
1900	8 / 26	(80) 20 / 60
1902	(42) 9 / 33	(94) 13 / 81
1904	4 / 38	4 / 90
1906	4 / 38	9 / 85
1908	3 / 39	6 / 88
1910	4 / 38	(97) 13 / 84

Affiliations	*Senate* *D / R / oth*	*House* *D / R / oth*
1912	9 / 27 / 6 Pg	19 / 49 / 29 Pg
1914	6 / 29 / 7 Pg	13 / 79 / 5 Pg
1916	5 / 37	14 / 83
1918	3 / 39	10 / 87
1920	1 / 40 / 1 FL	1 / 94 / 2 FL
1922	1 / 39 / 2 FL	9 / 84 / 4 FL
1924	2 / 40	5 / 92
1926	2 / 40	8 / 89
1928	1 / 41	6 / 91
1930	1 / 41	7 / 90
1932	(46) 25 / 21	(99) 70 / 29
1934	41 / 5	93 / 6
1936	37 / 9	91 / 8
1938	40 / 6	73 / 26
1940	37 / 9	68 / 31
1942	27 / 19	59 / 40
1944	32 / 14	63 / 36
1946	23 / 23	27 / 72
1948	19 / 27	67 / 32
1950	25 / 21	54 / 45
1952	21 / 25	41 / 58
1954	22 / 24	50 / 49
1956	31 / 15	56 / 43
1958	(49) 35 / 14	66 / 33
1960	36 / 13	60 / 39
1962	32 / 17	51 / 48
1964	32 / 17	60 / 39
1966	29 / 20	44 / 55
1968	27 / 22	43 / 56
1970	29 / 20	48 / 51
1972	30 / 19	(98) 57 / 41
1974	30 / 19	61 / 37
1976	30 / 19	62 / 36
1978	30 / 19	49 / 49
1980	24 / 25	42 / 56
1982	26 / 23	53 / 45
1984	27 / 22	53 / 45
1986	25 / 24	61 / 37
1988	24 / 25	63 / 35
1990	24 / 25	61 / 37
1992	28 / 21	66 / 32
1994	25 / 24	40 / 58
1996	23 / 26	45 / 53
1998	28 / 21	49 / 49
2000	25 / 24	49 / 49
2002	24 / 25	52 / 46
2004	26 / 23	55 / 43
2006	32 / 17	63 / 35

NOTES

1. Enacted by voter initiative.
2. Enacted by voter initiative; this reapportionment was modified by the legislature.

SOURCE

The State Archives supplied data for the elections of 1898, 1990 and 2000.

WEST VIRGINIA

Statehood: Following the secession of Virginia in 1861, representatives of approximately 50 counties in western Virginia met at Wheeling to voice their dissatisfaction with the state government. On June 19, 1861, a referendum was approved by the voters of those counties calling for the reorganization of the state government. A referendum calling for the creation of a new state was approved by the voters 18,408 to 781 on October 24, 1861. A constitutional convention convened at Wheeling on November 26, 1861, and met until February 18, 1862. When they finished their work, the document was approved by a vote of 18,852 to 514 on April 4, 1862. On May 13, 1862, the "restored" government of Virginia consented to the separation of what would become the state of West Virginia. President Lincoln signed a conditional statehood bill on December 31, 1862, requiring the new state to provide for the gradual emancipation of slaves. A reassembled convention met February 12–20, 1863, and amended the original document which was then approved by popular vote (27,749 to 572) on March 26, 1863. On May 28, 1863, the first legislature of West Virginia was elected. On June 20, 1863, statehood was achieved. The capital was located at Wheeling until 1870, when it was moved to Charleston. It was moved back to Wheeling in 1875 and reestablished at Charleston in 1885.

Term: Initially House members were elected annually. Senators originally were elected for two years, with one-half the body elected every year. Since 1872 senators have been elected for four years (one-half the body every two years), and House members are elected for a two-year term.

Districts/Elections: Senators have always been elected from two-member districts of one or more counties, but not more than one member can be elected from any county in a multi-county district. No county could be divided between districts. The House was apportioned among the counties and although initially smaller counties were not given separate representation, this became the practice beginning by 1900 and continued until the imposition of one person, one vote apportionment. Since 1966 House members have been elected from single- and multi-member districts of one or more whole counties. All members in multi-member districts were elected at large. In several of these districts there are restrictions on the number of members within the district a county may elect.

Membership/Size: the Senate originally had 20 members, increased on five occasions to reach the present total of 34 in 1964. The House started with 52 members, and six increases raised the total to 100 in 1952.

Reapportionment/Redistricting: 1872, 1882, 1892, 1902, 1916, 1938, 1952, 1964, 1966, 1972, 1976, 1982, 1992 and 2002.

Election Dates: Originally the fourth Thursday in October until 1876, when it was changed to the second Tuesday of October. It was changed to the first Tuesday after the first Monday in November in 1888.

Constitutions: There have been two constitutions in the state history, 1863 and 1872.

Affiliations	Senate D / R / oth	House D / R / oth
1863[1]	(20) —	(52) —
1864[1]	—	—
1865	1 / 19	8 / 48
1866	3 / 19	15 / 41
1867	2 / 20	14 / 42
1868	4 / 18	24 / 32
1869	5 / 4 / 13 LR	23 / 33
1870	12 / 10	40 / 16
1871	18 / 4	39 / 16 1?
1872	(24) 21 / 3	(65) 43 / 19 / 3?
1874	19 / 4 / 1 I	49 / 12 / 4 I
1876	19 / 5	46 / 19
1878	21 / 2 / 1 G	40 / 8 / 17 G
1880	20 / 3 / 1 G	46 / 17 / 2 G
1882	(26) 17 / 8 / 1 G	38 / 27
1884	15 / 11	37 / 28
1886	14 / 12	36 / 29
1888	12 / 13 / 1 UL	34 / 31
1890	16 / 10	44 / 21
1892	21 / 5	(71) 41 / 30

Affiliations	*Senate* D / R / oth	*House* D / R / oth
1894	12 / 14	22 / 49
1896	5 / 20 / 1 Pop	31 / 40
1898	9 / 17	37 / 33 / 1?
1900	8 / 18	26 / 45
1902	(30) 6 / 24	(86) 29 / 57
1904	5 / 25	25 / 61
1906	5 / 25	25 / 60 / 1 P
1908	6 / 24	26 / 60
1910	15 / 15	23 / 63
1912	15 / 15	33 / 53
1914	9 / 21	29 / 57
1916	10 / 20	(94) 52 / 42
1918	7 / 23	24 / 70
1920	4 / 26	21 / 73
1922	11 / 19	65 / 29
1924	14 / 16	39 / 55
1926	9 / 21	34 / 60
1928	6 / 24	31 / 63
1930	13 / 17	68 / 26
1932	24 / 6	79 / 15
1934	24 / 6	82 / 12
1936	24 / 6	72 / 22
1938	(32) 27 / 5	70 / 24
1940	26 / 6	74 / 20
1942	21 / 11	50 / 44
1944	21 / 11	65 / 29
1946	20 / 12	56 / 38
1948	20 / 12	78 / 16
1950	20 / 12	78 / 16
1952	22 / 10	(100) 67 / 33
1954	23 / 9	76 / 24
1956	21 / 11	58 / 42
1958	23 / 9	85 / 15
1960	25 / 7	82 / 18
1962	23 / 9	76 / 24
1964	(34) 27 / 7	91 / 9
1966	25 / 9	65 / 35
1968	22 / 12	63 / 37
1970	23 / 11	68 / 32
1972	24 / 10	57 / 43
1974	26 / 8	87 / 13
1976	28 / 6	91 / 9
1978	26 / 8	74 / 26
1980	27 / 7	78 / 22
1982	31 / 3	87 / 13
1984	30 / 4	73 / 27
1986	28 / 6	78 / 22
1988	29 / 5	79 / 21

Affiliations	Senate D / R / oth	House D / R / oth
1990	33 / 1	74 / 26
1992	32 / 2	79 / 21
1994	26 / 8	69 / 31
1996	25 / 9	74 / 26
1998	29 / 5	75 / 25
2000	28 / 6	75 / 25
2002	24 / 10	68 / 32
2004	21 / 13	68 / 32
2006	23 / 11	72 / 28

NOTES

1. Although party affiliation for these two elections could not be found, there is evidence, particularly for the 1863 election, that all members were Unionists.

WISCONSIN

Statehood: An enabling act was signed by President Polk on August 6, 1846, providing for the admission of Wisconsin into the Union. After an initial constitution was rejected by the voters, a second constitutional convention was elected on November 29, 1847, and convened on December 15 in Madison. On February 1, the document was finished; it was approved by the voters on March 13, 1848 (16,799 to 6,384). On May 8 the first legislature was elected; it convened on June 5. Statehood was formally granted on May 29, 1848. Madison has served as the capital throughout the state's history.

Term: Senators were originally elected for two years, with one-half the body elected every year. The term increased to four years in 1882, one-half elected every two years. Assemblymen were elected annually until 1882, when the term was increased to two years.

Districts/Elections: Members of both houses have been elected from single-member districts. Assembly districts have to be contained within a single senatorial district.

Membership/Size: The Senate had 19 members at its origin and three increases — in 1852, 1856 and 1861 — increased that body to its present total of 33. The Assembly originally had 66 members and, also in three increases, reached 100 in 1861. In 1972 it was reduced to its present size of 99.

Reapportionment/Redistricting: 1852, 1856, 1861, 1866, 1871, 1876, 1882, 1888, 1892, 1896, 1901, 1912, 1922, 1932,[1] 1954, 1964, 1972, 1982, 1992 and 2002.

Election Dates: Elections have always been held the first Tuesday after the first Monday in November.

Constitutions: The original constitution written in 1847 is in use today.

Affiliations	*Senate* D / W / oth	*Assembly* D / W / oth
1848	**(19)** 12 / 4 / 3 FS	**(66)** 35 / 16 / 15 FS
1849	12 / 4 / 2 FS, 1 ?	41 / 17 / 8 FS
1850	14 / 3 / 2 FS	46 / 11 / 9 FS
1851	13 / 5 / 1 FS	28 / 31 / 6 FS, 1 vac
1852	**(25)** 18 / 7	**(83)** 51 / 22 / 7 FD, 2 I
1853	20 / 5	50 / 25 / 8 FS

	D / R / oth	*D / R / oth*
1854	13 / 12	33 / 44 / 5 I, 1 ?
1855	12 / 13	45 / 35 / 1 I
1856	**(30)** 11 / 19	**(97)** 33 / 62 / 2 I
1857	18 / 12	48 / 49
1858	14 / 16	42 / 55
1859	13 / 17	39 / 58
1860	8 / 22	27 / 70
1861	**(33)** 11 / 22	**(100)** 33 / 44 / 23 U
1862	16 / 17	44 / 48 / 8 U
1863	11 / 22	25 / 75
1864	10 / 23	33 / 67
1865	9 / 23 / 1 I	32 / 59 / 9 I
1866	11 / 22	24 / 74 / 1 I, 1 ?
1867	15 / 18	41 / 59
1868	14 / 19	32 / 68
1869	11 / 19 / 3 I	38 / 55 / 7 I
1870	14 / 19	41 / 57 / 2 I
1871	9 / 23 / 1 I	38 / 58 / 4 I
1872	16 / 17	60 / 40
1873	15 / 17 / 1 I	35 / 64 / 1 I
1874	15 / 17 / 1 I	60 / 40
1875	12 / 21	49 / 47 / 4 I
1876	12 / 21	40 / 48 / 7 G, 4 I, 1 S
1877	9 / 24	42 / 48 / 7 G, 2 I, 1 S
1878	9 / 24	25 / 66 / 9 G
1879	8 / 25	29 / 70 / 1 G

Affiliations	*Senate*	*Assembly*
	D / R / oth	*D / R / oth*
1880	9 / 24	22 / 78
1881	10 / 23	34 / 64 / 2 I
1882	15 / 18	37 / 63
1884	13 / 20	39 / 61
1886	6 / 25 / 1 I, 1 Pe	30 / 57 / 6 Pe, 4 ID, 3 I
1888	6 / 24 / 2 UL, 1 I	29 / 71
1890	19 / 14	66 / 33 / 1 UL
1892	26 / 7	56 / 44
1894	13 / 20	19 / 81
1896	4 / 29	8 / 91 / 1 Fus
1898	2 / 31	19 / 81
1900	2 / 31	18 / 82
1902	3 / 30	25 / 75
1904	4 / 28 / 1 SD	11 / 85 / 4 SD
1906	5 / 27 / 1 SD	19 / 76 / 5 SD
1908	4 / 28 / 1 SD	17 / 80 / 3 SD
1910	4 / 27 / 2 SD	29 / 59 / 12 SD
1912	9 / 23 / 1 SD	37 / 57 / 6 SD
1914	11 / 21 / 1 SD	29 / 63 / 8 SD
1916	6 / 24 / 3 S	14 / 79 / 7 S
1918	2 / 27 / 4 S	5 / 79 / 16 S
1920	2 / 27 / 4 S	2 / 92 / 6 S
1922	0 / 30 / 3 S	1 / 89 / 10 S
1924	0 / 29 / 4 S	1 / 91 / 8 S
1926	0 / 31 / 2 S	3 / 89 / 8 S
1928	0 / 31 / 2 S	6 / 90 / 3 S, 1 I
1930	1 / 30 / 2 S	2 / 89 / 9 S
1932	9 / 23 / 1 Pg	59 / 13 / 24 Pg, 3 S, 1 IR
1934	13 / 6 / 14 Pg	35 / 17 / 45 Pg, 3 S
1936	9 / 8 / 16 Pg	31 / 21 / 46 Pg, 2 S
1938	6 / 16 / 11 Pg	15 / 53 / 32 Pg
1940	4 / 23 / 6 Pg	15 / 60 / 25 Pg
1942	4 / 23 / 6 Pg	14 / 73 / 13 Pg
1944	6 / 22 / 5 Pg	19 / 75 / 6 Pg
1946	5 / 27 / 1 Pg	12 / 88
1948	5 / 28	26 / 74
1950	7 / 26	24 / 76
1952	7 / 26	25 / 75
1954	8 / 25	36 / 64
1956	10 / 23	33 / 67
1958	13 / 20	55 / 45
1960	13 / 20	45 / 55
1962	11 / 22	47 / 53
1964	13 / 20	52 / 48
1966	12 / 21	47 / 53
1968	10 / 23	48 / 52
1970	13 / 20	67 / 33
1972	15 / 18	**(99)** 62 / 37

Affiliations	Senate D / R / oth	Assembly D / R / oth
1974	19 / 14	63 / 36
1976	23 / 10	66 / 33
1978	21 / 12	60 / 39
1980	20 / 13	59 / 40
1982	22 / 11	59 / 40
1984	19 / 14	52 / 47
1986	19 / 14	54 / 45
1988	20 / 13	56 / 43
1990	19 / 14	58 / 41
1992	18 / 15[2]	52 / 47
1994	16 / 17[3]	48 / 51
1996	17 / 16[4]	47 / 52
1998	17 / 16	44 / 55
2000	18 / 15	43 / 56
2002	15 / 18	41 / 58
2004	14 / 19	39 / 60
2006	18 / 15	47 / 52

NOTES

1. Redistricting of existing districts in multi-district counties only.

2. As a result of special elections the Republicans won control on April 20, 1993, 17–16.

3. As a result of a special election on June 16, 1996, the Democrats took control of the Senate, 17–16

4. As a result a special election on April 19, 1998, Republicans won control of the Senate, 17–16.

SOURCES

Michael F. Holt, *The Rise and Fall of the American Whig Party* (New York: Oxford University Press, 1999), p. 1081, for the years 1848–1851. Holt differs in 1851 (Senate 12 D / 6 W / 1 FS / Assembly 25 D / 35 W / 6 Fs) and also 1850 in the Assembly (48 D / 11 W / 7 FS) from the *Whig Almanac*. For years not located in the almanacs I used (Madison) *Weekly Argus & Democrat*, November 11, 1852; (Madison) *Daily State Journal,* November 12, 1852, January 12, 14, November 18, 1853, January 11, 17, 1854; (Milwaukee) *Daily Free Democrat,* November 17, 19, 22, 1852, (Milwaukee) *Weekly Wisconsin,* November 23, 1853; *Milwaukee Daily Sentinel,* November 21, 1853, January 16, 1854; (Madison) *Weekly Argus & Democrat,* January 20, 1857; *Madison Daily Democrat,* November 16, 1877.

From 1884 to 2000 all data was found in the *Wisconsin Blue Book 2001–2002,* p. 272.

H. Rupert Theobald, *Equal Representation* (Legislative Reference Bureau, 1970) was used for the data on reapportionment and elections.

WYOMING

Statehood: Territorial governor Francis E. Warren arranged for the election of delegates for a convention to meet in Laramie in September 1889. The delegates were elected on July 8, 1889. After a 25-day meeting the constitution was finished and submitted to the voters on November 5, 1889. It was approved 6,272 to 1,923.

After President Harrison signed a statehood bill on July 10, 1890, the voters of the state elected their first legislature on September 11, 1890. The legislature convened on November 12. The capital has always been located at Cheyenne.

Term: Senators have always been elected for four years, with one-half the body elected every two years. Representatives have always been elected for two years, since statehood.

Districts/Elections: Initially both houses were apportioned by county; each county was entitled to at least one senator and one representative. Counties were not divided into districts, so all members were elected countywide regardless of the number of members elected. Not until 1966 (one person, one vote apportionment) were counties combined to form a Senate district and in one instance was a county subdivided to form a district. Members still were elected at large as both single- and multi-member districts were used. This continued until 1992 when the apportionment provided for the first time only single-member districts, with many districts crossing county lines or taking in part of a county. The House until 1992 continued to be apportioned by county, and every county continued to have at least one member, all elected countywide. Since the 1992 apportionment both houses have been elected from single-member districts.

Membership/Size: From an initial membership of 16, the Senate increased four times, reaching 27 by 1908. The Senate was reduced to 25 in 1920 but increased to 27 in 1924. There have been two subsequent changes, a reduction to 25 in 1964 and an increase to 30 two years later. House; At statehood the House had 33 members; nine increases eventually produced a 62-member body in 1924. The House was reduced to 56 members in 1934. There have been four changes since then, the last of which reduced the House from 64 to 60 members in 1992.

Reapportionment/Redistricting: 1894, 1902, 1908, 1912, 1918, 1922, 1934, 1964, 1966 (Senate only) 1972, 1982, 1992 and 2002.

Election Date: Always the first Tuesday after the first Monday in November.

Constitutions: The constitution of 1889 is the only one in state history.

Affiliations	*Senate*	*House*
	D / R / oth	*D / R / oth*
1890	**(16)** 3 / 13	**(33)** 7 / 26
1892	5 / 11	16 / 12 / 5 Pop
1894	**(18)** 4 / 14	**(37)** 2 / 34 / 1 Pop
1896	**(19)** 4 / 14 / 1 SD	**(38)** 11 / 23 / 3 Fus, 1 Pop
1898	6 / 13	3 / 35
1900	2 / 16 / 1 Pop	2 / 36
1902	**(23)** 2 / 21	**(50)** 4 / 46
1904	3 / 20	3 / 47
1906	2 / 21	5 / 45
1908	**(27)** 3 / 24	**(56)** 7 / 49
1910	6 / 21	25 / 31
1912	8 / 19	**(57)** 28 / 29
1914	9 / 18	15 / 42
1916	11 / 16	25 / 32
1918	10 / 17	**(54)** 11 / 43
1920	**(25)** 3 / 22	1 / 53
1922	5 / 20	**(60)** 23 / 37
1924	**(27)** 11 / 16	**(62)** 23 / 39
1926	12 / 15	17 / 45
1928	10 / 17	11 / 51
1930	6 / 21	26 / 36
1932	12 / 15	42 / 20
1934	14 / 13	**(56)** 38 / 18
1936	16 / 11	38 / 18
1938	11 / 16	19 / 37
1940	11 / 16	28 / 28
1942	10 / 17	19 / 37
1944	6 / 21	28 / 28
1946	8 / 19	17 / 39
1948	9 / 18	21 / 35
1950	10 / 17	12 / 44
1952	6 / 21	24 / 32
1954	8 / 19	28 / 28
1956	11 / 16	26 / 30
1958	11 / 16	30 / 26
1960	10 / 17	21 / 35
1962	11 / 16	19 / 37
1964	**(25)** 12 / 13	**(61)** 34 / 27
1966	**(30)** 12 / 18	27 / 34

Affiliations	Senate D / R / oth	House D / R / oth
1968	12 / 18	16 / 45
1970	11 / 19	20 / 40 / 1 I
1972	11 / 19	17 / 44 / 1 I
1974	15 / 15	29 / 32 / 1 I
1976	12 / 18	29 / 32 / 1 I
1978	11 / 19	20 / 42
1980	11 / 19	23 / 39
1982	11 / 19	(64) 25 / 38 / 1 I
1984	11 / 19	18 / 46
1986	11 / 19	20 / 44
1988	11 / 19	21 / 43
1990	10 / 20	22 / 42
1992	10 / 20	(60) 19 / 4 1
1994	10 / 20	13 / 47
1996	9 / 21	17 / 43
1998	10 / 20	17 / 43
2000	10 / 20	14 / 46
2002	10 / 20	15 / 45
2004	7 / 23	14 / 46
2006	7 / 23	17 / 43

SOURCES

All data prior to 1972 was obtained from the Secretary of State, *Wyoming Official Directory 1971,* Cheyenne. For 1900 I used the *Cheyenne Daily Leader.*

Bibliography

Books and Articles

Adams, William H. *The Whig Party of Louisiana*. Lafayette: University of Southwestern Louisiana, 1973.

Allen, Don A. *Legislative Sourcebook: The California Legislature and Reapportionment 1849–1965*. Sacramento: Assembly of the State of California, 1965.

Anderson, Leon W. *To This Day*. Canaan, N.H.: Phoenix, 1981.

Asseff, Emmett. *Legislative Apportionment in Louisiana*. Baton Rouge: Bureau of Government Research, Louisiana State University, 1950.

Atkins, Jonathan M. *Parties, Politics and the Sectional Conflict in Tennessee 1832–1861*. Knoxville: University of Tennessee Press, 1997.

Barr, Alwyn. *Reconstruction to Reform: Texas Politics 1876–1906*. Dallas: SMU Press, 1971, 2000.

Carmony, Donald F. *Indiana 1816–1850: The Pioneer Era*. Indianapolis: Indiana Historical Bureau, 1998

Clark, Thomas D. *A History of Kentucky*. Lexington: John Bradford, 1960.

Clayton, John. *The Illinois Fact Book and Historical Almanac 1673–1968*. Carbondale: Southern Illinois University Press, 1970.

Clem, Alan L., ed. *South Dakota Political Almanac*. Vermillion: Dakota, 1969.

Coleman, John F. *The Disruption of the Pennsylvania Democracy 1840–1860*. Harrisburg: Pennsylvania Historical & Museum Commission, 1975.

Collins, Richard H. *History of Kentucky, Vol. 1*. Lexington: Collins & Co., 1878.

Cooper, William J. *The Conservative Regime: South Carolina 1877–1890*. Baltimore: Johns Hopkins University Press, 1968.

Corlew, Richard E. *Tennessee: A Short History*. Knoxville: University of Tennessee Press, 1969.

Cornwell, Elmer E. *The Rhode Island General Assembly*. Washington, D.C.: American Political Science Association, 1970.

Council of State Governments. *Book of the States*. Lexington, Ky.: 1935–(annual).

Creswell, Stephen. *Multi-party Politics in Mississippi 1877–1902*. Jackson: University of Mississippi Press, 1995.

Darling, Arthur B. *Political Changes in Massachusetts 1824–1848*. Reprint ed. Cos Cob, Conn.: John E. Edwards, 1968.

Dorman, Lewy. *Party Politics in Alabama from 1850 through 1860*. Reprint ed. Tuscaloosa: University of Alabama Press, 1995.

Dunbar, May, and Dunbar, Willis F. *A History of the Wolverine State*. Grand Rapids: William B. Eerdmans, 1980.

Fleming, Walter. *Civil War and Reconstruction in Alabama.* New York: Columbia University, 1905.

Fox, William Lloyd, and Walsh, Richard. *Maryland: A History 1632–1974.* Baltimore: Maryland Historical Society, 1974.

Friedelbaum, Stanley H. *Apportionment Legislation in New Jersey.* Proceedings of the New Jersey Historical Society LXX, 1952.

Garner, James W. *Reconstruction in Mississippi.* Reprint ed. Gloucester, Mass.: Peter Smith, 1964.

Hammond, Jabez D. *The History of Political Parties in the State of New York.* 2 vols. Albany: Van Benthuysen, 1842.

Harrington, Wynne P. *The Populist Party in Kansas.* Kansas State Historical Society, Collections. 16:403–450. 1925.

Harris, William C. *Presidential Reconstruction in Mississippi.* Baton Rouge: Louisiana State University, 1967.

Hart, Roger L. *Redeemers, Bourbons and Populists: Tennessee 1870–1896.* Baton Rouge: Louisiana State University Press, 1975.

Hatch, Louis C. *Maine: A History.* Reprint ed. Somersworth: New Hampshire Publishing Co., 1974.

Higginbottom, Sanford W. *The Keystone in the Democratic Arch: Pennsylvania Politics 1800–1816.* Harrisburg: Pennsylvania Historical & Museum Commission, 1952.

Hobbs, Edward H. *Apportionment in Mississippi.* University: Bureau of Public Administration, University of Mississippi, 1956.

Holt, Michael F. *The Rise and Fall of the American Whig Party.* New York: Oxford University Press, 1999.

Klotter, James C., and Tapp, Hambleton. *Kentucky: Decades of Discord 1865–1900.* Frankfort: Kentucky Historical Society, 1977.

Koontz, John, ed. *Political History of Nevada.* 10th ed. Carson City: 1997.

Kruman, Marc W. *Parties and Politics in North Carolina 1836–1865.* Baton Rouge: Louisiana State University Press, 1983.

Lamb, Karl A. *Apportionment and Representative Institutions: The Michigan Experience.* Washington, D.C.: The Institute for Social Science Research, 1963.

Lefler, Hugh T., and Newsome, Albert. *The History of a Southern State: North Carolina.* 3rd ed. Chapel Hill: University of North Carolina Press, 1973.

Lonn, Ella. *Reconstruction in Louisiana (after 1868).* Reprint ed. Gloucester, Mass.: Peter Smith, 1967.

Lucas, Melvin P. *The Period of Political Alchemy: Party in the Mississippi Legislature 1835–1846.* M.A. thesis, Cornell University, 1981.

Maddex, Jack P. *The Virginia Conservatives 1867–1879.* Chapel Hill: University of North Carolina Press, 1970.

Malone, Michael P., and Roeder, Richard B. *Montana: History of Two Centuries.* Seattle: University of Washington Press, 1976.

McCormick, Richard P. *The History of Voting in New Jersey.* New Brunswick: Rutgers University Press, 1953.

_____. *The Second American Party System.* Chapel Hill: University of North Carolina Press, 1966.

Morlan, Robert L. *Political Prairie Fire: The Non Partisan League 1915–1922.* Minneapolis: University of Minnesota Press, 1955.

Mueller, Henry R. *The Whig Party in Pennsylvania.* New York: Columbia University Press, 1922.

Overdyke, D. Darrell. *The Know-Nothing Party in the South.* Baton Rouge: Louisiana State University Press, 1950.

Niles, Hezekiah, ed. *Niles Register.* Baltimore: Hezekiah Niles, 1811–1849.

Page, Thomas. *Legislative Apportionment in Kansas.* Lawrence: Kansas Bureau of Governmental Research, University of Kansas Press, 1952.

Parrish, William E. *A History of Missouri 1860–1865, V III.* Columbia: University of Missouri Press, 1973.

Pease, Theodore C. *Illinois Election Returns 1818–1848.* Springfield: Illinois State Historical Society, 1923.

Poll, Richard D. *Utah's History.* Provo, Ut.: Brigham Young University Press, 1978.

Purcell, Richard J. *Connecticut in Transition 1775–1818.* Rev. ed. Middletown, Conn.: Wesleyan University Press, 1963.

Riker, Dorothy, and Thornbrough, Gayle, comps. *Indiana Election Returns 1816–1851.* Indianapolis: Indiana Historical Bureau, 1960.

Roger, William W., et al. *Alabama: The History of a Deep South State.* Tuscaloosa: University of Alabama Press, 1994.

Ross, Margaret. *Arkansas Gazette: The Early Years 1819–1866.* Little Rock: Arkansas Gazette Foundation, 1966.

Saye, Albert B. *A Constitutional History of Georgia 1732–1968.* Athens: University of Georgia Press, 1970.

Sellers, Charles G. *James K. Polk, Jacksonian, 1795–1843.* Princeton: Princeton University Press, 1957.

Shade, William G. *Democratizing the Old Dominion: Virginia and the Second Party System, 1824–1861.* Charlottesville: University of Virginia Press, 1995.

Smith, Joseph P. *A History of the Republican Party.* Chicago: Lewis, 1898.

Snyder, Charles M. *The Jacksonian Heritage: Pennsylvania Politics 1833–1848.* Harrisburg: Pennsylvania Historical & Museum Commission, 1958.

Spaw, Patsy McDonald. *The Texas Senate. V. 1, 1836–1861; V. 2, 1861–1889.* College Station: Texas A&M University Press, 1996, 1999.

Stamps, Norman L. *Political Parties in Connecticut 1789–1818.* Ph.d. diss., Yale University, 1952.

Staples, Thomas S. *Reconstruction in Arkansas 1862–1874.* Reprint ed. Gloucester, Mass.: Peter Smith, 1964.

Stokes, D. A. "First State Election in Arkansas 1836." *Arkansas Historical Quarterly,* 1961.

Tebeau, Charlton W. *A History of Florida.* Coral Gables: University of Miami Press, 1971.

Theobald, H. Rupert. *Equal Representation: A Study of Legislative and Congressional Apportionment in Wisconsin, 1970.* Legislative Reference Bureau, 1970.

Thompson, C. Mildred. *Reconstruction in Georgia.* Reprint ed. Gloucester, Mass.: Peter Smith, 1964.

Thornton, J. Mills. *Politics and Power in Alabama: A Slave Society 1800–1860.* Baton Rouge: Louisiana State University Press, 1978.

Titus, Charles H. "Voting in Kansas 1900–1932." *Kansas Historical Quarterly,* August 1935.

Turner, Lynn W. *The Ninth State: New Hampshire's Formative Years.* Chapel Hill: University of North Carolina Press, 1983.

Waldron, Ellis, and Wilson, Paul B. *Atlas of Montana Elections 1889–1976.* Missoula: University of Montana Press, 1978.

Walton, Brian. *Arkansas Politics During the Compromise Crisis 1848–1852.* Arkansas Historical Quarterly, v. 36, 1977.

Williamson, Chilton. "Rhode Island Suffrage Since the Dorr War." *New England Quarterly,* March 1955.

Williamson, Edward C. *Florida Politics in the Gilded Age 1877–1893.* Gainesville: University of Florida Press, 1976.

Whittemore, Arthur C. II. *An Analysis of the Problems of Legislative Representation in Mississippi.* M.A. thesis, State College, 1962.
Wiggins, Sarah Woolfolk. *The Scalawag in Alabama Politics, 1865–1881.* Tuscaloosa: University of Alabama Press, 1977.
Zornow, William F. *Kansas: A History of the Jayhawk State.* Norman: University of Oklahoma Press, 1957.

Almanacs

American Almanac. 1878–1889.
Argus Almanac. Albany: *Albany Argus,* 1870?–1893, 1898.
Baltimore Sun Almanac. Baltimore: *Baltimore Sun.*
Daily News Almanac. Chicago: *Chicago Daily News,* 1885–1937.
Doton, Hosea. *Vermont Almanac & State Register.* Woodstock, Vt.
Evening Journal Almanac. Albany: Weed Parsons & Co., 1858–1892, 1895, 1896.
Mathias, Benjamin R. *Politicians Register.* Philadelphia: 1835.
Providence Journal Almanac. Providence: *Providence Journal.*
Walton, E. P., and Walton, G. S. *Vermont Register & Almanac.* Montpelier.
Whig/Tribune Almanac. New York: Tribune Association, 1838–1914.
World Almanac. New York: New York World et al., 1868–1876, 1884.

State Manuals

Except where otherwise noted, all state government documents were published by the secretary of state.

Alabama: Department of Archives and History, *Alabama Official and Statistical Register, 1903–1977.*
Arizona: *Journal of the House of Representatives and the Senate.*
Arkansas: *Historical Report of the Secretary of State,* 1998.
Connecticut: *Register & Manual, 1889–.*
Delaware: *Delaware State Manual, 1940–1966.*
Idaho: *Idaho Blue Book, 2001–2002.*
Indiana: *Indiana Year Book,* 1900–.
Iowa: *Iowa Official Register,* 1888–.
Kentucky: Kentucky State Library, *Kentucky State Directory & Manual Kentucky Government Guide,* 1959–1973.
  Kentucky General Assembly Membership, v. 1 1900–1949, v. 2 1950–2000.
Maine: *Maine Register,* 1854–(published under various titles).
Maryland: *Maryland Manual,* 1900–.
Massachusetts: *Manual of the General Court,* 1875–.
  Massachusetts Election Statistics, 1892–.
Michigan: *The Michigan Manual,* 2002–.
Missouri: *Journal of the House Representatives,* 1863, 1865, 1867, 1869, 1871.
  Official Directory, 1935–6.
New Hampshire: *Manual,* 1890–.
  New Hampshire Register, 1863–1871.
New Jersey: *Fitzgerald's Manual of the Legislature of New Jersey,* 1877–.
  Results of the General Election, 1924–.
New York: *Manual for use of the Legislature,* 1892–1989.
  Red Book, 1892–.
North Dakota: *North Dakota Blue Book,* 1981.

Ohio: *Ohio Election Statistics*, 1918–.
    Ohio General Statistics, 1868–1927.
Oklahoma: *Directory of Oklahoma*, 1973.
Pennsylvania: *Smull's Legislative Hand Book* (became *The Pennsylvania Manual*), *1871–*.
Rhode Island: State Board of Elections, *Official Count* 1972–.
    Rhode Island Manual, 1885–.
Tennessee: *Manual* (published under various titles) 1892–.
Wisconsin: *Wisconsin Blue Book*, 2001–2002.
Wyoming: *Wyoming Official Directory*, 1971.

Websites

Kansas: *Legislators Past & Present.* http://www.Kslib.info/ref/legislators/index.html#A
Louisiana: *Louisiana List of House of Representatives 1880–.* http://house.louisiana.gov/H-RepsLA%20HOUSE%20%F
Missouri: *Historical listing of Missouri's State & Federal Officials.* http://www.sos.mo.gov/archives/history/historicallistings.asp
National Conference of State Legislatures. http://www.ncs/org/ncsldbelect98part comp.cfm?yearse=(+year)
Oregon: *Oregon Legislative Assembly Legislators.* http://arcweb.sos.state.or.us/legislative/histleg/statehood.htm
Pennsylvania: Cox, Harold E., Director. *The Wilkes University Election Statistics Project.* http: wilkes-fs1.wilkes.edu~hcox/

Newspapers

Alabama

Birmingham Times (Birmingham)
Democrat (Huntsville)
Independent Monitor (Tuscaloosa)
Jacksonville Republican (Jacksonville)

Arkansas

Arkansas Free Democrat (Little Rock)
Arkansas Gazette (Little Rock)

Connecticut

Connecticut Gazette (Hartford)
The Patriot (Concord)

Delaware

American Watchman (Wilmington)
Delaware Gazette (Wilmington)
Delaware Republican (Wilmington)
Eastern Shore Advertiser (Wilmington)
Every Evening (Wilmington)
Mirror of the Times (Wilmington)

Florida

East Floridian (Fernandina)
Florida News (St. Augustine)
Florida Republican (Jackson)
Florida Sentinel (Tallahassee)
Florida Whig (Marianna)
The Floridian (Tallahassee)
Herald (St. Augustine)

Georgia

Constitution (Atlanta)
Federal Union (Milledgeville)

Illinois

Illinois State Register (Springfield)
Illinois State Register (Vandilla)

Kansas

State Record (Topeka)

Kentucky

Daily Journal (Louisville)
Frankfort Argus (Frankfort)
Frankfort Commentator (Frankfort)
Kentucky Gazette (Lexington)
Kentucky Observer (Lexington)

Lexington Intelligencer (Lexington)
Louisville Public Advertiser (Louisville)
Spirit of 76 (Frankfort)
Reporter (Lexington)
Western Citizen (Paris)

Louisiana

Daily Picayune (New Orleans)
Weekly Advocate (Baton Rouge)

Maine

The Advertiser (Portland)
Eastern Argus (Portland)
Portland Gazette (Portland)

Maryland

Baltimore American (Baltimore)
Baltimore Sun (Baltimore)
Maryland Gazette (Annapolis)
Maryland Republican (Annapolis)
Republican Star (Easton)

Massachusetts

Atlas (Boston)
Berkshire Star (Berkshire)
Boston Press (Boston)
Columbian Centinel (Boston)
Commercial Gazette (Boston)
Essex Register (Salem)
Herald (Newburyport)
Independent Chronicle (Boston)
New Bedford Mercury (New Bedford)
Pittsfield Sun (Pittsfield)
Repertory (Newburyport)
Springfield Gazette (Springfield)

Michigan

Detroit Free Press (Detroit)

Minnesota

Pioneer & Democrat (St. Paul)

Missouri

Inquirer (Jefferson City)
Jeffersonian (Jefferson City)
Jefferson Republican (Jefferson City)
Missouri State Times (Jefferson City)
People's Tribune (Jefferson City)
Republican (St. Louis)

New Hampshire

Farmers Museum (Walpole)

Herald & New Hampshire Intelligencer (Concord)
New Hampshire Courier (Concord)
New Hampshire Statesman (Concord)
Oracle (Portsmouth)
Oracle of the Day (Concord)
Patriot (Concord)
Patriot & State Gazette (Concord)
New Hampshire Gazette (Portsmouth)
New Hampshire Spy (Portsmouth)

New Jersey

State Gazette (Trenton)
True American (Trenton)

New York

Albany Argus (Albany)
American Citizen (New York)
Columbian (New York)
Daily Advertiser (New York)
Evening Journal (Albany)
Journal Patriotic & Register (New York)

North Carolina

Raleigh Register (Raleigh)

North Dakota

Bismarck Tribune (Bismarck)
Fargo Forum (Fargo)

Ohio

Ohio State Journal (Columbus)
Ohio Statesman (Columbus)

Pennsylvania

American Daily Advertiser (Philadelphia)
American Sentinel (Philadelphia)
Crawford Messenger (Crawford)
Democratic Press (Philadelphia)
Farmers Register (Greensburgh)
Harrisburg Chronicle (Harrisburg)
Lancaster Intelligencer (Lancaster)
Pennsylvania Intelligencer (Harrisburg)
Pennsylvania Reporter (Harrisburg)
U.S. Gazette (Philadelphia)

Rhode Island

Providence Journal (Providence)
Rhode Island Republican (Providence)

Tennessee

Daily Union Nashville
Republican Banner (Nashville)

Texas

State Gazette (Austin)
Weekly Statesman (Austin)

Utah

Deseret Evening News (Salt Lake City)

Vermont

The Press (Burlington)

Virginia

The Enquirer (Richmond)
Richmond Whig (Richmond)

Wisconsin

Daily Democrat (Madison)
Daily State Journal (Madison)
Daily Free Democrat (Milwaukee)
Daily Sentinel (Milwaukee)
Weekly Argus & Democrat (Madison)
Weekly Wisconsin (Milwaukee)

Wyoming

Cheyenne Daily Leader (Cheyenne)